TOTAL QUALITY MANAGEMENT

The Portable MBA Series

TOTAL QUALITY MANAGEMENT

STRATEGIES AND TECHNIQUES PROVEN AT TODAY'S MOST SUCCESSFUL COMPANIES

Stephen George
Arnold Weimerskirch

37968

John Wiley & Sons, Inc.

New York • Chichester • Brisbane • Toronto • Singapore

Copyright © 1994 by Stephen George and Arnold Weimerskirch
Published by John Wiley & Sons, Inc.

Library of Congress Cataloging-in-Publication Data:
George, Stephen, 1948–
    Total quality management: strategies and techniques proven at
today's most successful companies / Stephen George,
Arnold Weimerskirch.
      p. cm. – (The Portable MBA series)
    Includes index.
    ISBN 0-471-59538-1
    1. Total quality management–United States–Case studies.
2. Malcolm Baldrige National Quality Award. I. Weimerskirch, Arnold, 1936–
II. Title. III. Series.
HD62.15.W44 1994
658.5′62–dc20   93-24465

Preface

We're all familiar with the customer's demand: *Higher quality at lower cost in less time*. And with the company's addendum: *At a reasonable profit*. The demand is wearing us down, the pace is too fast, and the expectations are too great. We're being pulled in too many directions—barely able to react when we should be anticipating and planning. On the verge of *dis*integration, we seek models of integration, examples of companies that have a clue about how everything they do fits together to the customer's delight and the company's benefit.

This book presents a model of integration, defined by the criteria for the Malcolm Baldrige National Quality Award and exemplified in the stories of 53 leading U.S. companies. Taken as a whole, this book demonstrates how all of a company's processes and people can be focused on meeting customer requirements and improving operating performance. For you, the reader, it provides some context for the roles you assume and shows you how others are redefining those roles to add value to the process of achieving their companies' goals.

Please understand that we're not talking about something you do *in addition to* what you are doing now, but about a way of understanding and organizing your activities—and those of your company—to be more efficient and effective. Such a holistic perspective allows you to stand back from the daily demands, study

v

the system in place that serves your customers, and develop a course of action that raises customer satisfaction. That is the greatest benefit of the new management model described in this book.

The idea for the book came from my coauthor. Arnie wanted to call it *The 1,000 Point Company* with the idea that we would create a composite company using the best practices of a host of real companies, and that the composite company could conceivably receive a perfect score in a Baldrige evalution: 1,000 points. That idea led to this book, although our research revealed that even a composite of the best practices would fall short of a thousand points. The companies who graciously agreed to be included in our book would be the first to admit that, though they aspire to be perfect, they still have a lot of work to do.

Arnie and I would like to thank all of the people quoted in this book for their cooperation. The men and women who agreed to be interviewed and who supplied us with valuable information helped bring the new management model to life. In particular, we would like to thank Joe Steinreich and his staff at Engelhard in Huntsville, Alabama, and Jim Medeiros and his staff at The New England in Boston.

I would also like to thank Arnie for his role in creating this book. His knowledge of total quality management and the Baldrige criteria helped anchor the book in sound principles, and his ability to explain them to me made the process both enlightening and enjoyable.

I would like to thank Daniel J. Rukavina for reading the first draft of the book and suggesting changes, Daniel M. Rukavina for his support during the research phase of the project, and publicist Stacey Miller for her unfailing optimism.

Finally, I dedicate my part in this book to my wife, Ellen Carroll George, and my children, Dan, Katie, Allie, and Zachary.

STEPHEN GEORGE
September 1993

I met Stephen George for the first time when he interviewed me for his book *The Baldrige Quality System*. The thoroughness of his research immediately impressed me. When I read the book, it was obvious to me that he has the ability to communicate ideas in living color. I suggested that we work together on this book.

I strongly believe in the power of the Baldrige criteria to bring about a fundamental change in the way America competes. I hoped we could combine Steve's ability to communicate with my experience in applying the criteria to help managers realize the full potential of their organizations. I felt that, if we could portray the "1,000 point company," we could create a vision of a new management model—management by quality. I hope we have done that in this book.

The Malcolm Baldrige National Quality Award has a very strict code of ethics, which has been strictly followed in writing this book. That code prevents me from discussing any applicant company except those that have won the award. Steve independently identified all the companies in this book through his diligent research, and they all willingly agreed to participate.

Finally, a word about my own company, Honeywell. Honeywell is working hard to apply the new management model. We could have used Honeywell as a role model to illustrate several points in this book. Somehow that seemed self-serving, so we did not.

I dedicate my part in this book to my wife, Anne. She has walked at my side for more than 33 years. We hope for many more.

ARNOLD WEIMERSKIRCH
September 1993

Contents

1 THE NEW MANAGEMENT MODEL

Some scientists believe they know why Adam and Eve left paradise: the tsetse fly. The insects carried "sleeping sickness," and since humans were easier to bite than the thicker-skinned animals around them, the tsetse fly drove man away. On the other hand, one animal that remained eluded the fly's bites: the zebra. A tsetse fly could starve to death while flying past a herd of "invisible" zebras. The fly's eyes cannot accept the black-and-white pattern of the zebra's skin. To the tsetse, the zebra does not exist.

Today's business leaders and managers face a similar quandary. Responding to intense competition in a rapidly changing world, they have been forced to seek ways to become more competitive. Many devour the closest "meals" first, laying people off, selling businesses, demanding more from those who remain. Eventually these sources run dry. At this point, leaders and managers turn their full attention to their companies, to the system they lead and manage, and while many notice the "hoofprints" of inefficiencies, errors, dissatisfaction, high costs, slow responses, and defecting customers, they cannot detect the sources of these problems. They cannot see the zebras.

When it comes to understanding the systems they lead and manage, most people see through tsetse eyes—and the zebras are frustrating the hell out of them. They *know* their companies could do significantly better if they could only focus everybody's attention on what was important, but what is important? Where do we look first? How do we make sense of this complex, confusing system we call our company? How do we attack something we cannot see?

Employees face similar frustrations with resignation, having been trampled by more than one invisible zebra. A problem that should have been solved reappears. A supplied component repeatedly fails. A time-consuming effort gets tossed aside when priorities suddenly change. For employees, the hoof-prints up their backs remind them that the system has serious problems.

But then, the system has always had problems—and it always will. What has changed is that companies are finding it harder and harder to survive their problems. What has changed is *change*. When American companies could capture markets by the sheer volume of their production, when they could compete just by working hard, and when they could sustain growth with a stream of innovative products, they could afford to follow a business theory built on capital, driven by profits, and organized by hierarchy. Change was slow and predictable, and the theory worked—for a while.

Global competition is quickly making this old management model obsolete. One of America's leading management experts, Peter Drucker, described the transition in an article in the *Wall Street Journal*. Inspired by the major turnarounds under way at General Motors, IBM, Westinghouse, and American Express, he wrote:

> To start this turnaround thus requires a willingness to rethink and to re-examine the company's business theory. It requires stopping saying "we know" and instead saying "let's ask." And there are two sets of questions that need to be asked. First: Who are the customers and who are the non-customers? What is value to them? What do they pay for? Second: What do the [successful companies] do that we do not do? What do they not do that we *know* is essential? What do they assume that we *know* to be wrong?

We will address both sets of questions in this book. Unlike the old model, the new management model is *customer driven*. The companies we will introduce make it their business to get and stay close to their customers. We will describe how they do it. In fact, we will tell you what 53 successful companies are doing to improve customer satisfaction and operational performance. Our "models of excellence" (Alcoa's definition of benchmarks) represent a wide variety of industries, including aluminum, steel, electronics, telecommunications, railroad, automobiles, hotels, office supplies, package delivery, ceramics, insurance, ice cream, photography, and baseball. They range in size from 80 employees to more than 300,000. They are at the leading edge of a sweeping transition from the old, inflexible management model to the new model we explore in this book.

To understand the transition, consider the contrasts between old and new, depicted in Table 1.1.

TABLE 1.1. Business in transition

Old Management Model	→	New Management Model
Vertical	*Organization*	Horizontal
Autocratic	*Leadership*	Cooperative
Profits	*Focus*	Customers
Self-serving	*Motivation*	Realistic altruism
Self-sufficient	*Structure*	Interdependent
Domestic	*Markets*	Global
Capital	*Resources*	Information
Cost	*Advantage*	Time
Homogeneous	*Work force*	Diverse
Security	*Worker expectation*	Personal growth
By individuals	*Work*	By teams
Imposed	*Quality*	Personal

Adapted from *Business Week*, "Reinventing America," 1992.

THE NEW MANAGEMENT MODEL
IS CUSTOMER DRIVEN

As Drucker suggests, the focus of the new model is not on how much we are making but on how well we are meeting our customers' requirements. The benchmark companies in this book—Motorola, Corning, Federal Express, Xerox, Solectron, the Ritz-Carlton Hotels, and others—make understanding and satisfying customer requirements their top priority. They have learned from experience that customer satisfaction determines financial success.

The Institutes for Productivity Through Quality in the College of Business at the University of Tennessee in Knoxville have more than a decade of experience in executive education and field research with a majority of *Fortune 500* companies. In an article in *Quality Progress*, associate dean Michael Stahl described two themes of primary importance to American competitiveness that have surfaced from the Institutes' experience:

> The first theme is that management should focus on creating and delivering the best net value to the customer, not maximizing stock price, return on investment, or shareholder equity—the typical measures of corporate performance. The second major theme is that managers must design and continuously improve organizational alliances and consensus thinking that will cut horizontally across vertical organizational structures; integrate corporate functions such as engineering, manufacturing, and finance; and foster teamwork.

Both themes fit the new management model. Both require a dramatic shift in thinking.

American businesses define themselves by financial measures. When *Fortune* announces its latest list of 500, it places the successes and the failures into three categories: biggest money makers and losers, biggest sales increases and decreases, and best and worst investments. Almost every article about company performance in business newspapers and magazines uses a financial yardstick, whether the article is about product innovation, quality improvement, customer service, or any other of the myriad issues companies are addressing. This system of financial measures has become the common language we use to assess and compare performance, but it shows only one part of performance, and as Stahl concludes, that part is not even the most important.

Our system of financial measurement is dragging us down, diverting our attention from what we really need to work on to become more competitive. Our tsetse fly's eyes are incapable of finding the zebras that are stomping all over the bottom line. Leaders who rely on these measures to evaluate their companies' performance will never understand what hits them.

By contrast, Stahl's themes point to a solution: *customer orientation, consensus thinking, integration, and teamwork*. To take advantage of this approach, leaders and managers must have a very good grasp of the system in which they work. You cannot take a haphazard approach to knowing your customers, turning your organization on its side, integrating functions, and working through teams. Those that have tried have failed. Studies by accounting and consulting firm Ernst & Young have suggested that companies have wasted millions of dollars on such quality initiatives as team building and benchmarking. You will read in this book about companies that have *saved* millions of dollars through similar quality initiatives. The primary difference is that the losers adopted programs they had seen work for others without understanding their own systems first. The winners become "systems thinkers" who integrate these initiatives into a broader process of quality improvement.

FOCUSING ON SYSTEMS THINKING

Peter Senge defines systems thinking, the focus of his book, *The Fifth Discipline*, as "a discipline for seeing wholes. It is a framework for seeing interrelationships rather than things, for seeing patterns of change rather than static snapshots." The new management model is nothing more than a discipline for seeing your entire organization, the interrelationships among people and processes that determine success, and the patterns of change that demand vigilance. *In an increasingly competitive marketplace, you cannot hope to survive in a system that is out of control.* And it *is* out of control if you do not:

- Know exactly what your customers require
- Have well-defined processes for translating those requirements into internal actions
- Align all of your tasks and processes along common goals and objectives
- Use key measures to manage by fact
- Involve everyone in continuous improvement
- Understand and improve all your critical processes
- Satisfy your customers

Most people are not used to thinking about their organizations in this way. We are dealing with complex structures here, from the operation of a company to the dynamics of a changing marketplace. People struggle to understand how it all fits together. They puzzle over where to begin. They lack the discipline for seeing wholes. "Systems thinking is the antidote to feeling overwhelmed and helpless," Senge writes. "It offers a language that begins by restructuring how we think."

USING THE BALDRIGE CRITERIA TO ASSESS QUALITY

The transition from the old management model to the new requires us to think differently. Chapters 2 through 17 each ends with a summary of the shift in thinking that our models of excellence have made in the areas common to every system. These areas have been identified by the criteria for the Malcolm Baldrige National Quality Award. *We believe the Baldrige criteria define the new management model because they provide the best guide to understanding, assessing, controlling, and improving your organization.*

No other model has gained such widespread global acceptance. As evidence, consider these facts:

- Since the Baldrige program was introduced in 1988, the National Institute of Standards and Technology has distributed more than a million copies of the criteria. It estimates that people have made at least that many copies for their own use.
- More than half the states in the country now have state quality award programs based on the Baldrige criteria.

- Several countries including Argentina, Australia, Brazil, Canada, and India are developing or have implemented quality award programs based on the Baldrige criteria.

- The criteria for the European Quality Award, first presented in 1992, are patterned after the Baldrige criteria.

- Companies such as Honeywell, Intel, IBM, Carrier, Kodak, and AT&T have adopted the Baldrige criteria as their internal assessment tool and criteria for their corporate quality awards. Many other large companies are asking suppliers to assess their organizations by the Baldrige criteria.

All these influences have helped expose thousands of companies to the Baldrige model.

In *The Baldrige Quality System: The Do-It-Yourself Way to Transform Your Business*, Stephen George explains how the criteria evolved and how companies of all types and sizes are using them to improve. The book includes a statement by Joe Rocca, one of the leaders of IBM Rochester's 1990 Baldrige Award–winning application effort: "It's really a genius document, as far as I'm concerned, because it allows you to go back to the basics and see the common thread that exists in everything you do. Things get down to some very basic fundamentals that you know are at work. If you can put your finger on them, you look at life with a clearer vision of what it's about and why things are happening."

Rocca is describing a shift in thinking. *In our experience with companies that use the Baldrige criteria to improve, people who examine their organizations from a Baldrige perspective acquire a discipline for seeing wholes, for seeing interrelationships rather than things, for seeing patterns of change. They become systems thinkers.*

The Baldrige system was created to promote an understanding of the requirements for quality excellence. That the system also defines a new management model surprises no one who has been active in the implementation of total quality management (TQM). TQM has long been misunderstood as some kind of limited add-on program that may help improve quality but does not affect the rest of the organization. Our benchmarks and other quality leaders demonstrate that quality *is* the system.

Quality has been widely defined as "meeting or exceeding customer expectations," a criterion that also happens to be the focus of the new management model. *The best system for meeting or exceeding customer requirements is defined by the Baldrige criteria.* Speaking to the Canadian Life Insurance Association in 1992, Robert Shafto, president of the New England Mutual Life

Insurance Company, said, "I've become more and more convinced that the Baldrige is a management guide for business success, and if you meet all the requirements, you'll end up satisfying the customer—hence, grow the business." Shafto's conclusion is shared by a host of leaders who have made the Baldrige criteria their new management model. In the Baldrige model, they find a system that:

- Focuses on the customer
- Aligns internal processes with customer satisfaction
- Puts everybody in the company to work on shared goals
- Facilitates a long-term approach to continuous improvement
- Demands management by fact
- Promotes prevention rather than reaction
- Seeks ways to be faster and more flexible throughout the organization
- Looks outside the company for opportunities to form partnerships with customers, suppliers, and other companies; to benchmark; and to fulfill the company's responsibilities as a corporate citizen
- Values results

For leaders who have been looking for a way to get their arms around their organizations—to round up the zebras—this description of the new management model offers hope. The companies featured in this book are living proof of the benefits of systems thinking.

QUALITY IMPROVEMENT INCREASES PROFITABILITY

For leaders who are reluctant to turn their attention away from the bottom line, the final Baldrige characteristic offers a back door: *The new model values results.* The pursuit of quality excellence does not come at the expense of financial excellence. Rather, financial results are another way of measuring the effectiveness of the system. The difference is that the goal of the new model is not profits, it is customer satisfaction, with the understanding that profits will improve as quality improves. Figure 1.1 shows how conformance quality (meeting customer requirements) and perceived quality (exceeding customer requirements) improve profitability.

Figure 1.1 reflects the experiences of quality leaders worldwide. Reducing waste and increasing productivity are natural by-products of a systematic process of quality improvement. Less waste and greater productivity lower costs, which improves both margins and the use of assets. With respect to perceived quality,

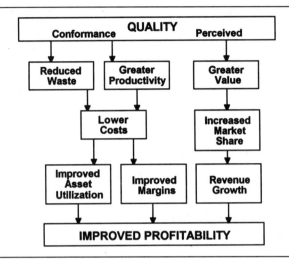

FIGURE 1.1.   How quality contributes to profitability.

products and services that exceed customer requirements are of greater value to customers than competitors' products and services. Increasing numbers of customers are likely to purchase such quality, and that improves margins and grows revenues. Revenue growth and improvements in asset utilization and margins mean improved profitability—and higher projected cash flows, higher stock prices, and greater shareholder value.

That is one way to look at the financial benefits of implementing the new management model. However, the connections between improving quality and improving profitability are not always this evident. We have all read about quality leaders that have stumbled financially. The business media are quick to hold these companies up as proof that the quality movement is a passing fad with limited value, which is like saying a baseball team finished the season in last place because it had a poor spring training. A company's financial success depends on many different factors, not the least of which is the company's leadership. *The new management model gives leaders the ability to control and improve their entire company, but it does not make the decisions for them.* Even the best management models are subject to the skill of the people who use them.

That having been said, skilled leaders are embracing the new management model because it makes them more effective. Financial performance depends on how well a company does in three areas: strategy development, market performance, and internal performance. The new model strengthens a company's position in all three:

- It contributes to more efficient strategies and better business decisions, which improves the development of strategies and helps companies respond to a changing environment.

- It increases customer retention, market share, and revenues, which improves performance in the marketplace.

- It improves asset utilization and productivity and lowers operating costs, which improves internal performance.

The new management model accomplishes all this by focusing the entire company on the customer, then identifying and improving the processes that lead to customer satisfaction. We will outline how companies are doing this in the chapters that follow, but before we present the elements in the system, it is important to "see the whole," to understand how the new management model works as a system before studying the parts in that system.

Figure 1.2 identifies the key elements in the new model and the ways in which they are interconnected. The model is driven by *customer requirements* and directed toward *customer satisfaction*. Leadership and information affect every part of the organization: *Leadership* commits everyone in the company to meeting customer requirements through continuous improvement; *information* is gathered from all critical points to evaluate and improve current operations and to help people make decisions based on fact. The *planning* process involves leaders, managers, employees, customers, and suppliers in charting a course that every department, team, and employee can translate into daily actions. *People*—leaders, managers, supervisors, and employees—are at the center of the new model, involved in planning, managing and improving processes, and serving customers (see Figure 1.3). The new model is also *process-oriented*, a horizontal organization aimed at fulfilling customer requirements (see

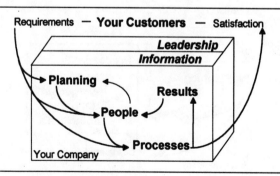

FIGURE 1.2.   The new management model.

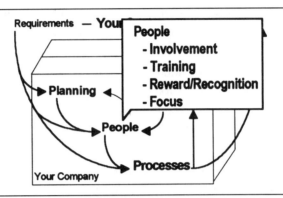

FIGURE 1.3. How people contribute to the new management model.

Figure 1.4). And the measure of success, whether of processes, products, services, or performance, is the *results* that are then used to develop or modify plans, improve processes, and predict customer satisfaction.

The new model is directed toward results, which provide the link between customer requirements and the company's system. As the Baldrige criteria booklet points out: "Through this focus, the dual purpose of quality—superior value of offerings as viewed by the customer and the marketplace and superior company performance reflected in productivity and effectiveness indicators—is maintained." Successful companies use results to assess progress and to keep people focused on company goals. Paul Noakes, a vice-president at Motorola and director of external quality programs, has talked to hundreds of companies since Motorola won the first Baldrige Award in 1988. He says, "The fundamental reason total quality management fails is that no level of expectation is set. You need results or people get disillusioned." Motorola expects its people to realize

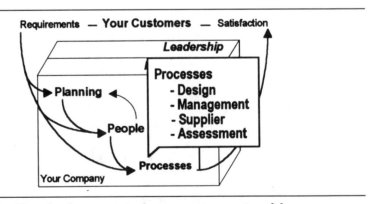

FIGURE 1.4. The role of processes in the new management model.

a 68% improvement in their critical measures *every year*, which leaves little time for disillusionment. Since results are the measure of every element in a company's system, they are inherent in every chapter in this book.

HOW THIS BOOK CAN HELP YOU MEASURE EVERY ELEMENT OF YOUR BUSINESS

Leaders rely on results more than any other group. In Chapter 2, we explore how senior executives lead the transition from traditional management to systems management. Senior executives are the gatekeepers for this cultural change, the only ones in the system with the power to facilitate it or squash it. As quality pioneer J. M. Juran said, "To my knowledge, no company has attained world-class quality without upper management leadership."

Once the gates are open, a company's first task is to know its customers. Chapter 3 shows how companies determine their customers' requirements, then use that knowledge to drive their entire systems. The customer connection at the top of our model closes the loop in your system, the source of the requirements you need to meet and the results of your success in meeting them.

Chapter 4 examines how companies internalize customer requirements. Our benchmarks integrate strategic quality and business planning to create one strategic planning process for the entire system. They involve people from throughout the company in this process, translating customer requirements into short- and long-term plans that guide the activities of every division, department, team, and individual.

Although management of the system is the subject of this entire book, Chapter 5 looks specifically at the roles of managers and supervisors in communicating customer and company requirements throughout the organization and making sure those requirements are met. The roles require new skills: an ability to listen, persuade, coach, train, facilitate, and serve.

One reason for the change in roles is the new model's emphasis on employee involvement. Quality leaders have discovered that the planning process improves when more employees are involved in it. They have realized that the people most qualified to manage and improve processes, including the processes that satisfy customer requirements, are the employees involved in them. Chapter 6 reveals how companies are giving their employees the authority and responsibility for continuous improvement. Chapter 7 describes how companies are giving employees the knowledge and skills they need to be effective in their expanded roles. Chapter 8 considers the role that rewards and recognition play in supporting employees' efforts to improve quality and satisfy customers.

Chapter 9 puts the focus on employee satisfaction, the result of the initiatives in Chapters 6–8 and of a company's pervasive belief in the value of its employees. Many believe employee satisfaction is a key indicator of customer satisfaction and company performance. People are at the center of the new management model.

This pivotal position is especially important when it comes to building relationships with customers. In the new management model, companies work very hard at bringing customers into their organizations because such contact makes it easier to understand and meet the customers' requirements. Chapter 10 looks at how our benchmarks stay close to their customers.

Staying close to customers involves several different processes and subprocesses. The new management model is process oriented, viewing everything a company does in terms of the processes involved. Sorting through these processes is often one of the first tasks a company undertakes as it breaks out of the traditional management model. Chapter 11 examines the processes used to translate external customer requirements into internal company requirements. The design of products and services is a critical link between customers and company. Chapter 12 focuses on how companies manage and improve all processes in all areas of the company. In the new management model, companies are organized around the core processes that meet customer requirements. Process management is about identifying and improving those core processes, then addressing all the other processes that feed into them. A number of those processes exist outside a company's control, with the suppliers of goods and services. Chapter 13 describes how companies are continuously improving supplier quality. (The final process element, assessments, is covered in Chapter 17.)

To manage processes, achieve company goals, and satisfy customers, a company must measure what it wants to manage, then analyze the information it collects and use that analysis to improve. Chapter 14 shows how people are using companywide measurement systems to help them align and integrate their systems and to manage by fact. Chapter 15 looks at how companies put their measures and performance into perspective by benchmarking industry and world-class leaders. Our models of excellence excel at "borrowing shamelessly" from the best to encourage breakthrough thinking.

Successful companies do not look outside their walls solely to feed their internal processes; they also look outside to fulfill their public expectations and to take the lead in publicly important issues. Chapter 16 explores the relationship between companies and their communities, clarifying the connections between the new management model and a company's public responsibilities.

Chapter 17 describes how companies check the health of their systems. Companies that use the Baldrige criteria to define their management systems use the same criteria to identify their strengths and weaknesses for every area discussed in this book. The assessment process becomes an annual booster, rocketing companies to new levels of quality and performance.

Chapter 18 presents approaches your company can use to make the transition from traditional to systems management. As the companies in this book demonstrate, the transition does not follow any single path. Some companies use strategic planning to initiate the new order. Others begin by empowering, training, and involving their employees in continuous improvement. Still others turn to process management as the key to their cultural transformation. In this final chapter we will outline how these approaches can help your company shift to the new management model.

QUALITY LESSONS FROM 53 SUCCESSFUL COMPANIES

One of the basic tenets of the new model is the idea of learning from successful companies. We have applied the same idea to this book. Our goal was to bring each element in the new model to life through the experiences of three or more models of excellence. Each chapter features at least one manufacturing company, one service company, and one small business ("small" usually meaning less than 1,000 employees). No company is featured in more than one chapter, primarily because we wanted this book to present as wide a variety of corporate cultures and experiences as possible.

We selected the companies through a benchmarking process similar to those described in Chapter 15: We identified the areas to benchmark and the questions we wished to ask, talked to people and researched written material to come up with a list of candidates, conducted phone interviews to ascertain interest and qualifications, narrowed the list to our top choices, and interviewed our benchmarks. The initial list of more than 150 companies was narrowed to an impressive group of 53, including 14 of the 17 Baldrige Award winners, several others that have received Baldrige site visits, and companies that are leaders in their industries. As with any such list, ours is neither perfect nor definitive. No company in this book can claim that all its processes run without problems or that it satisfies its customers all the time or that it achieves its corporate goals without fail. You may be able to think of others you believe would have been better examples. That is not the point. Each of our 53 benchmarks has something to teach us, depending on the nature of our business and the challenges and opportunities before us.

That is the point of this book: to teach by example. We invite you to explore the new management model not as a business theory but as a business reality. Consider how the lessons learned by our models of excellence could be applied to your organization, but be careful about copying any one particular piece. Quality has gotten a bad name because of all the companies that have tried to lift a single element, such as team building or benchmarking, and plug it into their old management models. The new model requires *systems thinking*, which means you must understand all the elements in your company—and how changes in one affect the others—to systematically improve it.

The following chapters introduce you to the different approaches companies are taking in these areas and to the ways the areas are interconnected. It is a thorough examination of the system, but not of the elements in that system. Other books have been written about each of the chapters in this book. Our purpose was to show how all these elements fit together, how companies are using systems thinking to transform their organizations.

Systems thinking is a discipline for seeing wholes. As you explore the elements in your system, you will begin to acquire this discipline, and it will change how you view your organization. The shift in thinking is as dramatic as the transition from old model to new, a process of discovery that is exhilarating and enlightening.

And startling, when all those zebras begin to materialize.

2 LEADERSHIP

Corning
Federal Express
Marlow Industries

Here is the one question every Baldrige Award winner hears too often:

"How do I get my company's leaders involved in the quality improvement process?"

People ask because they know they must return to a company where quality improvement is not a priority—because senior management has not made it one. They ask because they are tired of fixing pieces of the system, only to have apathy and resistance to change swallow up their efforts. They ask because they recognize the power the company's leaders have to change the entire system by making quality improvement a cultural attribute.

Leadership holds the key to the door of continuous improvement. If it keeps the key in its pocket, the organization has no chance of becoming a quality leader. None. Zero. The company may implement scattered improvements through the diligence of a quality champion. It may train everyone in the fundamentals of quality and urge their involvement. It may achieve ISO certification for the documentation of its processes. It may even win an award from a customer. But without clear, consistent leadership, the company will never be a quality leader, its management system will never be sound and efficient, and its improvement efforts will eventually be replaced by an intriguing new management fad.

For a contrast, look at the Baldrige Award winners. They are driven by the quality zealousness of their senior executives, leaders who meet with employees frequently to inspire and recognize their best efforts, who visit with customers regularly to find out what they need and expect, who track quality improvements religiously, who take and teach quality courses, who demand excellence (100% customer satisfaction 100% of the time), and who preach quality to every audience that will listen—and that includes civic groups, schools, government agencies, foreign companies, and trade associations, among others. They lead the quality improvement process because they are responsible for making the company more competitive and profitable, and the only way to do that consistently and for the long term is through continuous improvement of the entire system. That's not a one-speech, quick-fix kind of commitment; it is a relentless, all-consuming desire to make the company the best it can be.

So how do you make your leader a quality leader? You can't. You can no more make a CEO walk the quality path than you can make him or her convert to a new religion. In fact, the analogy to a religious conversion often surfaces in the way leaders talk about becoming quality believers. Many describe it as a "leap of faith." J. M. Juran likes to say that quality leaders have "the faith of the true believers," a faith they got by "witnessing the miracles."

Like those who experience a religious awakening, quality leaders are eager to spread the gospel. "When you get into quality, you become intolerant of the lack of quality in business, education, government, and other organizations," says James R. Houghton, chairman of Corning Incorporated. "I make a lot of outside speeches because I think quality is now in a spillover phase in our society."

Houghton does more than give speeches. Six months after he took the reins at Corning in 1983, he announced that the company would spend $5 million to set up a Quality Institute. "We were barely breaking even at the time," Houghton remembers, "and the cynics thought this was my new toy. Today there are very few cynics for two reasons: I've never stopped promoting quality and people now realize that quality means survival."

The survival issue is prominent in the minds of quality leaders. Federal Express founder Fredrick W. Smith compares the awakening to quality to "a near-death experience. A lot of times it's brought on by trauma." Leaders often embrace total quality management because they see no alternative: Improve or die. Whatever inspires them—the fear of failure, the promise of success, the achievements of other companies, the belief that there must be a better way to manage a company—triggers a "leap of faith." Once they are on the quality path, the cultural changes they see all around them frequently breed a missionary zeal about the need for, and the benefits of, the quality improvement process.

In the process of becoming quality leaders, they seek to identify the words and actions that will bring everyone into the fold:

- What can we do as senior executives to personally lead the quality improvement process?
- What are our company's quality values?
- How can we communicate those values to our customers, employees, suppliers, and other groups?
- How can we improve as quality leaders?

In this chapter we will see how the senior executives of three world-class companies—Corning, Federal Express, and Marlow Industries—answer these questions. Although much of the chapter will focus on the highest-ranking officials of these three companies, their methods of leadership are shared by the senior executives who report to them. If you are a leader at your company, the perspectives of these senior executives will inspire you. If you wonder about the thought processes and actions of such leaders, their stories will enlighten you. If you wish to influence your leaders to embrace the quality improvement process, *good luck*! Our three benchmarks will give you some powerful ammunition, but you are probably facing a long campaign.

MODELS OF EXCELLENCE

Corning is an international corporation operating in four broad market sectors: specialty materials, telecommunications, laboratory sevices, and consumer housewares. It supplies more than 60,000 products, plus advanced laboratory and engineering services, to these sectors. Headquartered in Corning, New York, the company has more than 30,000 employees at over 100 locations around the world. Corning chairman Jamie Houghton is regularly featured in business magazines and newspapers as a quality advocate. He chaired National Quality Month in 1987.

Federal Express created the overnight air express business in 1973. Ten years later it was the first U.S. company to top $1 billion in revenues in its first decade. The company currently has more than 94,000 employees moving over 400 million packages a year on the largest air cargo fleet in the world. In 1990 Federal Express became the first service company to win the Baldrige Award. CEO Fredrick W. Smith chaired National Quality Month in 1992.

Marlow Industries manufactures customized thermoelectric coolers—small, solid-state electronic devices that heat, cool, or stabilize the temperature of electronic equipment—for commercial and defense applications. Located in Dallas, Marlow employs 150 people and has total annual sales of $13 million. Marlow

Industries won the Baldrige Award in 1991. CEO and president Ray Marlow founded the company in 1973 and initiated a systematic quality improvement process in 1987, even though Marlow's market share was more than 50 % at the time.

LEADING THE TRANSITION

Step One: Commit to Quality

The first step in leading the transition to systems management for any company president, chairman, or CEO is committing himself or herself and the company to the process. Jamie Houghton took this step in 1983, shortly after he became chairman. Fred Smith and his top executives founded a company on the idea of providing the highest-quality service, then participated in quality training in the first year of Federal Express's existence. Ray Marlow initiated a systematic approach to quality improvement in 1987. All did it thoughtfully and deliberately, knowing that such a commitment would redefine their roles for as long as they remained leaders.

"When you start things as a leader," says Houghton, "you've got to make up your mind, then you've got to do it—even though you may not have one clue how effective it's going to be." In speeches, interviews, and articles, Houghton talks about leadership as a lonely art. Speaking to the Economic Club of Detroit, he said, "You're out front, the color guard, deliberately visible, encouraging and cheering on total quality, and you don't break stride for a second."

Step Two: Know Your Company's Systems and Values

Being "out front" can make you vulnerable to questions of substance about your new management system. The second step in leading the transition is to know your way around your system, because you will be looked upon as the point person for continuous quality improvement.

Jamie Houghton, Fred Smith, Ray Marlow, and their executive staffs created their companies' visions, missions, policies, and values. To do that, they looked at other companies' visions, studied their customers and their competition, assessed their own companies' strengths, and pinned down exactly what their companies stood for and aspired to achieve. Their values are presented later in this chapter. Each of the leaders has had to explain these values again and again and again, in myriad ways, to make sure the message sticks.

The explanations are often one-on-one. Fred Smith visits Federal Express facilities and employees every week; he invites their questions about any topic. Jamie Houghton visits 40 to 50 different Corning locations every year on a rotating basis. He has lunch or dinner with the unit manager and his or her staff and a two-hour meeting with about 150 employees, representing all groups at the location, during which he fields their questions. After Ray Marlow introduced his company's quality policy, he went over it a phrase at a time at six straight monthly all-employee meetings. In recent monthly meetings he has been reviewing the policy and talking about the company's quality pledge and quality tools. "You've got to keep it in front of people," he says.

At the end of one meeting, during which he had been stressing the understanding and use of Marlow's eight quality tools, an hourly employee asked for the microphone, then asked Marlow if he could name the tools. "I got 'em," he says proudly. In so doing, he showed his people that he could "walk the talk."

That is what quality leaders are asked to do every day. As the embodiment of their company's values they are under constant surveillance to see if they "break stride." If they do, people become cynical about the value of the quality improvement process, and that cynicism poisons the process. We have all had leaders who say one thing and do another, and we are smart enough to know that what they do is what is really important. Leaders who talk about quality and actively participate in the quality improvement process leave no doubt about where the company's priorities lie.

Step Three: Participate in Your Company's Quality Processes

Active participation, the third step in leading the transition, can take many forms. At Federal Express, Fred Smith has been directly involved in the development of every major quality process and system the company has implemented. He founded the company with the belief that customers would value a time-definite express delivery service, then used on-time delivery as the company's primary measure of performance. In the late 1980s, he helped develop a more comprehensive, proactive, customer-oriented measure of customer satisfaction and service quality called the Service Quality Indicator (SQI).

SQI measures 12 indicators that Federal Express has determined are most important for customer satisfaction and service quality (see Table 2.1). As Smith said, "We believe that service quality must be mathematically measured." The company tracks these 12 indicators daily across its entire system, individually and in total. Each indicator is weighted; the greater the weight, the greater the impact on customer satisfaction.

One of Federal Express's service goals is to reduce the SQI every year. Service is one of the company's three overall corporate objectives: *people-service-profit*. Every manager at Federal Express, including Fred Smith and his senior executive staff, has annual objectives for each of these three corporate objectives.

TABLE 2.1. Federal Express Service Quality Indicators

Indicator	Weight
Damaged packages	10
Lost packages	10
Missed pickups	10
Complaints reopened	5
Overgoods (lost and found)	5
Wrong-day late deliveries	5
Abandoned calls	1
International	1
Invoice adjustments requested	1
Missing proofs of delivery	1
Right-day late deliveries	1
Traces	1

Smith sets his personal objectives with input from the board of directors, and the process cascades through the organization from there. Managers are evaluated on how well they achieve their objectives.

To develop and implement such broad measures and objectives, Smith and his staff had to understand the company's quality objectives, its customers' needs, and the potential effectiveness of SQI as a measure and motivator. Although many companies, especially service companies, are still trying to figure out what to measure, Smith led the development of a measure that tells all Federal Express employees every day exactly how they are doing on customer satisfaction and service quality. That is active participation in the quality improvement process.

Jamie Houghton talks about quality improvement at Corning in terms of phases. "First, you've got to get your organization up and running and understanding the concepts. The second phase, we began moving out to customers and suppliers. The third phase came in 1990 when we decided to pursue world-class quality. We adopted the Baldrige Award criteria as our roadmap and set up a system of key results indicators of customer deliverables." Houghton and his staff review 260 companywide key results indicators quarterly.

It is important to note that subsequent phases do not replace their predecessors. Corning is still training its employees in quality concepts and tools, and it is still carrying its quality message to customers and suppliers. In fact, Houghton and his staff—and their direct reports—all spend significant time with major Corning customers. At Federal Express each officer is assigned responsibility for the major customers in a sales district. Smith and his staff talk to customers continuously at the executive level to make sure their needs are being met.

Quality leaders reinforce a customer focus by investing their own time in improving customer relationships. Marlow Industries has a standing rule: Every customer (which means anybody from a customer's company) that visits Marlow meets with either Ray Marlow or Chris Witzke, the chief operating officer. "We're not like Xerox," Marlow says. "We don't have something we sell to thousands of customers. Our products are customized for a select group, and we develop relationships with those customers. In fact, I keep track of how many customer contacts I have."

Leaders such as Marlow, Smith, and Houghton spend a great deal of their time discussing quality with employees, customers, suppliers, distributors, and other groups that affect and are affected by their companies. We will look at how they do this later in the chapter.

Step Four: Integrate Quality into the Company's Management Model

Once a leader is committed to management by quality, understands its basics, and physically participates in the transition, the fourth step is to institutionalize systems management as the company's business management model.

"You can't do quality as a separate job," says Houghton. "You've got to integrate it. We want our business units to integrate quality so that it becomes part of what they do. Units used to talk about their plans for growth and profitability and their plans for quality separately. That's not happening now."

Federal Express has been integrating quality into the way it runs its business from the beginning. "Like many service companies, we're widely dispersed," says Anne Manning, marketing specialist, Business Logistics Services. "Half of our people—almost 45,000 employees—are front-line, customer-contact employees, and they're all expected to deliver the same standard of quality." Federal Express's senior executive leadership created the system that makes customer satisfaction and service delivery a corporate strength.

Marlow Industries hails integration as a breakthrough for the company. "We made the mistake of having two structures—business and quality—when we started to pursue quality," says Witzke. "We kept moving quality into the business area until we collapsed business and quality into one structure. Our agenda for quality is now the way we run our business." At Witzke's suggestion, Marlow is considering changing the name of its Total Quality Management Council to Total Business Management Council, reflecting its broader scope.

"As a Baldrige Award winner, we get a lot of requests about how to start this process," Witzke adds. "We recommend using the Baldrige criteria as a roadmap for your business from day one."

Notice he said "for your business," not just for improving quality. To follow that advice, leaders must buy into the Baldrige criteria: They must demonstrate commitment, knowledge, and participation before integration can occur. And leaders must take all these steps all the time. "You have to be at least a zealot in your commitment to the quality improvement process to be effective," says Smith. "You've got to speak it and reinforce it at every opportunity."

EXPRESSING YOUR COMPANY'S VALUES

Federal Express, Corning, Marlow Industries, and other quality leaders build their quality improvement processes on clear and precise quality values. These are not some idealistic wish lists to be framed and hung in every conference room. The values of our three quality role models guide their quality efforts in tangible, measurable ways.

Federal Express has three corporate goals: *people-service-profit*. As Smith summarizes, "When people are placed first, they will provide the highest possible service, and profits will follow." The three corporate goals are translated into measurable objectives throughout the corporation. Progress on the *people* goal is determined by the Leadership Index, a statistical measurement of subordinates' opinions of management's performance. *Service* is based on the Service Quality Indicator described earlier in this chapter. The *profit* goal is a percentage of pretax margin determined by the previous year's financial results. Success in meeting the objectives for each area determines the annual bonuses for management and professionals; this can account for up to 40% of their total compensation.

Federal Express has two primary corporate quality goals:

- 100% customer satisfaction after every interaction and transaction
- 100% service performance on every package handled

Many people doubt the ability to achieve 100% of anything. "We acknowledge that 100% is impossible," says Smith, "but that doesn't keep us from striving to achieve it. We have to be wary of being satisfied with 99% performance because the law of large numbers catches up with us. When you're handling millions of packages a day, a 1% failure rate is totally unacceptable. We believe the road toward 100% is worth the effort."

The business philosophy of Marlow Industries is expressed in its quality policy: *For every product or service we provide, we will meet or exceed the customers' requirements, without exception. Our standard of performance is: Do It Right Today, Better Tomorrow.*

Marlow's quality pledge is each employee's personal commitment to quality: *I pledge to make a constant, conscious effort to do my job right today, better tomorrow, recognizing that my individual contribution is* critical *to the success of Marlow Industries.*

The policy and pledge are further defined by Marlow's quality values:

- Senior executives must be the leaders.
- Employees have the authority to make decisions and take actions on their own.
- Honesty with our customers, employees, and suppliers.
- Meeting the customers' requirements.
- Quality comes from prevention.
- Anticipate problems and take appropriate action before the problem happens.
- Do it right the first time.
- Continuous improvements toward customer satisfaction.

Nothing earthshaking here. Many companies espouse similar values. The difference is that Marlow Industries actually lives by them. The company's leaders will allow nothing less.

When Corning started its quality initiative in 1983, one of its first tasks was to identify the principles, actions, and strategies upon which its system would be built. It introduced the foundation of its system in January 1984. Here are Corning's four principles:

1. *Meet the customer's requirements.* This defines quality and drives the entire system.
2. *Error-free work.* This sets the standard for meeting the requirements: the first time, every time.
3. *Manage by prevention.* This defines the method of work and dictates that processes be designed with errors anticipated and designed out.
4. *Measure by the cost of quality.* This states that the cost of not doing things right the first time can be measured.

Here are the ten actions Corning identified:

- Commitment
- Teams
- Education
- Measure and display
- Cost of quality
- Communication
- Corrective action
- Recognition
- Event
- Goals

Finally, these are Corning's strategies for achieving its quality goals:

1. Provide visible, unquestioned leadership
2. Focus on customer results
3. Training
4. Achieve and recognize employee participation
5. Communication
6. Provide a quality process and quality tools

Building on this foundation, Corning offered training in quality awareness and tools. It formed teams around each of the ten actions and asked each department to confirm that it had a plan in place to carry out the actions. Since then the company has performed Baldrige assessments and established key results indicators to measure and improve the elements that contribute to its quality values. It is currently focusing on three corporate initiatives: performance, quality, and diversity.

COMMUNICATING VALUES THROUGHOUT THE COMPANY

"I don't talk about anything else," says Houghton, referring to Corning's initiatives. To follow Jamie Houghton, Fred Smith, or Ray Marlow around for a week is to hear the same message repeated—often in the same way—to a wide variety of audiences. "You have to be persistent," says Marlow. "You've got to keep talking about quality every chance you get."

All three of our role models excel at communication. Ray Marlow and Chris Witzke use monthly all-employee meetings to reinforce the company's customer focus and values. During these meetings Marlow hands out the Employee of the Month Award and Witzke presents the training awards. They frequently talk to employees in the manufacturing area, go to lunch with different employees, and act as mentors for employee effectiveness teams. They are involved in quality training: "If we're not teaching the class ourselves, we're there as students," says Witzke. They talk about quality regularly with their customers and suppliers and have been strong quality advocates outside the company. Ray Marlow helped found the Texas Quality Consortium, a group of small companies that meets to discuss W. Edwards Deming's 14 principles of management. Marlow and his staff made 25 presentations on quality the year before they won the Baldrige Award; they have made many more since then.

Unlike Ray Marlow, Fred Smith does not have the luxury of communicating his quality values to 160 people in one building. To provide what Smith calls "timely communication of the company's quality goals to our far-flung work force," Federal Express invested $8 million in FXTV, a television network that connects 1,200 downlink sites in the United States and Canada and six facilities in Europe. Each weekday morning a five- to seven-minute morning news program is broadcast from Federal Express's Memphis headquarters. The program includes features on company products and services, stock prices, package volume and service performance, forecasts of the day's volume, and frequent segments on company quality goals and initiatives.

"Open, two-way communication is absolutely essential to achieving our quality goals," says Smith. In the company's early days Smith and his senior executive staff held regular meetings at a local hotel. Any employee could attend these "family briefings." When Federal Express outgrew such meetings, the television network became the vehicle for continuing two-way communication. Smith appears on the network live every six months or so to discuss the state of the company and to field questions from employees throughout the Federal Express network.

Employees are not afraid to ask tough questions; open communication is part of the company's culture. During Smith's weekly forays to Federal Express facilities he asks for input and questions from the employees he meets. He and his staff also reinforce the company's customer focus and values by establishing and monitoring measures tied directly to each. On a quarterly basis representatives of about a dozen employee teams come to Memphis to share their "quality success stories." Smith frequently opens these meetings, then he and his staff remain to hear about the improvements being made—and to show by their presence that quality efforts at every level are important to Federal Express.

Communication about quality extends to Federal Express's customers and suppliers. "Fred Smith talks to customers continuously," says Tom Martin, managing director of public relations, "and he encourages his direct reports to do the same. Being assigned a sales district (which every senior executive is) certainly encourages communication with customers." "I try to take a business trip to a different district every month," says Smith, "and to schedule one or two customer visits per trip."

What Federal Express called a family briefing, Corning calls a "coffee klatsch." When Jamie Houghton meets with 150 employees at a Corning facility, that's a coffee klatsch. The executives who report to Houghton hold their own coffee klatschs with their people, who have them for their people, down through the levels of management. It is a distinctly Corning form of two-way communication, part of a broader commitment to face-to-face discussions. "I spend about 50 percent of my time meeting with people," says Marty Mariner, director of quality management. "If you do that, a lot of administrative paperwork goes away."

Jamie Houghton's calendar shows that he spends about 40 percent of his time on quality-related matters, including 30% on creating a quality environment and values. "You simply cannot communicate enough on the subject of quality," Houghton says. "It is as essential to the quality process as oil in an engine."

Like the executive leadership at Federal Express and Marlow Industries, Houghton and his staff spend significant time communicating about quality with their customers, suppliers, and distributors, and with outside groups. "It tells our employees that if quality is important enough for the chairman to talk about it in public, then they should get on with it," says Houghton.

The cumulative effect of this unrelenting communication about quality is the creation of a quality organization. Marlow describes it as "consistency of purpose," the leader's responsibility to nurture an environment where excellence is everyone's goal.

In an article in *Total Quality Management* magazine Houghton describes what leadership means to him:

> In the end, quality is something that becomes deeply personal. It is a commitment to a way of life—to a way of interacting with others. Quality isn't just a little pool for wading. It is an ocean. If you don't take the plunge, if you don't totally immerse yourself, you can't hope to coax a whole organization to jump in. That's why quality starts at the top, with the leaders of an organization.

IMPROVING AS A LEADER

According to the new business management model, the key to improving as a leader is to establish key indicators of performance, track those indicators, and develop actions to improve. Ray Marlow monitors how many customer contacts he has, studies customer service measurements to determine how well he is leading in that area, and regularly reviews charts and graphs posted throughout his facility to see if the company is improving. Jamie Houghton calls his senior management team "the quality improvement team at the top of the organization." Like any QIT, it has goals and measures of success.

Quality leaders tend to apply what they say about quality to what they do. "I'm always trying to find ways to engineer out rework," says Fred Smith, "and to be more effective in dealing with my external and internal customers. Not a quarter goes by that we don't formally evaluate that." Smith believes the ultimate measures of his effectiveness as a leader are Federal Express's measures of customer satisfaction and service quality. "The name of the game is driving the Customer Satisfaction Index up and the Service Quality Indicator score down."

In addition to working to improve their own leadership skills, both Smith and Houghton have helped develop a set of criteria or attributes that define leadership for their organizations. These leadership qualities show what Smith and Houghton value in and expect from themselves and from other leaders in their companies.

In 1989 an internal Federal Express task force implemented a Leadership Evaluation and Awareness Process (LEAP). An employee must complete this process before becoming a first-line manager. Since Federal Express implemented the process, its manager turnover rate has dropped from 10.7% to 1.7%.

LEAP identified three "transformational leadership behavioral dimensions" and six "leadership qualities" as the most important attributes in a candidate for management in a people-first work environment. The dimensions are:

1. *Charismatic leadership.* Charisma derives from an ability to see what is really important and to transmit a sense of mission to others. It is found in people throughout business organizations and is one of the elements that separates an ordinary manager from a true leader.

2. *Individual consideration.* Managers who practice the individualized consideration concept of transformational leadership treat each subordinate as an individual and serve as coaches and teachers through delegation and learning opportunities.

3. *Intellectual stimulation.* Leaders perceived as using intellectual stimulation successfully are those who encourage others to look at problems in new ways, rethink ideas, and use problem-solving techniques.

The leadership requirements are:

- *Courage.* A courageous leader stands up for unpopular ideas, does not avoid confrontations, gives negative feedback to subordinates and superiors, has confidence in his or her own capability, desires to act independently, and does the right thing for the company or subordinates in spite of personal hardship or sacrifice.

- *Dependability.* A dependable leader follows through, keeps commitments, meets deadlines, takes and accepts responsibility for actions and admits mistakes to superiors, works effectively with little or no contact with supervisor, keeps supervisor informed on progress.

- *Flexibility.* A flexible leader functions effectively in a changing environment, provides stability, remains objective when confronted with many responsibilities at once, handles several problems simultaneously, focuses on critical items, and changes course when required.

- *Integrity.* A leader with integrity adheres to a code of business ethics and moral values, behaves in a manner that is consistent with corporate climate and professional responsibility, does not abuse management privilege, gains trust/respect, and serves as a role model in support of corporate policies, professional ethics, and corporate culture.

- *Judgment.* A leader with judgment uses logical and intellectual discernment to reach sound evaluations of alternative actions, bases decisions on logical and factual information and consideration of human factors, knows his or her own authority and is careful not to exceed it, uses past experiences and information to gain perspective on present decisions, and makes objective evaluations.

- *Respect for others.* A leader with respect for others honors rather than belittles the opinions or work of others, regardless of their status or position in the organization, and demonstrates a belief in each individual's value regardless of each individual's background.

These dimensions and qualities define leadership at Federal Express. They prove that the senior executives at Federal Express have thought carefully about what a leader is, using Fred Smith and other corporate leaders as their best examples. For any company, this is an awesome list of attributes that any leader can use to guide his or her improvement.

Corning's criteria for leadership were outlined in a presentation made by Jamie Houghton. He identified the five key leadership traits as honesty, vision, caring, strength, and change, then described ten key traits a person *must* have to be a leader within the Corning network and ten more traits he or she *should* have.

To be a leader one *must:*

1. Believe in and live our corporate values
2. Develop and communicate a rallying vision
3. Be a strategic thinker
4. Be a risk taker
5. Have a proven track record
6. Be a catalyst for change
7. Have earned the trust of the organization
8. Be a listener and an enabler
9. Develop good, strong subordinates for succession
10. Be an optimist and have a sense of humor

To be a leader one *should:*

11. Have had different work experiences
12. Have developed an international orientation
13. Be financially adept
14. Understand and know how to deploy technology
15. Be able to deal with ambiguity
16. Be skilled at alliance management
17. Have a balanced, healthy lifestyle
18. Contribute to the local community, both personally and financially
19. Be active in at least one business activity outside Corning
20. Be active in at least one nonbusiness, nonlocal activity

This list, drawn from more than 140 leadership characteristics identified during research, reflects Corning's culture and the values of its leadership. Like Federal Express's dimensions and qualities, Corning's criteria remove leadership from the realm of the mysterious and make it tangible and measurable. And what can be measured can be improved.

The lists also redefine leadership for the new business management model. "The way I see it, leadership does not begin with power, but rather with a compelling vision or goal of excellence," says Smith. "One becomes a leader when he or she is able to communicate that vision in such a way that others feel empowered to achieve success."

THE SHIFT IN THINKING

The new business management model requires a dramatic shift in thinking for senior executives who resist a systems view of their organizations. The model is not something you can fit into the way your company operates, nor is it something you can do in addition to your normal operations. It is a different way of leading and managing that will change your view of your company—your "system"—and of your role in improving that system.

This new paradigm is the reason leaders talk about taking a "leap of faith" when they embrace its principles. Despite evidence that the new model works, you confront the task of changing a culture—and many within the culture will hate it. Like Smith, Houghton, and Marlow, you will need to be a tireless advocate of daily, continuous improvement.

This means that you must first accept *your* responsibilities in the new management model. We have discussed many of those responsibilities in this and other chapters; a summary shows how you affect and are affected by the new model:

- *You lead the quality improvement process.*   No one else in the organization can lead it as effectively.

- *You are a quality zealot.*   The leaders that appear throughout this book do not lead the improvement effort by spending all their time on financial matters; they walk, talk, and think quality.

- *You understand your customers' needs and expectations.*   Because quality is defined by the customer, you need to spend time with your customers and compare what you learn with what others in your company know about them and about your markets. Only then will you know if your system is truly being driven by customer needs and expectations.

- *You empower everyone in the company to meet those needs and expectations.*   You get all employees involved in improving quality and customer satisfaction. You promote training so that they can achieve their objectives. You establish rewards and recognition that encourage employees to work together toward common goals. And you create a culture in which every person is considered a valuable resource, where employee satisfaction is seen as an indicator of customer satisfaction.

- *You manage by fact.*   If you think of your business system as a car, you have within view all the gauges and indicators you need to assess the condition of the system and to decide what to do next.

- *You promote process improvement.*   If you were to step back and observe any part of your company for any period of time, you would notice that work follows different processes. The better you manage those processes, the more productive people are and the higher their quality of work is. You can help your company focus on process improvement by studying the processes you are involved in.

- *You use the strategic planning process to keep the company focused.* Quality leaders establish clear missions, goals, and objectives for their organizations, then use the planning process to translate corporate objectives into team and individual action.

- *You demand rapid, continuous improvement.* A business exists to meet customer requirements and to achieve superior operational performance. By setting ambitious goals for each, you challenge people to change and improve, to channel their energy, knowledge, and determination toward a shared vision.

Leaders such as Ray Marlow, Jamie Houghton, and Fred Smith run their companies according to this new paradigm. As the results of Marlow Industries, Corning, and Federal Express demonstrate, such a systems approach to leadership results in profitable, successful organizations.

3 CUSTOMER FOCUS

Xerox

IBM Rochester

L.L. Bean

Staples

Louisville Redbirds

The new business management model is customer driven. *Stop!* You have read and heard this philosophy so much in the past few years that it rarely even registers anymore. After all, you deliver products and services to your customers, who buy what you sell and keep you in business. It is easy to assume that this means your company is customer driven. Such assumptions are wrong.

A company that is customer driven is fundamentally different from a company that is not. Consider IBM Rochester. "In the past, all we did was monitor customer satisfaction, but now customer satisfaction drives all we do," says Greg Lea, director of market-driven quality. "Most of the actions we take as an organization are the result of a need identified by customer satisfaction or a problem with customer satisfaction. Whether it's how we deliver our products, how we provide service, how easy we are to do business with, the quality of our products—everything we are doing now points to some customer satisfaction item."

"Satisfaction used to be something that validated the way we did business," Lea says. "Now it drives it. That is a dramatic change."

In this chapter we will explore how customer requirements and satisfaction dictate a company's direction and actions. IBM Rochester is one of the benchmarks that will provide insight into how a system of customer satisfiers can be the foundation for continuous improvement.

Companies that build their systems on a foundation of customer satisfaction must be careful that the foundation is secure. This requires a thorough and accurate knowledge of customer requirements. L.L. Bean, another of this chapter's models of excellence, found that its customer satisfaction data were not good indicators of its customers' actual buying behavior. Its surveys asked, "All things considered, how satisfied are you with the merchandise and service at L.L. Bean?" The company scored high because of its reputation for superior service, but the scores did not mean that people would buy from them again. L.L. Bean is changing how it segments its market and surveys its customers to get more predictive information.

We will look at how Xerox relies on "customer obsession" to sustain a competitive advantage. Xerox believes that such an obsession is critical for four reasons:

1. *It improves financial returns.* This is how Xerox sees it: Customer obsession leads to fully satisfied customers, which produce superior customer loyalty, which improves market share, which improves financial returns. (For a more thorough discussion of this point, see Chapter 1.)

2. *It fulfills certain needs of Xerox's people.* Employees have a basic human need to receive positive feedback from those they serve. Giving them permission to be obsessed with customer satisfaction enables them to provide the quality of service their customers will value. (For examples of how this looks, see Chapters 6 and 10.)

3. *It provides an integrating focus for empowerment.* Customer obsession is a unifying vision that guides everyone's efforts toward shared goals. (For more information about companies guided by a unified vision, see Chapters 2, 4, and 5.)

4. *It can be institutionalized to provide a sustainable competitive advantage.* When customers perceive that the entire organization is obsessed with satisfying their requirements, they become loyal, not because of the product's features and price, but because they know Xerox supports their business goals.

Staples, a chain of office products superstores and another of our benchmarks, founded its industry. As competitors flocked to this new business opportunity, it quickly became apparent that anybody could build a new superstore around the same branded products. Staples decided early to differentiate itself by its customer focus.

The Louisville Redbirds have no trouble differentiating their entertainment product from others. Where else can you see Billy Bird vault over the centerfield fence, hear classic rock-and-roll tunes between innings, win 10 grand when a Redbird hits a grand slam, or get your kids in for $1.75 each? We will show how the Redbirds are driven to success by customer satisfaction.

We will use these five models of excellence to answer the following questions:

1. Who are our customers?
2. How do we determine their requirements?
3. How do we use customer satisfaction to drive our business?

In the new business management model total customer satisfaction is the goal of the entire system, and a pervasive customer focus is what gets you there. *The system is organized around customer satisfaction, which makes knowing what your customers expect and require the most important job your company has.*

MODELS OF EXCELLENCE

Xerox's Business Products and Systems, one of two Xerox Corporation businesses, makes more than 250 types of document-processing equipment, including copiers and other duplicating equipment, electronic printers and typing equipment, networks, workstations, and software products. The Business Products and Systems' U.S. Customer Operations Division, featured in this chapter, employs nearly 35,000 people and is the largest group within Xerox. The Business Products and Systems organization won the Baldrige Award in 1989.

IBM Rochester manufactures intermediate computer systems, nearly a half-million of which have been installed worldwide. The Rochester, Minnesota, facility also makes hard disk drives. It employs 7,000 people who are responsible for product development and U.S. manufacturing. IBM Rochester won the Baldrige Award in 1990.

Staples is an office products chain of more than 7,000 employees and 200 stores, based in Framingham, Massachusetts. Its stores, located in the northeastern United States, southern California, and southern Florida, provide office supplies, computers, printing, electronics, furniture, and other goods primarily to white-collar businesses with fewer than 100 employees. Staples founded the office superstore industry in 1986. In its first six years, its sales soared to $890 million.

L.L. Bean is the world's largest cataloger in the outdoor specialty field. It employs nearly 7,000 people during peak times. Headquartered in Freeport,

Maine, the company distributes more than 100 million catalogs in North America each year, creating $662 million in catalog sales in 1992. Of the more than 18,000 items stocked for catalog sales, 94% carry the L.L. Bean label.

The Louisville Redbirds are the Triple-A minor league baseball club of the St. Louis Cardinals. One of 28 Triple-A teams, the Redbirds play a 144-game schedule, plus any postseason play-off games. The Redbirds were the first minor league franchise to attract a million fans in one year, establishing their leadership in providing entertaining events for their customers. The focus on the event proved necessary because the Redbirds have no control over their primary product: the Redbirds team.

IDENTIFYING YOUR CUSTOMERS

Most companies assume they know who their customers are, and they are probably right. But there are degrees of knowledge here, and the greater the knowledge, the better your chances of satisfying customer requirements.

The Louisville Redbirds maintain a data base containing 90% of their customers' names, addresses, and phone numbers. They use the data base for target marketing and frequent direct mailings. The primary targets: children and their parents. "Kids on the weekend probably have 80 percent of the say in where the family goes," says Dale Owens, general manager. "Parents want to do something with their children. Our goal is to entertain and to provide a sense of community." Owens targeted children because of his own memories of going to Louisville Colonels games when he was a child. The focus seems to be paying off: Attendance at Redbirds games has grown steadily since Owens became general manager in 1987.

Few people have the luxury of being able to relate so directly to their customers. Employees who are making, selling, or servicing computers, copiers, or office products have to work a little harder to put themselves in the customers' shoes. Some companies are making it easier by involving customers in such activities as strategic planning, product design and development, process management, and benchmarking. They are encouraging employees to participate in customer teams, interact with their peers at the customers' companies, and be aware of customer satisfaction measurements and results. They know what Owens has acted on: *The better you understand your customers, the more likely you are to satisfy their requirements.*

Like the Redbirds, Staples maintains a customer data base that is unusual in its business. Unlike the Redbirds, Staples' data base tracks almost 5 million customers representing 1.8 million businesses. It updates the data base weekly and uses the information in it all the time. "Capturing customer-based marketing data on an ongoing basis gives us a unique advantage over other retail businesses," says Staples president Henry Nasella. "We're always trying to understand what our customers want, measuring their response to Staples' initiatives. We know what marketing contacts, what mechandise, what price levels, what services our customers care most about and are most responsive to."

Staples asks all its customers to become superstore members, which entitles them to lower prices on about 200 items and, if they use their membership cards, frequent mailings that include product announcements, coupons, and discounts. In exchange, Staples gets a customer name, company name, address, industry, and number of people who buy office supplies.

It uses this information to segment its customers by frequency of purchase, type of business, size, and other criteria. "We have the ability to understand what a customer's primary purchases are," says James Forbush, vice-president of marketing. "We can use that information in several ways. For example, if customers aren't buying from other areas of the store because they aren't aware of them, we try to educate them about all that we offer. If we know people have been purchasers of higher-priced business machines and the technology changes, we can tell them about that. Or, if we find out we're doing well with doctors' offices, we may send a mailing to other doctors' offices."

Staples also uses the data base to determine the lifetime sales and profit stream it can expect from a particular type of customer. It relies on this information to determine how much to invest in attracting new customers in that market segment.

L.L. Bean is changing the way it segments its customers. Traditionally, it grouped customers by the frequency, size, and timing of their purchases. Frequent buyers, big spenders, and recent customers attracted more of the company's attention.

The segmentation was based on L.L. Bean's financial goals, which provided little guidance when it came to customer satisfaction. The company is shifting to customer-defined segmentation. It has identified a half-dozen customer groups based on what they generally purchase from L.L. Bean. For example, a customer who usually buys sporting goods will be placed in that segment. Perhaps more importantly, the company is aligning its customer satisfaction surveys and other monitoring systems to the new segments. This will allow L.L. Bean to identify and track the specific requirements for each segment, and that information will help the company improve customer satisfaction.

Xerox segments customers according to their environment, geography, and type of decision making, then maps that information back to Xerox's core competencies. This process involves lengthy discussions with customer groups during which Xerox listens to their requirements and checks to make sure it has heard them accurately. It also involves market analysis to understand the general field Xerox is competing in, the problems people have, and the ways in which Xerox can help solve them. The goal is to find the best synergy between where the customers have problems and where Xerox's competence lies, "the sweet spot that will be good for both our customers and Xerox," as John Swaim, vice president of quality and customer satisfaction, puts it.

He offers an example. Productivity is a big deal now, especially for people working in teams, and a major problem is speeding up their work and sharing information. "It seemed to us that they were saying they would like to improve productivity by improving their work processes," says Swaim. "We discussed this with our customers and they agreed. One way to improve work processes is to improve the way information flows; then you can improve or reengineer the work process by the information flow."

One of Xerox's core competencies is understanding document technology: how it is formed, developed, used, revised, thrown away, collaborated on, and so forth. Another core competency is work flow. These core competencies combined with the customers' need to improve their work processes revealed the "sweet spot": helping customers improve their information flow for work processes that are document intensive. "We're about helping people solve productivity problems or take advantage of marketplace opportunities, and our focus is on document intensive work processes. That gives us the shape of the market we are after."

Xerox's process for identifying its customers and market segments gives it great insight and flexibility. Rather than fall into the trap of assuming it knows who its customers are, it searches for needs that it is well suited to meet, then verifies the validity of those needs and the promise of the market as it talks and listens to its potential customers. Getting close to customers, talking and listening, checking, verifying, testing—the dialogue is endless, and priceless. There is no other way to know your customers.

DETERMINING CUSTOMER REQUIREMENTS

"Setting up the organization to gather customer information is *hard work*, but your business changes so fast you could be out of business before you realize customer satisfaction has gone in the ditch."

IBM Rochester's Greg Lea sails an ocean of data in search of anything that might tell him more about his customers. His group casts a wide net, regularly hauling in an abundant catch of information:

- IBM surveys its customers quarterly. The survey asks how customers feel about its six key satisfiers (described in the next section).
- It does product-specific surveys, talking to customers of a particular product after anywhere from 90 days to a year after purchase.
- It calls all its U.S. customers 90–120 days after installing its products. This customer contact is different from the product-specific surveys.
- It has a closed-loop process for responding to customer complaints, feeding the complaint information into its customer management data base.
- Its marketing teams conduct a win/loss analysis for every competitive bid.
- It holds customer roundtables, bringing in present and potential customers to discuss their requirements. The roundtables are held annually for worldwide customers and every three or four months for regional focus groups.
- It has a competitive analysis team that buys, uses, and studies competitors' products.
- It validates all its customer information with independent surveys and double-blind surveys conducted by its marketing department.

When Lea was asked about sources of information, these are the items that came to mind, but it is not a complete list. There are many other meaty morsels IBM Rochester tosses into its customer satisfaction soup. When that soup is what feeds your system, you want to make sure that nothing essential is missing.

Like IBM Rochester, Xerox collects customer information from a variety of sources, including:

- 40,000 customer surveys every month
- Regular focus groups in which Xerox is not identified as the sponsor
- Ongoing customer panels with which the company shares ideas and asks for input
- Roundtables with salespeople to determine problems and solutions
- Market research focused on potential product opportunities
- Collaborative development with customers in which Xerox installs prototypes at a few customer locations to see how the prototypes meet their needs
- Competitive analysis
- Discussions with industry experts
- Conjoint analysis with customers of specific product and service features

- Problems and usage reported in real time by 30,000 copiers linked by phone lines to Xerox service offices
- Collaboration with cosuppliers (such as computer hardware and software developers)

The information from these different listening posts is aggregated and used to evaluate and refine Xerox's market segments and facilitate continuous improvement. Both IBM Rochester and Xerox spend considerable time collecting, comparing, and correlating information. This is partly because of the changeable nature of the high-tech industries in which they compete, but the primary reason is that their management models are built on customer satisfaction. They have set up their businesses to move in the direction their customers point them. By aggregating and comparing information, they can feel confident that they have chosen the right path.

Staples relies on its huge data base to determine its direction. It validates the customer information in the data base and enhances it through primary research, tracking customer purchases, and soliciting customer information through its store managers, who are a key connection between customers and the corporation.

Staples uses an independent research firm to survey 5,000 customers and noncustomers each year, asking them who they buy from and why. The results have shown a strong correlation with Staples's own data. Customer orders, either of the 5,500 items carried in its superstores or the 25,000 catalog items, indicate what types of products customers are currently buying. Staples distributes these data within the company weekly; it also maintains constant communication with its store managers, who are encouraged to talk to customers daily.

These sources and others supplement the customer data base, which remains the most popular tool for understanding and serving customer needs. "The fabulous thing about our data base is that you can test things by groups of customers," says Forbush. "We call it closed loop marketing because we can tell what the stimulus/response mechanism is. That puts us a good deal closer to our customers."

Staples uses the data base to identify sites for new superstores by determining what kinds of people are likely to buy at a Staples store. It also uses the data base to set up the new stores, analyzing key data to anticipate buying trends and types of services that will appeal to potential customers in the area.

One of the great advantages of pulling everything into a data base is that it gives you the ability to manipulate the information, to use it as IBM Rochester, Xerox, and Staples do to group their customers into major markets, then extract the precise customer requirements for each. However, the data base is not a prerequisite for collecting, organizing, and using information to understand your customers. You may choose to have these functions performed by teams in the senior staff, marketing department, or customer service department. You may decide to identify key measures of customer satisfaction for each requirement, then post results on these measures so that every employee knows how things are going. The critical factor is not the data base but the aggregation and use of all available customer information in a timely manner.

L.L. Bean can speak to the issue of timeliness. It used to do annual customer satisfaction surveys, but now conducts them monthly. "As a direct result of our involvement with the quality movement, customer focus has taken on a more significant role in our overall management," says Greg Sweeney, director of customer retention. "For example, we used to contact 9,000 customers by phone or mail. This year we had more than 100,000 contacts, and that number will grow with our new monthly customer satisfaction surveys."

The information fuels a new focus on customer-defined segmentation. "In the past, we had limited information about what we wanted to do—and we hoped the customer would go along with us," Sweeney says. "Now we are getting a better profile of our customers that allows us to develop better strategies to meet their needs."

Companies intent on staying close to their customers make it a point to factor information about dissatisfaction into the equation. L.L. Bean compiles all customer complaints and distributes that information within the company. "We have a Product Suggestion Report we use to note all comments, suggestions, and complaints, broken down by area," says Susan Dale, vice-president of customer satisfaction. "The report allows us to aggregate customer feedback from a variety of sources and get it to the people who can identify the root causes of any problems."

The company also asks customers to compare its performance to that of its competitors. "We monitor in absolute numbers how we're doing and how the competition is doing," says Sweeney, "then act on what we learn about our strengths and weaknesses."

Staples closely monitors indicators of customer dissatisfaction. Customer complaints and compliments are aggregated and reported weekly. Purchasing patterns are reported monthly. Its regional call center reports any negative feedback daily. Customer retention and defections are tracked through the customer data base and reported monthly. All these reports are distributed to senior and middle managers. In addition, Staples sends "mystery shoppers" to its stores, then reviews their findings with the individual store managers.

Looking back through this section at all the different types of customer information our role models collect, it is easy to agree with the statement by

Greg Lea of IBM that setting up such an information-gathering organization is hard work. Gone are the days when you can assume you know your customers' requirements. Xerox's Swaim talks about the "science" of understanding customer requirements: "A lot of times they can't tell us what problems they have in specific terms, only vaguely, so we must listen carefully and use our knowledge of their work processes, any new technologies, and our core competencies to guide us."

Know your customers. Know your business. Know yourself. The degree of knowledge in all three of these areas will shape your success.

USING CUSTOMER SATISFACTION TO DRIVE YOUR BUSINESS

In 1991 Louisville Redbirds management spent $300,000 to rebuild the stadium's concession stands. They have spent $1 million on the state-owned stadium since 1987. The latest changes were hardly imperative, since the old area was very good, with wide, clean halls and large, eye-catching signs, but the Redbirds are in the business of customer satisfaction. They made the ice cream stand bigger (so the kids could get back to the game faster), and they added closed circuit television (so the parents would not miss the action). Parents and their children are the Redbirds' target customers, and the Redbirds' business is satisfying those customers. General manager Dale Owens and his staff circulate at every home game, talking to customers to find out what they like and dislike, then using that information to make each game fun, safe, and memorable.

The Redbirds developed mascot Billy Bird to appeal to their young customers. Before Owens came along, the mascot was a beady-eyed cardinal that scared small children, which is not exactly the response you want. Owens hired one of this country's most popular mascots, the San Diego Chicken, to redesign Billy Bird (which is why the mascot now looks like a red chicken), and the children adore him. Three- and four-year-olds who are easily bored with baseball love Billy Bird. When he "leaves" in the seventh inning, he races up a ramp in centerfield, leaps onto a trampoline, and flips over the fence, then goes to the concession area to sign autographs and talk to fans.

The Redbirds also target parents. They hired a great rock-and-roll organist to play music that couples would like. They hire off-duty policemen to provide excellent security. They have a doctor on duty at the stadium for every game. Attendants check the bathrooms three times a night to make sure they are clean and well stocked. Such attention to details helps create a positive experience that brings customers back.

The Redbirds run a lot of contests to keep fans entertained during games. For example, if a Redbird player hits a grand slam home run on a Friday night, some lucky ticket holder wins $10,000. The team also holds promotions for 50 to 60 of its 72 home games. (By comparison, the Minnesota Twins have only 20 promotions over their 81-game home schedule.) For example, the Redbirds have Quarter Night, when everything costs a quarter and the Redbirds staff tapes quarters to 10,000 seats (which is as much work as it sounds). "I throw all of our promotions out every year, with a few exceptions," says Owens. "Typically, we determine next year's promotions, then match sponsors with them. There are thousands of companies you can approach about supporting these events."

The Redbirds' focus on satisfying its customers drives its business. According to Owens, the average minor league team run in the traditional way—with a few promotions, basic concessions, and the game itself as the sole entertainment—can make money drawing 250,000 people. In 1992 the Redbirds drew nearly 650,000 fans. "We run it as a community asset," Owens says. "We want to pass it on to the next generation of Louisville youth. And it also happens to be a way to make money."

Few companies have the luxury of focusing on customer satisfaction to the point where making money is almost an afterthought. Even though efforts to satisfy customers obviously cannot be allowed to wipe out a company's financial resources, improving customer satisfaction can still be the company's driving force. The Louisville Redbirds are making money. They could also make money while doing far less for their customers. They have chosen their course because they want satisfied customers. As a result, the Redbirds have a shared vision of what they wish to be—a company with a much sounder customer base, a strong competitive position in their marketplace, and a clear understanding of their customers' requirements. And they're making 650,000 customers happy in the process.

Owens and his staff get feedback from these customers at least 72 times a year, when the Redbirds play at home. They learn from them what works, what does not, and what they would like to see. Owens uses that knowledge to improve. He understands that customers' requirements constantly change—usually becoming more demanding—which is one reason the Redbirds offer a fresh slate of promotions each season and continually update their facilities.

Larger companies recognize the same dynamics at work in their customer base. "We believe that managing to satisfy customer requirements is a little like the hierarchy of needs," says Xerox's Swaim. "We look at the basics people expect to have, understanding that the line keeps going up." He gives an example. People expect Xerox to be easy to do business with. Two years ago the company began offering a customer satisfaction guarantee that basically said, "If you're not happy with a Xerox product, we'll replace it at your request with no hassle, period." Swaim says, "At the time, the guarantee was a differentiator, but now others are trying to follow, and it's becoming more of an expected service."

Xerox aggregates all the customer information it gathers (described in the previous section of this chapter) in a data base that is then used to generate customer satisfaction levels and trends. This information is updated weekly and reviewed during regular management meetings. Always one of the first topics on the agenda, customer satisfaction data are used to identify gaps and develop action plans that address them. The levels and trends are also communicated to employees. Control charts for overall customer satisfaction and the supporting internal process measures are prominently displayed on walls and in work areas throughout the organization, including the boardroom where the top management of U.S. Operations meets.

Of course, it is much easier to show trends when you can show them off:

- Xerox's overall customer satisfaction has improved more than 40% since 1985.
- In the category of low-volume copiers Xerox improved 33%, compared to a 16% improvement for its competitors.
- In the category of both mid- and high-volume copiers, Xerox is the leader.

Outside research companies confirm these trends and levels. At the same time adverse indicators, such as sales returns and accommodation adjustments, have declined.

IBM Rochester tracks customer satisfaction in six general categories it calls "customer satisfiers": administration, marketing/sales offerings, technical solutions, delivery, maintenance and service support, and image. Like Xerox, IBM Rochester recognizes that the items that satisfy a customer are constantly changing. "Image" only recently made the list when Rochester's information showed that its customers were factoring a company's image into their buying decisions. Other items, such as "ease of doing business," have become attributes a company is expected to have. "An element may be a satisfier today, but when everyone is doing it, it is no longer a satisfier; it is expected," says Lea. Figure 3.1 shows how customers' expectations (shown in the top block) combine with satisfiers to produce the "customer solution."

A different executive is in charge of each of these six areas. IBM Rochester's goal is to be the undisputed leader in all six. Under these general headings are 35 to 40 more specific satisfiers. Monthly customer surveys ask for input on all 35 to 40, except for those not valid for a particular customer. The executive team

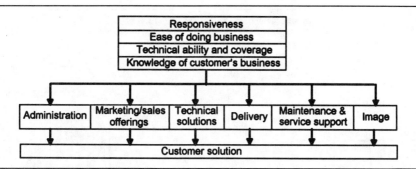

FIGURE 3.1. The customer's view of IBM Rochester. (Reprinted with permission of IBM Rochester.)

reviews the results monthly. If a particular area shows a potential problem, the executive in charge of the general satisfier establishes an action team to address it. Figure 3.2 shows how IBM Rochester uses customer satisfaction information to drive its business.

Hardware quality is a key quality indicator under the "technical solutions" satisfier indentified in Figure 3.1. The closed-loop process shown in Figure 3.2 follows six steps, beginning with the measurement of hardware quality:

Step 1:   Measure and benchmark the key quality indicator.

Step 2:   Prioritize the key elements that affect the indicator (Pareto analysis).

Step 3:   Use a leverage matrix to determine which elements to work on.

Step 4:   For each element you choose, perform a root cause analysis to identify the drivers of dissatisfaction or the satisfaction inhibitors. Choose the key drivers you will address.

Step 5:   Measure the driver and establish an improvement target.

Step 6:   Identify actions to reduce the driver defects. Assign owners to each action. Track the impact of the actions.

The process continues with measurement of the key quality indicator to gauge the effects of the improvement actions—the return to Step 1 that closes the loop.

By institutionalizing customer satisfaction, IBM Rochester steers an entire organization along a course charted by its customers. It acts on one agenda: *customer satisfaction.* It analyzes and improves its processes to improve performance in its six primary satisfiers. It is not in the business of making computers or servicing computers or selling solutions; *it is in the business of satisfying customers better than anyone else.* That is what it means to use customer satisfaction to drive your business.

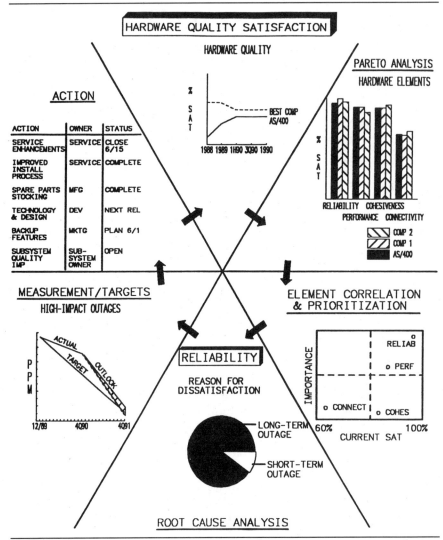

FIGURE 3.2. IBM Rochester's 6–step process for improving customer satisfaction. (Reprinted with permission of IBM Rochester.)

THE SHIFT IN THINKING

In the new management model, business begins with a *customer focus* and ends with *customer satisfaction*, which are two sides of the same coin. The customer requirements that you focus your business on are the same requirements you measure satisfaction on. Changes in customer satisfaction or requirements trigger changes in how you do business, which affects customer satisfaction.

The new management model is a closed loop system driven by customer satisfaction.

The remainder of the book demonstrates how the desire to satisfy customers translates into action. Companies that are accustomed to defining their activities by other criteria (such as departmental goals, financial targets, or quality measures) find that the shift in thinking to a total customer focus requires *deep-rooted cultural change*.

"What we are learning about customer requirements and satisfaction affects our measuring, planning, processes, results—our entire system," says IBM's Lea. "We saw a little of that in 1990 when we won the Baldrige Award, but we did not see all of the connections." As our models of excellence show, the closer a company gets to being customer driven, the clearer the connections are among all its actions—and the more efficiently and effectively the system operates.

4 STRATEGIC PLANNING

Zytec

Cadillac

Southern Pacific

The function of strategic planning in the new management model is to align all the efforts of the organization to customer satisfaction, quality, and operational performance goals. Deployed to its fullest, a world-class planning process would make it possible for all employees to match their tasks to specific company objectives, as the employees at Zytec, Cadillac, and Southern Pacific Transportation Company can do. All three companies use their strategic planning processes not only to align quality improvement activities within their organizations but to drive the whole improvement process.

Zytec calls its process (which is patterned after the Japanese *hoshin kanri*) management by planning. Cadillac states that its business plan is its quality plan. Southern Pacific chose its planning process as the primary vehicle for a dramatic turnaround. All blend business and quality planning into a single strategic plan.

MODELS OF EXCELLENCE

In this chapter we will show how Zytec, Cadillac, and Southern Pacific integrate quality and business planning and use their planning processes to align their business and quality improvement activities. Zytec designs and makes power supplies for the manufacturers of computer, medical, office, and testing equipment. It is also the largest power supply repair company in the United States. The company has more than 600 employees at two locations in Minnesota and one in California. At the company's first strategic planning meeting in the summer of 1984 its senior executives committed to follow the concepts of W. Edwards Deming as the basis for its drive for quality improvement. In 1991 Zytec won the Baldrige Award and the first Minnesota Quality Award.

Cadillac Motor Car Company is a division of General Motors North American Automotive Operations. A Baldrige Award winner in 1990, Cadillac earned quality recognition as early as 1908, when it was the first American company to win the prestigious Dewar Trophy. Cadillac's quality leadership declined in the early 1980s, but a reorganization in 1987 spurred a transformation built on three strategies: a cultural change; a constant focus on the customer; and a disciplined approach to planning.

Southern Pacific Transportation Company is the largest privately owned transportation company in the United States, with more than 23,000 employees in 15 states. It owns, operates, and maintains 15,000 miles of track in the West and Midwest. In 1869 Southern Pacific's parent, Central Pacific, helped drive the golden spike on a transcontinental railroad that served the needs of a growing country. Today Southern Pacific is using its strategic planning process to drive dramatic improvements in customer satisfaction.

We first introduce the planning processes of these companies separately to show how they work. We then examine the manner in which they address the following issues:

- Who is involved in the planning process?
- What data and information, including customer requirements and company capabilities, feed the planning process?
- How does the planning process address continuous improvement?
- How is the plan deployed throughout the company?
- How is the planning process improved?

ZYTEC: MANAGEMENT BY PLANNING

Zytec's long-range strategic planning process boils down to three steps:

1. Data are gathered.
2. Cross-functional teams set goals.
3. Departmental management-by-planning (MBP) teams implement the goals by developing detailed action plans.

Zytec gets most of its data from three sources: customer feedback (primarily on a factory-to-factory basis), formal and informal market research, and benchmarking. The data must be consistent from year to year, within the control of the area doing the collecting, and able to be presented using statistical methods. Examples of the types of data collected include:

- Customer on-time delivery
- Customer reliability (mean time between failures)
- Production cycle time
- Employee quality training
- Supplier dock-to-stock percentage

The planning cycle begins when senior management identifies the company's strategic issues. Each issue is assigned to strategic planning groups in marketing, technology, manufacturing, materials, the product renewal center, and corporate administration. Each strategic planning group consists of eight to ten employees from throughout the company. Over a three-month period, the groups research their issues using the data that have been collected and interviews with internal experts, customers, and suppliers, then prepare reports that identify what has been examined and lay out a five-year plan.

The reports are discussed at two off-site, one-day planning meetings attended by all managers, all exempt employees, representatives of the rest of the work force, customers, and suppliers. In 1992 more than 200 people participated in these meetings. Following the meetings, a consensus document is written that identifies Zytec's long-range (five-year) goals. The people who attended the meetings share the results with and request reactions from employees, major customers, and key suppliers who did not attend.

When agreement is reached on the company's vision, which is Zytec's long-range strategic plan (LRSP), attention turns to short-term planning. *At this point the company's strategic planning process translates its vision into action plans.* Senior management uses the LRSP to set broad corporate objectives for the company to address. For 1993 Zytec's objectives were to:

1. Improve the quality of products and services to become a Six Sigma company by 1995
2. Reduce total cycle time
3. Improve service to customers
4. Reduce the cost of products and services to improve profitability

With these objectives and the LRSP as their guide, MBP teams in every operating department develop their departmental objectives for the year and create detailed action plans with measurable and specific monthly goals. "We're getting the people closest to the processes involved in setting goals for what those processes produce," says Doug Tersteeg, director of quality, reliability, safety, and employee development. Tersteeg adds that Zytec's internal yield of power supplies since implementation of the management-by-planning process has risen from 65% to 92%.

The MBP teams complete a standardized matrix to show how they have translated corporate objectives into team objectives and measurements. They use a standardized action plan to identify activity steps, resources required, measures, and time of completion. The standardization of these techniques, combined with a common set of problem-solving tools all employees have been trained to use, keeps everyone in the company on the same path toward shared goals.

To prevent conflicts between departments, senior executives play "catchball" with the MBP teams. "Catchball" involves meeting with the teams to exchange information and negotiate specific objectives and actions that fit with those of the other teams and with the LRSP. The senior staff then signs off on the teams' objectives, plans, and measurements. Zytec then establishes detailed department budgets, staffing plans, and capital plans to support the objectives.

After the plan is implemented, all departments review their measurements and action plans with senior management monthly. These meetings reinforce interest in and support for the departments' efforts to improve quality while giving management an opportunity to help departments that are not performing according to plan.

After completing the LRSP process, Zytec asks participants how each major step in the process could be improved. Senior management evaluates the suggestions and initiates changes for the next planning cycle. The feedback has generated continuous improvement: increasing the number of employees participating in the process, bringing customers and suppliers into the process, and expanding training to give employees more tools for meeting their objectives.

CADILLAC: BUSINESS PLANNING PROCESS

Once a week Cadillac's Detroit-Hamtramck assembly center shuts down completely for a half-hour plant meeting, during which an employee reviews the plant's performance to its annual plan. The review reinforces the employees' understanding of the division's and plant's business (read *quality*) plan, as do the single-page daily progress sheets that track six key indicators. It is all part of a strategic planning process Cadillac calls "Aligning the Arrows."

In its Baldrige Award–winning application, Cadillac Motor Car Company wrote, "At Cadillac, the Business Plan is the Quality Plan." The business planning process spurs quality improvement at Cadillac because:

1. It drives an *annual review* of the division's mission and strategic objectives to make sure they are aligned with the business environment and the mission of General Motors.

2. It guides the development and implementation of *key processes* such as simultaneous engineering and the labor/management quality network.

3. It builds *discipline* into the ongoing process of creating and achieving short- and long-term quality improvement goals.

Figure 4.1 illustrates Cadillac's planning process. The planning process begins every June when the executive staff reviews current objectives to make sure they are aligned with corporate objectives. The staff then gathers relevant data from throughout the organization to assess Cadillac's strengths and weaknesses. The data include benchmarking of competitive products and processes used by world-class companies. Key suppliers and dealers also contribute to the planning process.

On the basis of this situational analysis, the executive staff proposes business objectives for the next year. In 1992 Cadillac had 29 business objectives in six major areas: leadership, people, quality, customer satisfaction, cost, and speed to market. The proposed objectives are reviewed across the division, and the feedback generated by this review is used to develop the final business objectives. The executive staff shares the objectives with top union and management leaders of the company and division at the business planning kickoff meeting.

Now it is up to the functional staffs, plant quality councils, and human resource management to develop goals and action plans that support the business objectives. "Just about everybody in Cadillac gets involved in this process," says William Lesner, superintendent of manufacturing. "Plants and departments come up with their own plans to meet the division's plans." The executive staff reviews all plans for alignment and adequacy. In December the entire business plan is presented to all Cadillac employees at the annual state-of-the-business meeting. Implementation begins in January.

For example, Cadillac identified three business objectives for quality in its 1991 plan. The first, labeled Q1, was: "Cadillac will continuously improve the quality of our processes, products, and services." The Detroit-Hamtramck assembly center developed five goals to achieve this objective (all labeled Q1 also):

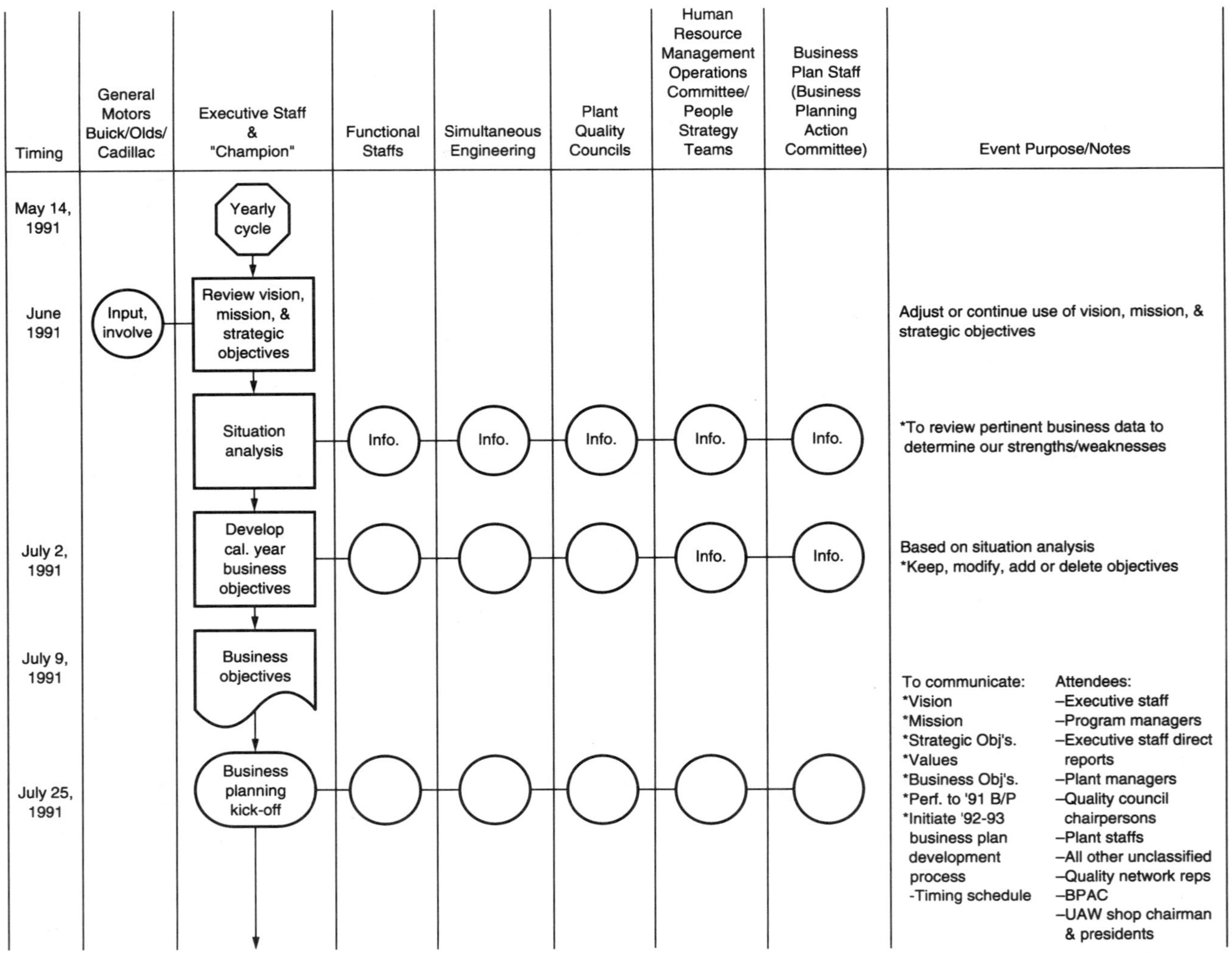

FIGURE 4.1. **Cadillac planning process model.**

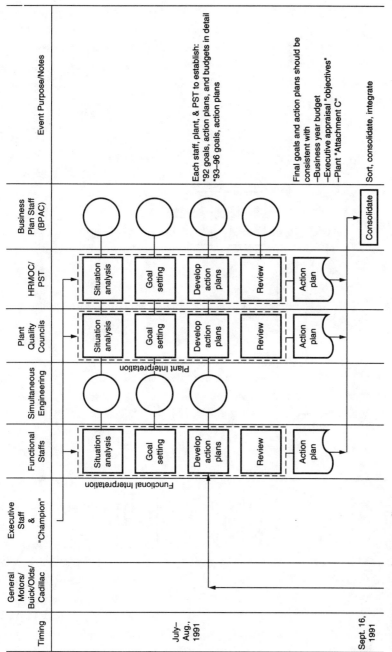

FIGURE 4.1. (continued)

55

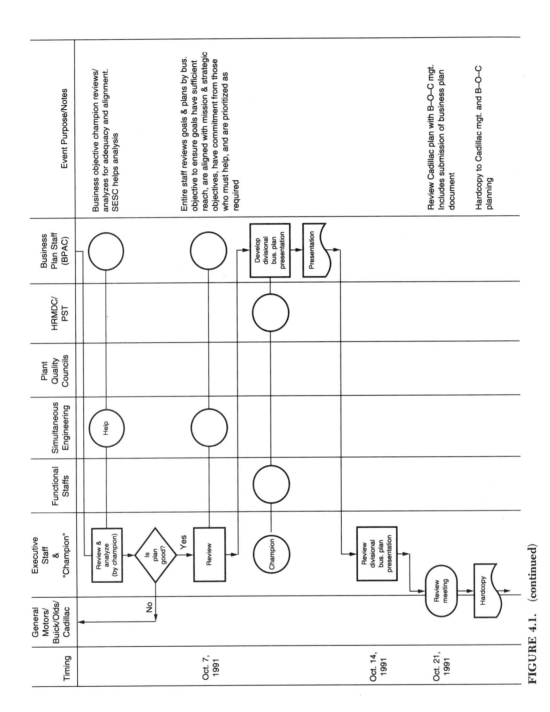

FIGURE 4.1. (continued)

56

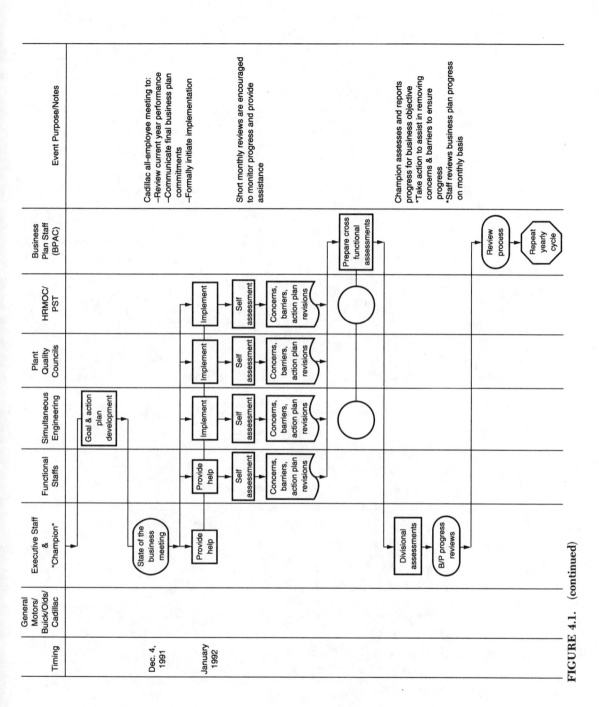

FIGURE 4.1. (continued)

57

Detroit-Hamtramck will:

- Continually improve first-time quality through the Quality Planning process.
- Achieve greater awareness and responsiveness to internal customer expectations.
- Continually implement the approved Quality Network action strategies.
- Expand implementation of the Pull System throughout general assembly and Allanté.
- Establish a Level Schedule Index (LSI) to measure variation in scheduling of vehicles to assembly.

The Detroit-Hamtramck plant simplified its 1992 plan to focus more on fewer key goals and measures. Every day, management distributes a single-page handout: On one side of the page are Cadillac's vision, mission, and business objectives and the plant's vision and problem-solving process, and on the other are six critical measures. The first five minutes of each day's quality audit meeting are spent reviewing three of the critical measures: two measures for daily audits and one for daily production. Weekly team meetings include reviews of progress on the business plan. Monthly division management meetings focus on performance relative to the business plan. "All plant objectives are on a wall at headquarters," says Lesner, "with different-colored circles showing their status. During the meeting, champions from the executive staff have to explain the current status and what's being done to achieve the objectives."

By using a variety of communication tools to keep its key goals and measures in front of people, Cadillac focuses everyone's efforts on activities that contribute to achieving its business objectives.

SOUTHERN PACIFIC: STRATEGIC PLANNING

In May 1991 the senior staff at Southern Pacific Transportation Company heard the results of the company's first-ever customer satisfaction survey. Only a few months earlier Southern Pacific had initiated an aggressive quality improvement process. The company's leadership hoped the survey would tell them what they needed to focus on first.

The answer was *everything*. Of 17 critical areas Southern Pacific finished last compared to its competitors in all but one. The results did not surprise anyone; the company had embraced quality improvement because it was losing $100 million a year and was one of only two large railroads that did not have a formal improvement process in place. However, it did solidify management's commitment to a complete and rapid cultural change.

Eighteen months later Southern Pacific's customer survey showed the company moving toward the top in all 17 areas. Customer displeasure had turned into customer delight—and the annual loss had turned into a profit—because of the company's quality improvement process. And the basis of that process is strategic planning.

The process is managed by a quality steering committee consisting of Southern Pacific's senior executive staff and a few others. Beginning in mid-June, the steering committee develops the company's strategic plan for the next five years. Data and information upon which the plan is based come from throughout the system and include:

- Southern Pacific's mission
- Current and future customer needs
- Levels of customer satisfaction
- Benchmarking
- Government regulations
- Local needs
- Environmental issues
- An analysis of current performance

The five-year strategy for 1993 focused on nine key areas:

1. Continuous improvement in ability to meet or exceed customer requirements
2. Continuous growth of revenues
3. Improvement of revenue collections
4. Continuous reduction in the cost of nonconformance
5. Strengthening of operation effectiveness
6. Improvement of asset utilization
7. Improvement of safety
8. Development of human resources
9. Establishment of a management system focused on continuous quality improvement

Figure 4.2 is a flowchart overview of Southern Pacific's quality improvement process.

The steering committee meets four times with department managers to discuss and finalize the strategies, corporate objectives that will improve quality and performance in each of these areas, action plans for each objective that in-

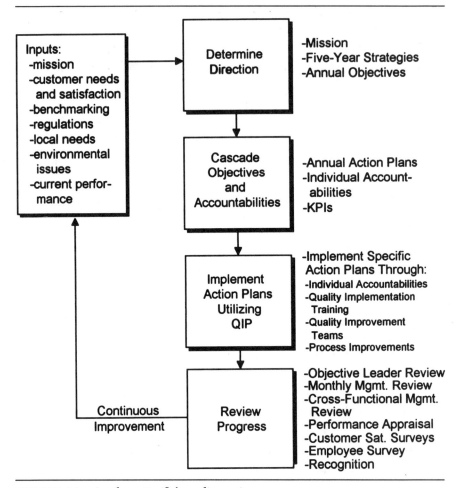

FIGURE 4.2.   Southern Pacific's quality review process.

clude accountabilities and delivery dates, and key performance indicators (KPIs) that will measure progress on the objectives. The plan is organized to show the logical progression from strategies to objectives to action plan to KPIs. Each corporate objective is assigned to corporate officers for accountability. Each item on the action plan lists the department, team, or people responsible for getting it done. Each key performance indicator that is represented numerically includes starting, baseline, and target figures. Figure 4.3 provides a segment of a plan showing strategy, objectives, action plans, and KPIs.

The plan is reviewed with middle management and union leadership at a two-day meeting. "The meeting is designed to allow everyone to review and react to the overall plan," says Kent Sterett, executive vice-president of qual-

"Road to '93"
Action Plan Summary

5-Year Plan Strategy: Establish a Management System Focused on Continuous Quality Improvement.			
"Road to '93" Objective: 9C1. Encourage Our Employees to Contribute to Continuous Improvement.			
"Road to '93" Objective Leader(s): Dept. Heads*, W.K. Sterett			
Problem/Opportunity Statement: Ensure 50% of All Employees Have Received Some Training in the Quality Improvement Process.			
Causes:			

Action	Schedule Date:	Completion Date:	Who?
ACT			
• Develop and distribute first quarter training schedule.	11/15/91	11/15/91	QID/HR
• Complete first quarter training schedule.	12/13/91	12/13/91	Dept Hds
PLAN			
• Cascade corporate training objective and course offerings.	1/15/92	1/20/92	QID/HR
• Provide up-to-date report on those trained in QIP.	1/15/92	1/20/92	QID/HR
• Identify training needs and develop department training plan.	2/10/92		Dept Hds
• Identify instructor candidates.	TBD		Dept Hds
DO			
• Develop and distribute second quarter training schedule.	2/15/92	2/18/92	QID/HR
• Ensure employees attend courses when scheduled.	Ongoing		Dept Hds
• Develop and distribute third quarter training schedule.	5/15/92	5/15/92	QID/HR
• Develop and distribute fourth quarter training schedule.	8/15/92		QID/HR
• Train instructors.	TBD		QID/HR
CHECK			
• Monitor quarterly progress (plan vs. actual) and provide feedback to Department Heads.	2/15/92 5/15/92 8/15/92 12/15/92	2/18/92	QID/HR
• Monitor quality of courses and instructors.	Ongoing	Ongoing	QID/HR
ACT			
• Adjust quarterly training plan based on plan vs. actual reports.	2/15/92 5/15/92 8/15/92	2/18/92 5/15/92 8/27/92	Dept Hds
• Identify 1993 training needs.	10/15/92		Dept Hds

Key Performance Indicators	Baseline 1991	Target 1992
9C1. % of Employees Trained in QIP	6.5%	50%

FIGURE 4.3. Action plan summary.

ity. "All senior managers are involved in the presentation, and there are also presentations by first-level quality teams and a customer."

Following the meeting, the quality department assembles a package that includes a video synopsis of the information presented at the meeting, along with supporting slides and written material. *Approximately 150 managers and*

50 union leaders use this package to cascade the strategies to all management employees, an effort that involves several hundred meetings across the entire system. "They sit down with their folks and say, 'Here's what we learned. Here's how the rest of it fits together. And here's what we're going to do in the next year at this location,'" says Sterett.

The meetings are completed by Christmas. By the end of January every Southern Pacific manager knows what his or her area is doing that year to achieve the company's objectives—which is good, because in February Southern Pacific's senior executives visit major work locations to find out how the plan is being implemented. They expect to see measures up on the wall and to hear about specific actions being taken by the 60 to 70 managers invited to make presentations.

For the rest of the year the senior staff reviews progress on the corporate objectives on a monthly basis. This is possible because there are timely data to work with. For example, service reliability is an ongoing measure available on demand, while another measure, accidents, are reported to headquarters from anywhere in the system within 24 hours. The collected data are interpreted for senior management in an extensive report that includes a general overview of the percentage of KPIs achieved and changes in KPIs from the previous month, and a specific performance report for each individual KPI. And next to every KPI is the name of the senior executive responsible for the related corporate objective. "This clear accountability not only encourages the rate of improvement but the velocity of improvement as well," says Sterett.

Southern Pacific refines its planning process annually by surveying participants down to the department level to find out what worked well and what could be done better. The chief financial and quality officers use this input to recommend improvements in the planning process for the coming year.

WHOM TO INVOLVE IN STRATEGIC PLANNING

At Zytec, Cadillac, and Southern Pacific, senior management initiates the planning process. Leaders are responsible for identifying strategies that reflect their company's long-range vision, which typically reaches five years into the future. *They develop those strategies with input from people throughout the company, primarily from managers and from finance and sales and marketing, although teams, departments, and work units may also contribute. They may get feedback from key customers and suppliers.*

Once the corporate strategies and objectives have been determined, the planning process involves more employees. Departments, teams, and work units must translate the corporate vision into specific goals, action plans, and measures. The more employees involved in the process, both in developing and carrying out the strategic plan, the greater the understanding and deployment.

The completed plan may be circulated among major customers and suppliers for their input. The advantage of involving external people in the process is one of *alignment:* You are sure the plan reflects what your customers need and expect and what your suppliers are able to provide and support.

Once the plan has been implemented, managers and employees report progress on action plans and objectives. The employees participate in the reporting process as members of teams that work on related issues or as representatives of their departments.

WHAT DATA AND INFORMATION TO USE

As with any decision a company must make, the better the data and information available to understand the situation and evaluate options, the better the decision—in this case, what to focus the company's resources on—will be.

The data come from many sources, which may include the following:

- Customer service, sales, and marketing functions usually report on customer satisfaction and current and future needs.
- The human resources department describes what talent and skills are available to achieve the company's vision and how those talents and skills can be enhanced through involvement, training, and reward and recognition.
- The quality and finance departments outline the company's condition and the resources available for the coming year.
- Other departments may provide relevant data on such areas as environmental issues, government regulations, process capabilities, and supplier capabilities.
- Ongoing teams formed to address major issues or problems summarize their progress and their needs and expectations for the year ahead.

The data they provide include performance on key measures over the past year, the results of competitive comparisons and benchmarking studies, survey results, and their perceptions and ideas about current and future capabilities.

Senior executives and others involved in developing the plan use all these data to establish corporate goals, objectives, strategies, action plans, and key indicators. Data collected on the key indicators during the year are used to evaluate progress on the plan. For example, Southern Pacific publishes a monthly report that shows how the company is doing on all its key performance indicators for the year. Senior management can immediately see where improvements are being made and where help may be needed.

ADDRESSING CONTINUOUS IMPROVEMENT

The best strategic plans include specific measures for achieving every objective, a means for gathering and publishing data on these measures, and a process for timely review by management. It is critical to identify, collect, and use the right data; otherwise, continuous improvement on the company's most important areas cannot be made.

At Zytec, Cadillac, and Southern Pacific, the strategic plans focus the organizations' resources on a few key processes. Key indicators for these processes include current levels and targets for the end of the next year. Progress on the indicators is communicated regularly and frequently:

- Cadillac's Detroit/Hamtramck plant distributes a page of graphs showing daily performance on six critical measures, discusses three of those measures at daily quality audit meetings, and reviews progress on the business plan at weekly team and plant meetings and at monthly division management meetings.

- Zytec's and Southern Pacific's senior management reviews all key indicators and action plans monthly. At Zytec, departments track performance on their key measures and report progress at the monthly meetings. Southern Pacific has senior executives accountable for each of its key indicators.

As someone once said, "What gets paid attention to, gets done." Many companies find that just posting trend charts in a department immediately improves performance because people naturally want to see that their efforts are making a positive impact. By assigning responsibility for moving those trends in the right direction, a company institutionalizes continuous improvement on those areas considered most important to the company.

Deploying the Plan

The most effective strategic plan would be so well implemented that every task performed by every employee would support one or more corporate objectives. And the connections would be traceable. And the employees would understand the connections.

As our quality role models show, world-class planning processes are only half over when the plan is complete. The second half is turning plans into action. This involves identifying the steps necessary to achieve the objectives at a corporate, division, department, work unit, team, and individual level. It is not a particularly mysterious or difficult process, but it does require a deployment process for each level to translate corporate goals and objectives into action items and an evaluation process for management to monitor performance and assist those units that are having trouble.

At Zytec the plan is deployed by MBP teams using a standard matrix and action plan to show the translation of corporate objectives into team objectives, measurements, and actions. Cadillac translates corporate and division objectives into plant objectives, then uses a few visible, broad measures to focus everyone's attention on what is critical. Southern Pacific cascades the corporate plan throughout the organization by having 200 managers and union leaders discuss the plan with all Southern Pacific managers, who are then responsible for identifying and tracking relevant measures at their facilities.

Deployment is complete when management checks to make sure plans are in place at the local level to accomplish the corporate objectives. This is done primarily through monthly senior staff meetings at all three companies.

Improving the Planning Process

All three models for this chapter can point to improvements in their planning processes because they solicited input from those involved, through either feedback sessions or surveys. Zytec asks for feedback after each major step in its planning process; Southern Pacific conducts an annual survey when the process has been completed. Senior management analyzes the information and incorporates changes into the next planning cycle.

THE SHIFT IN THINKING

Early in their quality improvement process many companies attempt to do quality planning separately from business planning. *This doesn't work.* Baldrige Award–winner Marlow Industries (profiled in Chapter 2) is quick to point out the mistake it made by trying to have two structures, one for quality and the other for the rest of their business. "We kept moving quality into the business area," says Chris Witzke, chief operating officer, "until now we can't make any distinction. We make quality part of our business by integrating it into our business plan."

Leading companies affirm Cadillac's claim that "the business plan is the quality plan." Treating the two as separate entities suggests to employees that quality exists outside the rest of the business, that they can work on quality over here and everything else over there. Senior executives create an environment for continuous improvement by demonstrating that quality is inherent in *everything* that *every* employee does.

Leading companies also show that the planning process can benefit from a wide variety of inputs. They involve more employees in the process, which typically involves additional training and is another method of increasing employee involvement. Some invite customers and suppliers to participate, which improves both customer satisfaction and supplier quality. They pull in a host of data and information to make sure they understand their customers' needs and their companies' capabilities. These inputs produce a plan that accurately reflects the real world, with goals and objectives that everyone in the company can support. As a result, efforts to improve processes can center on those that are identified as most important to the company.

Finally, leading companies have proven that the strategic planning process can be used to coordinate and fuel rapid quality improvement. Southern Pacific has been able to attack a number of quality issues on several fronts because it has a unified plan. Key performance indicators measure progress on action plans that address corporate objectives derived from nine key areas most important to the company's success. Employees know what is important—to the company, to their departments and teams, and to themselves.

The alignment of activities through the strategic planning process makes it possible for a company of any size to focus all its resources on the strategies and objectives that are critical to its success.

5 MANAGEMENT

Ritz-Carlton Hotel Company

Motorola

Engelhard-Huntsville

Since 1988, when Motorola won the first Baldrige Award, its people have given thousands of speeches about how Motorola became and remains a successful company, the "big company that acts like a small company," as some have called it. The standard presentation includes a slide that states:

We have been successful because of our management process.

There is no vacillation here, no all-encompassing list of reasons Motorola succeeds. It is the management process. Put simply, Motorola's process is:

1. Have a set of metrics.
2. Determine results.
3. Pick a problem.
4. Address the problem.
5. Analyze the solution.
6. Move on.

The process is far from earthshaking. "This is no magic solution," says Paul Noakes, vice-president and director of external quality programs for Motorola and the man responsible for a good portion of those speeches. "The basic tools are there for everyone to use. The rest is a management process."

How you manage your company—your system, your quality improvement process—determines your success. Such a statement sounds so obvious it is almost trite, but somewhere between thinking it and actually believing it lies a wall of disclaimers. Management is the key *except* when competition is unfair. Management is the key *except* when employees don't do their jobs. Management is the key *except* when the market goes bad. Motorola accepts no exceptions. "If we don't make a goal," says Noakes, "we've learned it's because management isn't involved enough in the process."

This chapter focuses on managing the quality improvement process. It will look at how three successful organizations convert their customers' and company's requirements into goals and standards for their managers, supervisors, and other employees. The processes they have developed respond to three critical management questions:

- How do we translate our customer focus and quality values into requirements for our managers, supervisors, and other employees?
- How do we communicate these requirements throughout the organization?
- How do we make sure the requirements are being met?

As we answer these questions, we will try to pin down the changing roles of managers and supervisors. The new business management model has not been kind to old-style bosses, the type who would have bluntly answered our questions with one simple command: "Do it." With the advent of total quality management, managers and supervisors have had to learn how to listen to their subordinates, encourage their feedback, support their initiatives, persuade rather than demand, coach, train, facilitate, and serve. This is not the job many envisioned. As if these expectations were not enough, the specter of "self-directed work teams" threatens to eliminate their jobs altogether.

All this seems to suggest a contradiction: If the key to success is the management process, what exactly should management be doing? Answers to that question appear in this chapter and in every other chapter in this book. Managers need to understand the *system* in which they work and for which they are responsible. They need to tune that system to customer requirements and get every person and process they are responsible for humming the same tune.

And no, they cannot do it with a glare and a threat.

MODELS OF EXCELLENCE

The Ritz-Carlton Hotel Company is a management company based in Atlanta that develops and operates luxury hotels for W. B. Johnson Properties. The company operates 23 business and resort hotels in the United States and two hotels in Australia. It also has nine international sales offices and two subsidiary products: restaurants and banquets. It employs 11,500 people. The Ritz-Carlton Hotel Company targets primarily industry executives, meeting and corporate travel planners, and prestigious travelers. In 1991 the company received 121 quality-related awards and industry-best rankings by major hotel-rating organizations. In 1992 Ritz-Carlton won the Baldrige Award.

Motorola is one of the world's leading providers of electronic equipment, systems, components, and services for worldwide markets. Its products include two-way radios, pagers, cellular telephones, semiconductors, and automotive and industrial electronics. Motorola employs more than 100,000 people in facilities around the world. In 1988 Motorola won the first Malcolm Baldrige National Quality Award.

Engelhard-Huntsville is a major manufacturer of catalytic parts for controlling air emissions from automobiles, forklifts, and stationary pollution sources. It also produces silver chemicals. Engelhard invented catalytic converters in the early 1970s and built a plant in Huntsville, Alabama, to manufacture them. By the early 1980s productivity and quality were so bad the plant was close to being shut down. Today the Huntsville plant's 270 employees proudly point to their dramatic productivity gains, incredible safety record, and low turnover rate as indicators of their success. Among the many quality awards and citations it has received, two of the most notable are the Ford Total Quality Excellence award (only eight of Ford's 3,300 suppliers have won this award) and the United States Senate Award for Productivity, which it won in 1991.

MAKING THE SYSTEM HUM

Leadership sets the company's values. Customers tell you what to focus on. Strategic planning converts quality values and customer requirements into company goals. And the system stands ready to pursue those goals. But first the *goals* must be translated into *requirements* that rivet the attention of all employees on the specific improvements they can and must make. Without these shared requirements, clearly communicated and reviewed for progress, the system is out of sync, clanking and wheezing instead of humming along with continuous improvement.

The primary methods our role models use to make their systems hum are:

- Set challenging goals.
- Develop action plans to pursue those goals.
- Train people to achieve the goals.

Motorola: Setting "Stretch" Goals

Motorola is a very goal-oriented company. In 1987 it announced aggressive corporate quality goals:

- 10 times improvement by 1989
- 100 times improvement by 1991
- Six Sigma performance by 1992 (Six Sigma roughly equates to 3.4 defects per million opportunities)

Such ambitious goals clearly define the level of improvement that Motorola expects from every business unit, division, department, work team, and individual in the company. "I believe the fundamental reason total quality management fails is because no level of expectations has been set," says Noakes. "You need *results* or people will get disillusioned—and that includes management."

Motorola has produced results: From 1987 to 1992 its cumulative savings from quality improvement was $3.15 billion—and the company had done little in the nonmanufacturing areas, where its data suggested it could save another billion dollars. Over the same period, sales increased 126% and sales per employee increased 100%, while the number of employees increased only 13.3%. This translates into an average increase in employee productivity of 12.2% per year.

To achieve these goals, Motorola changed its system. Keki Bhote, senior corporate consultant on quality and productivity for Motorola, listed the changes in an article in *National Productivity Review:*

- Reducing the number of managerial and supervisory layers and increasing spans of control.
- Organizing to a more manageable size to build teamwork and give employees a greater sense of control.
- Integrating related functions to break down artificial department walls and overcome the "vertical silo" syndrome.
- Changing the organization's traditional role of policing to that of coaching.
- Enhancing every standard, expectation, process, and system in a few businesses that have now become the models for others to follow.
- Making quality the first order of attention on meeting agendas, reviews, plans, compensation, and rewards.

Notice that every change affected the way in which managers and supervisors managed the process. The fundamental change in Motorola's system was to redefine management's roles and responsibilities. Only then could the management process achieve the company's "stretch" goals.

Motorola's current "stretch" goal is ten times improvement in quality every two years, which works out to a 68% annual improvement in whatever is being measured. Managers and supervisors are expected to reduce the amount of defects in the products and services for which they are responsible by 68% this year. Then they must do it again next year, and the year after that. They are also expected to reduce cycle times by ten times in five years—approximately 40% per year. Through clearly defined goals Motorola focuses the efforts of its managers, supervisors, and other employees on *five initiatives* that capture the company's customer focus and quality values:

- Six Sigma quality.
- Total cycle time reduction.
- Product, manufacturing, and environmental leadership.
- Profit improvement.
- Empowerment for all in a participative, cooperative, and creative workplace.

Ritz-Carlton: Striving for "Gold Standards"

By comparison, the Ritz-Carlton Hotel Company translates customer requirements into employee requirements through its Gold Standards and its strategic planning process. The Gold Standards include a credo, motto, three steps of service, and 20 "Ritz-Carlton basics." The credo states:

> The Ritz-Carlton Hotel is a place where the genuine care and comfort of our guests is our highest mission. We pledge to provide the finest personal service and facilities for our guests who will always enjoy a warm, relaxed yet refined ambiance. The Ritz-Carlton experience enlivens the senses, instills well-being, and fulfills even the unexpressed wishes and needs of our guests.

The company's motto is: "We are ladies and gentlemen serving ladies and gentlemen," and its three steps of service are:

1. A warm and sincere greeting. Use the guest name, if and when possible.
2. Anticipation and compliance with guest needs.
3. Fond farewell. Give them a warm good-bye and use their names, if and when possible.

The 20 "basics" include understanding and following the credo, motto, and three steps, and other requirements.

Employees are expected to adhere to these standards, which describe processes for solving problems guests may have as well as detailed grooming, housekeeping, and safety and efficiency standards. "We've taken the things our customers want most and come up with the simplest ways to provide them," says Patrick Mene, corporate director of quality. "And then we continuously emphasize them. We define our employees' behavior." The Ritz-Carlton's data show that its employees' understanding of the Gold Standards is directly correlated with guest satisfaction.

Ritz-Carlton employees are charged with mastering the basics first, then improving. The requirements for improving are set through the strategic planning process. Teams that include corporate leaders, managers, and employees set objectives and devise action plans, which the corporate steering company reviews. Quality goals draw extensively on customer requirements determined by travel industry research and the company's customer reaction data, focus groups, and surveys.

Employees also determine and respond to customer requirements at the individual level because, as Mene points out, "this is a highly personal, individual service." Ritz-Carlton's 11,500 employees are trained to read customers' reactions and to detect their likes and dislikes. "You're fully deploying customer reaction detection," says Mene. Customer likes are documented on a simple piece of paper and entered in a computerized guest history profile that provides information on the preferences of 240,000 repeat Ritz-Carlton guests. "When the customer returns, we know his or her personal preferences, which are distributed to the employees providing the service," Mene says. "What's unique is that employees correct and use customer reaction data to deliver premium service at the individual level. Our business management system is almost driven by the individual employees, running the business at the lowest levels."

If an employee detects a dislike, he or she is empowered to break away from the routine and take immediate positive action, to "move heaven and earth" to satisfy the customer. Any employee can spend up to $2,000 on the spot to make the customer happy. Or the employee can call on any other employee to assist. The Ritz-Carlton refers to this as "lateral service." Such a system depends on trained, empowered, and involved employees, which is why the Ritz-Carlton is careful to hire perceptive people, define their behavior, and train them to serve. With more than a million customer contacts on a busy day, the Ritz-Carlton understands that its customer and quality requirements must be driven by each individual employee.

Engelhard-Huntsville: Aiming for "Exceptional Quality"

Both Motorola and the Ritz-Carlton use formal processes to translate customer requirements and quality values into requirements for managers, supervisors, and other employees. The scope of their operations demands goals, action plans, and performance reviews for the companies to make sure their requirements are being deployed and met. At Engelhard's Huntsville operation, customer requirements and quality values are converted into employee requirements through its Quality Operating System, which includes measures and requirements for three areas identified as customer focus, internal focus, and prevention focus. However, the size of the Huntsville plant makes it easier for managers and supervisors to communicate, review performance on, and help meet these requirements. Leadership deploys its customer and quality requirements by giving clear direction about what is expected, serving as examples of what customer service and quality improvement mean, and promoting training.

Engelhard's version of total quality management is called *Exceptional Quality*. The entire plant has been trained in Exceptional Quality, which formalized what Huntsville had been doing since the mid-1980s. There are twelve principles that support the commitment to EQ, including pledges to be flexible and adaptable, work together, train and empower each other, encourage innovation, and promote long-term relationships with customers, suppliers, and fellow employees. The twelfth principle is a pledge to "provide management support and accountability for the quality commitment and principles through direction, example, and appropriate resource commitment."

The Huntsville operation knows from experience that management is key to success. When Joseph Steinreich became general manager of the plant in 1981, it had 590 employees. In 1982 they filed 82 grievances and lost 22 work days because of accidents. Turnover was at 150% per year. Eighteen percent of its products were being wasted because of poor quality. Not surprisingly, the plant was losing money. Engelhard gave Steinreich six months to turn things around or the plant would be closed.

Steinreich began by ditching the plant's confrontational management style. He instituted a supervisor training program to foster a more people-oriented management culture. Managers and supervisors changed or were replaced. "We focused on skill building, on how to get along and solve problems," says Carl English, human resources manager.

Ten years later, employees recognize the dramatic changes that have occurred. Asked to list the changes during recent training sessions, employees came up with more than 500, only two of which were negative. Many items on the list described how the new management style has contributed to the operation's success, such as "management is concerned about everything," "people will listen to you," "a good job is recognized," and "we're partners with each other and with our customers and suppliers."

And Engelhard-Huntsville *has* been successful:

- Turnover has been reduced from 150% to less than 3% annually.
- Waste has dropped from 18% to less than 1% of total product.
- Rework has been cut from 12% to 0.5%.
- Productivity has increased 324%. The plant produces more than 40,000 catalysts a year per employee, compared to slightly more than 8,000 in 1980.
- Not one work day has been lost because of an accident in nine years (nearly 4.5 million labor-hours).
- The plant provides 70% of the automotive catalysts for the Japanese market.
- From October 1990 to October 1992, the plant shipped more than 9 million catalysts to Ford without a single defect.

Engelhard-Huntsville has achieved these successes by setting specific requirements through its Quality Operating System and by empowering its managers, supervisors, and other employees to meet these requirements. As we will describe in the next section, it also uses training to translate customer requirements and quality values into requirements for its employees, then relies on frequent communication through meetings and personal contact to clarify and reinforce these requirements.

COMMUNICATING REQUIREMENTS THROUGHOUT THE COMPANY

When asked how to manage quality, the first thing Joe Steinreich says is, "Set an example." As the man responsible for initiating the turnaround at Engelhard's Hunstville operation, Steinreich knows how important it is for managers and supervisors to exemplify the attitudes and behaviors they wish to encourage.

For example, Steinreich meets with his staff weekly. At one of these meetings every month, he asks five "monthly EQ (Exceptional Quality) questions" he carries with him on a laminated card the size of a credit card:

1. What are you personally doing to improve EQ?
2. What are your plans for improving the work climate in your area?
3. What are your plans for empowering your people?
4. What have you identified that needs to be fixed and how can I help you fix it?
5. What successes have you had with EQ in your area?

"I go around the table and ask each person to respond," says Steinreich. "After I answer them first." In this way Steinreich communicates what is important to him as a leader and to his operation. The managers take the five questions to their direct reports, cascading the requirements throughout the organization.

Steinreich also communicates directly, frequently, with employees. Every quarter he meets with all employees to discuss the state of the business, which includes customer requirements and quality issues. In addition to these meetings, Steinreich and one of his human resources department managers conduct 16 to 18 roundtable meetings each year. "We select a group of hourly people to participate, and they always ask their co-workers what they want or need to know" says Steinreich. "We meet for lunch or dinner. I talk briefly about the state of the company, then we go around the table for discussion and questions. If we can't answer a question, we write it up and post the answer."

Employees make a habit of checking bulletin boards. "We do a lot of communicating," says Carl English, human resources manager. "A well-run company communicates well. We have about 40 new postings every month on customers coming to the plant, recognition, promotion, policy statements, company stock prices and general information." Every new posting has a blue "NEW" sticker on it to catch employees' attention.

Another form of communication helps managers and supervisors understand what employees go through to meet their requirements. The program is called "Working with the Folks." Once a month, managers and supervisors work with people in the plant for two to four hours. "You get a new appreciation for the lack of control workers must face," says English. The work takes place in noisy, dusty areas, in jobs where all you do is lift fragile ceramic substrates off conveyors and place them on another conveyor or in a box. "Working with the Folks" helps managers and supervisors see their requirements in a different light.

Engelhard-Huntsville emphasizes working together to satisfy customers and achieve goals. It teaches employees how to contribute ideas and get along with their supervisors, peers, and subordinates in a training course called "Working." "It's designed to teach people how to work with facts instead of personalities," says Steinreich. "Employees can't concentrate on quality work if they're constantly stressed out from battling managers." One or two people from all areas of the plant, including supervisors, attend 16 two-hour sessions. The class takes 10 months to a year to complete. "We begin by talking about customers and suppliers, so that people start seeing the connection," says trainer Stan Creekmore. "This leads to being a team player, to building trust and sharing values."

All three companies profiled in this chapter emphasize *constant communication of shared values and expectations*. At the Ritz-Carlton, service standards are continuously emphasized during all work activities, beginning on day one. "On the first day of work for every employee, our president and chief executive officer personally and aggressively communicates our vision, values, and methods," says Mene. "You are expected to internalize those values and vision and to use our methods quite naturally." Service standards are reinforced during training and daily "line-ups," brief meetings between managers and employees. The constant communication about requirements is effective. In a 1991 survey, 96% of all employees identified guest services as a top hotel and personal priority—and 3,000 of those employees had been with the company less than three years.

Like Engelhard-Huntsville and the Ritz-Carlton, Motorola communicates its requirements through extensive training (Motorola spent $120 million on education in 1992) and shared goals (Six Sigma quality and its other initiatives). Motorola also believes that management accountability is critical. "We want to involve people in the improvement process," says Noakes, "but we must change ourselves first."

One way Motorola encourages change and communicates customer and quality requirements is through rewards and recognition. Since the early 1980s Motorola has tied 25% or more of its managers' bonuses to improvements in quality, customer satisfaction, and cycle time. The goal of 68% improvement per year clearly communicates management's requirements.

In 1987 Motorola began paying a bonus twice a year for performance on one measure: return on net assets. If a business unit does not make its goal, no one in the unit receives the bonus. If the company does not meet its goal, no one in the company gets the bonus.

In 1990 Motorola began a worldwide competition among teams, an idea it picked up from the Japanese. As long as a team is working on something that relates to one of Motorola's five initiatives, it can enter the competition. More than 3,700 teams competed in 1992.

Through rewards and recognition, frequent meetings, personal contact, and training, successful companies tell managers, supervisors, and other employees exactly what is expected from them. Quality leaders make sure every message reflects the same central themes and key requirements; the Ritz-Carlton has its Gold Standards, Motorola its five initiatives, and Engelhard-Huntsville its Quality Operating System. By communicating the same basic requirements over and over, in a variety of venues and situations, leaders help their people internalize those requirements and act upon them naturally. And their systems hum as many voices become one.

REVIEWING AND BOOSTING PERFORMANCE

Our role models review performance to requirements frequently, in many ways, to make sure the requirements are being met and to identify and help those who need assistance. In the new management model the purpose of the review is not to fix blame, scare people into action, or punish. Quite the opposite. Managers and employees mutually discuss the working relationship, ever mindful of the need to enable and empower everyone in the organization to achieve their goals.

That does not mean our benchmarks do not evaluate individual performance. We discuss this subject in more detail in Chapter 8, but to close the loop here, consider what the Ritz-Carlton does. Individual performance is judged by the employee's ability to master the company's gold standards. The performance is measured, evaluated constantly, and assessed through opinion surveys. "We evaluate people's performance because we're coaching them every day," says Mene. "We're constantly evaluating the process."

Service companies have long resisted the idea of measuring their performance. When Federal Express became the first service company to win the Baldrige Award, an honor it received in no small part because of its measurement system (see Chapter 2), other service folks were quick to claim that Federal Express was really no different from a manufacturer: It handled commodities, in this case, packages. Not at all like an insurance company. Not one bit like an ad agency. Nothing like a bank. Nope, they said, we cannot measure what we do.

"People who haven't measured," says Mene, "haven't tried. They're making excuses." The Ritz-Carlton gets information from training, observing performance, employee evaluations, customer evaluations, and assessments by independent groups. Mene emphasizes that the measurement of performance does not have to be statistics controlled; it can be behavior controlled. "The difference between us and high-tech firms is that, when they do analysis, they have more data and more strident analysis. But even without hard data, you can still meet and talk through data analysis and prevention. Nobody said you had to have Deming in your plant to look at a control chart. The only difference I find from manufacturing to service is how detailed you're going to be. Managing people isn't always detail data, it's judgment."

Process data stay at the hotels, where they are used to evaluate and improve performance. The only results that get to the corporate level are data on key products, customer satisfaction, customer complaints, market share, turnover, profits, safety, and employee satisfaction. "If a hotel is worse than the norm, there's some special reason unique to that hotel," says Mene. "Usually, they can find it themselves and get it in control. If they can't, we try to help."

Based on results, the Ritz-Carlton Hotels are doing an exceptional job of translating customer requirements and quality values into requirements for all employees, then communicating those requirements. Ninety-seven percent of the Ritz-Carlton's customers report having a "memorable experience" while staying at one of the hotels.

Engelhard's Huntsville operation relies on fewer data to review performance, but then, with only 270 employees at one plant, its managers are getting constant feedback on performance. Senior management reviews performance during its weekly meetings. Performance is also studied as part of its Quality Operating System and in employee opinion surveys.

At Motorola, business units submit charts on their quality and cycle time performance monthly to the corporate quality division, which selects which ones to discuss during the corporate reviews. Corporate performance reviews occur eight times a year. During these four-hour meetings quality is the first item on the agenda, and issues of quality and cycle time typically take up half the meeting. (When Robert Galvin was chairman, he would leave the meetings at this point, before the group discussed financial issues. The message: If quality and cycle time are improving, the bottom line will improve with them.)

The heads of all major organizations are accountable for their performance. The goal is 68% improvement. If they are meeting the goal, there is no discussion. If the trend is on target, there is little discussion. If the trend is flat, the group identifies the causes and develops an action plan to address the most important. The action plan lists who is going to make it happen and when.

Divisions hold quality review meetings at least monthly, but it is common to see weekly and daily quality review meetings—and even hourly meetings in the factories.

Motorola conducts quality system reviews of its major business units and suppliers every two years. Seven-person teams spend a week auditing the unit's system. Ninety days after the audit, the team presents its finding. The general manager must then respond with plans for improvement.

Motorola also uses the Baldrige criteria as an internal system assessment. (Chapter 17 explains how companies are using Baldrige assessments to improve.) In 1991–1992 every business unit wrote and submitted a full Baldrige application, identifying how they would address areas for improvement. Motorola is now working on uniting its quality system reviews and Baldrige assessments into a single tool. (For more about data collection and analysis, see Chapter 14.)

THE SHIFT IN THINKING

At the beginning of this chapter we referred to a slide in Motorola's standard quality speech that says, "We have been successful because of our management process." It is a statement any role model in this book could make, a summary of the single, overriding factor contributing to continuous improvement and long-term success.

It is also the subject of this book. In the new business management model the management process is a *systematic approach* to meeting and exceeding customers' expectations. The approach includes every element in the system, as described in the chapters in this book. The shift in thinking is as dramatic as driving out of the narrow tunnel of daily department supervision to discover a panorama stretching from suppliers on one horizon to customers on the other, across an ever-changing landscape populated with planning, extensive measuring and analysis, and process improvement, and employee involvement as far as the eye can see. In this new horizontal organization managers manage processes, not results. They become process owners in charge of the processes that lead to customer satisfaction.

To manage quality is to manage the process is to manage the system. As Motorola's standard presentation summarizes on its final slide:

Quality is not an assignable task. It must be rooted and institutionalized in every process. It is everyone's responsibility.

Management's job is to do the rooting and institutionalizing, to manage the system. As self-directed work teams have shown, people can pretty much manage themselves. It's the system that causes the problems—and that is management's responsibility.

6 EMPLOYEE INVOLVEMENT

Lyondell Petrochemical

Paul Revere Insurance Group

Dana-Minneapolis

In the last chapter we looked at managing the system to make it hum. The sweet music that results does not come from factory lines or computers or stock market tickers, but from the people who make the system work. Employee empowerment, responsibility, and innovation produce long-term success.

However, before managers grab this concept off the shelf and install it as the latest symbol of their company's dedication to quality, a word of warning: *If management is not prepared to give employees control over their activities, freedom to make important decisions, and responsibility for their actions— forever—they should put this idea back on the shelf.* Employee involvement is a long-term commitment, a new way of doing business, a fundamental change in culture. Employees who have been trained, empowered, and recognized for their achievements see their jobs and their companies from a different perspective. They no longer punch a clock, do what they are told, and count the minutes until the weekend rolls around. They "own" the company, in the sense that they feel personally responsible for its performance. As Shirley Helms, a lab technician at Lyondell Petrochemical (one of the role models described in this chapter) says, "If I see something that needs to be done, I do it or find someone who can. That's empowerment to me."

Managers who try to take some of that power back end up with bitter, frustrated, and disillusioned employees. Performance will suffer, and future attempts to revive it will be met with cynicism.

Employee involvement works, but only as a way of running a business. It is not something you dabble in. It does not work as a short-term solution or an intriguing experiment. It is truly a Pandora's box, tempting to open but powerful enough to change your "world" forever.

The main difference is that instead of releasing all the ills that could plague humanity, unlocking this box produces a torrent of positive energy, enthusiasm, ideas, and improvements. In this chapter we will describe how three quality leaders benefit from employee involvement. All three have been at it for several years with notable successes; two have had Baldrige site visits, and one has won the prestigious Shingo Award for manufacturing excellence. We will explore how they address these key questions:

- How do we get people involved in the quality improvement process?
- How do we keep them involved?
- How can we use teams to improve?

Employee involvement, like managing quality, touches every other part of the business management model, as described throughout this book:

- Employees nurture relationships with customers (see Chapters 3 and 10).
- Employees translate customer expectations into products and services (see Chapter 11).
- Employees manage and improve a company's processes (see Chapter 12).
- Employees work with suppliers (see Chapter 13).
- Employees determine and use measurements to improve (see Chapter 14).
- Employees compare their processes to others (see Chapter 15).
- Employees contribute to their communities (see Chapter 16).

They are empowered to do all this by management (as discussed in Chapters 2 and 5). At some companies, like our role models in Chapter 4, they are empowered through the strategic planning process to contribute individually and in teams to corporate objectives. In this chapter we will briefly discuss how the Paul Revere Insurance Group uses a system of key performance indicators to empower all employees to work toward shared goals.

Companies also empower people through training and rewards and recognition. We mention these briefly in this chapter, then devote more time to training in Chapter 7 and rewards and recognition in Chapter 8.

In this chapter we focus on how to initiate and sustain employee involvement. One of the fastest growing methods is through teams, with many companies (including this chapter's three quality leaders) moving toward self-directed work teams. We will look at how our role models use teams to get the most out of their human resource.

In the process they have permanently changed their corporate cultures. "We haven't had a supervisor on our shift for seven years," says Helms. "I don't think it's ever going backwards." After seven years it is hard to imagine how it could—or why Lyondell would want it to.

MODELS OF EXCELLENCE

Lyondell Petrochemical Company produces a wide variety of petrochemicals, including olefins (ethylene, propylene, butadiene, butylenes, and specialty products), methanol, MTBE, low-density polyethylene and polypropylene, and refined petroleum products (gasoline, heating oil, jet fuel, aromatics, and lubricants). It has more than 2,300 employees at four sites in the Houston area. Since the company was formed in 1985, cumulative earnings have exceeded $1.7 billion.

The Paul Revere Insurance Group is the largest producer of individual, noncancelable disability income insurance for professionals and small business owners. It also markets group long-term disability insurance, life insurance, and financial products. Founded in 1895, Paul Revere has 1,500 employees at its headquarters in Worcester, Massachusetts, 1,500 in field offices, and 400 in Canada. The company received a Baldrige site visit in 1988.

Dana Corporation's Mobile Fluid Products Division is a leading manufacturer of hydraulic control valves. Its Minneapolis plant, one of six plants and the facility we will feature in this chapter, has 300 employees. From 1987, when the plant began its focus on team building, to 1991, when it won the Shingo Prize for excellence in manufacturing, the Minneapolis plant improved productivity 32%, reduced the cost of quality 47%, improved on-time deliveries to the 95% range, and reduced inventory 50%.

INITIATING AND SUSTAINING EMPLOYEE INVOLVEMENT AT LYONDELL

In the early 1980s, Atlantic Richfield executive Bob Gower was on a team that suggested that the company lump together the petrochemical and refining operations that were losing money and form a new company. Atlantic Richfield called the company Lyondell Petrochemical and asked Gower to run it. Choosing to think of an organization that had lost a total of $200 million each year for the past three years as a challenge, he accepted.

Serious red ink was not Gower's only problem. The new company had no assets that set it apart from the competition. It had no unique technologies, nor did it enjoy any special advantages in the marketplace. The only way it could differentiate itself, the only way to return to profitability, was to improve productivity. But as Gower notes, "morale was low and costs were way too high."

To make matters worse, Gower had to build a new management team. "I was told that I could have anybody I could talk into joining me." No doubt Atlantic Richfield's leaders felt pretty safe with such a generous offer, but then, they did not count on Gower's persuasive powers. He not only pulled together a management team, "but the people who came were risk takers who believed as I did that people are the key to a successful turnaround."

And Lyondell has succeeded. In 1989 *Fortune* ranked Lyondell first in sales per employee among all industrial companies in the United States. It earned the same honor again in 1990 and 1991. It received Baldrige site visits in 1991 and 1992. And in 1993 it was identified as one of the 100 best companies to work for in the book by that name. The key to Lyondell's success has been employee involvement.

Employee involvement begins with a change in management's attitude. As Gower says, "You can only have empowerment if the top person makes the decision to have it." He and his management staff turned to employee involvement as the key to continuous improvement because they knew Lyondell would have continued to lose money without it, and because they believed that most people want to do their jobs well, are proud of their work, have valuable ideas to share, and want responsibility.

The Process of Empowerment

Empowerment at Lyondell begins with:

- A willingness by managers and supervisors to give others responsibility
- Training supervisors and employees in how to delegate and accept responsibility
- Communication and feedback to tell people how they are doing
- Rewards and recognition

Giving Employees Responsibility

Here's how they do it. Lyondell helps its managers and supervisors turn over responsibility through a two-day training course called "Managing the Lyondell Way." The course identifies 10 key management behaviors that Lyondell values:

1. Low-cost production
2. Quality
3. Entrepreneurship and innovation
4. Action orientation
5. People are the difference
6. Responsibility and accountability in all jobs
7. Teamwork
8. Communication
9. Safety of people
10. Social responsibility and ethics

The course covers what to communicate for each behavior, what actions to take, and how to follow up and monitor progress. Many of the actions encourage employee involvement. For example, one of the "quality" actions "involves employees in achieving and improving quality performance." For "entrepreneurship and innovation," managers are told to "encourage others to use sound, creative thought and action that can lead to innovations." For "people are the difference," managers must "assure that people understand their responsibility to make the greatest, most positive difference they can."

The behaviors and actions overlap, forming a cultural web that defines continuous improvement for Lyondell. "One of the greatest strengths of 'Managing the Lyondell Way' is integration. It works as a whole," says David Lindsay, manager of quality process.

Training Employees to Accept Responsibility

This second part of empowerment at Lyondell is often overlooked in a company's eagerness to empower. Managers soon discover that most people lack the skills or experience they need to take responsibility, make decisions, and act confidently. "It was a revelation to me that not everyone knows how to do this," says Gower.

People need to be trained in their new roles, given opportunities to succeed, supported, and encouraged. The transition will be faster for some than others, while a few will never make it. "It's scary for some people," says Shirley Holman-Unger, a member of Lyondell's safety committee. "When you become empowered, you get additional responsibility, and some people don't want that."

Communicating and Giving Feedback

Lyondell provides feedback, the third part of empowerment, frequently and in a variety of ways. Teams are given feedback at every meeting. Each team has a management sponsor who provides support and advice. Managers and supervisors are trained in giving feedback during the "Managing the Lyondell Way" course. Teams make presentations on their progress to management, which offers on-the-spot feedback. All these opportunities and more are encouraged as integral to continuous improvement.

Giving Rewards and Recognition

Lyondell ties its rewards and recognition, the fourth part of empowerment, to the behaviors identified in "Managing the Lyondell Way." Every employee's annual performance review includes an evaluation of performance on these behaviors, and improvement spurs increases in merit pay. A host of recognition programs honors employee contributions to Lyondell's quality and performance objectives.

Making the Transition to Employee Involvement

All these actions establish employee involvement as a way of doing business at Lyondell, even though the transition to total employee involvement continues. Employees who are naturally suspicious of management's motives often reserve their support until they feel comfortable that the change is permanent. This is especially true for union shops.

"We've had a long tradition of having clear lines drawn between management and the work force," says David Taylor, union committeeman and a member of the employee safety team. "But we're trying to change that." Union leaders are often torn between the promise of empowered workers and the possibility that management is empowering only to get people to do more in less time for less money—as some have. As adversarial relationships are replaced by participative management, unions' roles will change from a necessary preoccupation with arbitration to a focus on other areas of concern to their members, such as health care and job skills.

ALIGNING EMPLOYEES' ACTIVITIES WITH CUSTOMER SATISFACTION AT PAUL REVERE

The change in attitude from adversarial to cooperative is no short journey. For years companies that have wanted to learn what such a participative management culture might look like have studied the Paul Revere Insurance Group, where employees work cooperatively with management to improve the way they do business and better satisfy customer needs.

Employee involvement is the cornerstone of Paul Revere's quality improvement process. "Responsibility is inbred, to the point that each person feels responsible for what goes on in the company," says Diane Gardner, quality consultant. "New employees are usually surprised at that. All of a sudden, people are asking for their opinions, or they suggest things and are told it's a good idea, run with it. We don't even think about it anymore."

To strengthen its competitive advantage in the marketplace, Paul Revere established a Quality Has Value Process in 1984. The process takes advantage of a Paul Revere strength: *quality teams.* All employees, including executives, managers, and supervisors, participate in quality teams. We will describe their team activity later in this chapter.

More recently, Paul Revere has reorganized its strategic planning process to focus its employees' activities on common goals. The goals, called key performance indicators (KPIs), are developed through customer feedback. Programs and activities are then planned to help the company achieve its KPIs, which, in turn, increase customer satisfaction.

Senior management develops corporate KPIs and communicates them to the organization. The corporate KPIs fit into three basic areas:

- Financial leadership
- Disability income leadership
- Service leadership

Within these three areas, Paul Revere has quantifiable goals it wishes to reach:

- Four financial indicators
- Four disability income indicators
- A varied number of service indicators, depending on input from external surveys

Managers use these KPIs to develop divisional and departmental indicators. They also work with employees to determine how each can contribute to meeting the corporate KPIs. Once the individual KPIs are in place, every employee at every level is working toward customer satisfaction improvements. The KPIs are continually reviewed, measured, and revised. As customers' needs change, the indicators change.

Departments within Paul Revere used to look at division operating plans as a team and develop quality goals to achieve them. The new, interlocking system of key performance indicators has changed the focus from operating plan to customer satisfaction.

Paul Revere did not change the way it *treated* its employees; rather it changed the way it *focused* them. Paul Revere built on its history of teamwork and empowerment to align everyone's activities toward customer satisfaction. As companies hurry to empower, they will do well to set their employees loose on meeting customer requirements.

DANA CORPORATION'S TEAMWORK APPROACH

As a corporation, Dana determined to meet customer needs by introducing its Excellence in Manufacturing (EIM) program in 1986. The keys to the program are teamwork, employee involvement, and the elimination of waste. The primary tool is cellular manufacturing, which localizes the responsibility for production, from raw castings to finished products, in a single area.

Dana's Minneapolis plant has 34 semi–self-directed EIM teams. Management's role is to supply information, offer assistance, and provide encouragement, to build consensus rather than dictate direction. "All we do is manage the momentum," says plant manager Thomas Neusiis. "People have to be empowered. I have to lobby hard to get changes made. I have to build respect and trust, and they still don't take everything I suggest."

As documented earlier, that momentum has carried the Minneapolis plant to dramatic improvements. Managers have seen their roles change from running the show to seeking out barriers to empowerment. Every day they communicate informally with cell and team members to identify these barriers and offer their help. On a more formal basis three teams share what they have accomplished with the management staff every month. The staff goes to their areas, learns what they are working on, and finds out what barriers they are facing. Managers applaud their progress and offer assistance with the challenges ahead.

Communication is the key. Neusiis holds six monthly meetings scheduled at different times so that all employees can attend. The one-hour meetings cover financial performance, return on sales, return on investment, upcoming orders, and quality concerns. "People need to know where we are today to get us where we want to be tomorrow."

COMMUNICATION IS CRITICAL

As organizations get flatter by empowering front-line people to take more responsibility, communication needs change. The process of moving information must also be analyzed and improved if that information is to reach the right people when they need it. For example, it is typical for a company to make decisions at the top, then go to the next level to get consensus, then on down through the organization. At Dana's Minneapolis plant and at Lyondell Petrochemical management decisions are communicated directly to all employees during monthly meetings. More frequent informal communication helps assure managers that everyone in the system is humming the same tune.

One of the oldest methods of communication, the suggestion system, has been rejuvenated by companies intent on empowering their employees. The new systems fit the new model well: They are easily accessible, employee initiated, and geared for quick and serious attention. For example, Lyondell's mechanism for encouraging individuals or teams to contribute ideas is called Quality Improvement Ideas (QII). Feedback on each suggestion is given within 48 hours of receipt, and employees are updated on progress until the idea is implemented. Ideas submitted to QII have saved Lyondell more than $41 million since 1985.

The primary difference between the old systems, characterized by suggestion boxes that gathered more dust than ideas, and the new systems is that now employees know their suggestions are valued and valuable. High-performance companies act on them quickly, keep the contributor in the information loop, announce implementation and cost savings, and recognize the contributor. At some point the suggestion system becomes a widely accepted method of communicating ideas.

Here is a more measurable comparison of old and new. U.S. companies currently average about one-half suggestion for improvement per employee per year. Milliken, a 1989 Baldrige Award winner, averaged 52 suggestions per employee in 1991. Milliken does not pay for suggestions, but it does have a 24/72 policy: A supervisor must respond to an idea within 24 hours and show a plan to act on the idea within 72 hours. And that, it seems, is all the empowered employee requires.

USING TEAMS FOR CONTINUOUS IMPROVEMENT

Like suggestions systems, teams have been around for some time. Work groups are teams. Departments are teams. Quality circles are teams. Some companies even like to claim that their entire organization is a team.

Today, however, what it means to be a team has changed. Based on its extensive experience with the subject, Paul Revere has identified the following basic elements of a successful quality team:

- Team goals are as important as individual goals.
- Team goals are the responsibility of all the team members.
- Individual competitiveness must be reduced.
- Communication is a *must*.

- Mutual understanding, respect, and cooperation are emphasized.
- 100% team participation is required.

Many companies are moving toward *team-driven organizations* in which teams are responsible for determining what to work on, when to work on it, how to improve it, and what to do next. As we wrote earlier, all of Paul Revere's employees participate on quality teams. In fact, employees are assigned to quality teams on their first day of work, and every department is organized as a team. "I'm in a department and I'm on that team," says Gardner. "If I also have expertise in another area, I can jump on another team working on a related project. But I'll always have my department team." In addition to their focus on customer requirements, the teams constantly study functions within the department to determine how they can be more efficient and effective.

"The point we're trying to get across is that your department is quality," says Gardner. "It's your quality team and it's also your department team, with no line between the two. Quality isn't separate from your job, it *is* your job."

Another type of team, the process analysis team, works to improve a specific process. All employees have been trained in process analysis with their co-workers so that everyone on a process analysis team shares the same understanding of the team's goals and process. "Many people have been doing this all along but didn't know it. Now they have the tools to improve the process and they're excited about it," Gardner says. The people involved in the process to be improved are asked to join the team, whether the process exists within a department or across departmental lines.

Paul Revere currently has a few *self-directed work teams* in its customer service departments. They meet daily to schedule their work, spreading it out on a table and taking responsibility for the different pieces.

Self-directed work teams are typically groups of 4 to 25 people, drawn from within a function or department, who work with a high degree of autonomy to produce a complete component or to perform a particular service. The concept of self-directed work teams was introduced in the mid-1920s and more thoroughly developed in the late 1950s. The Japanese have been leaders in institutionalizing the concept, having learned about it from IBM. In 1984 Toyota had 5,800 self-directed work teams.

The members of self-directed work teams are typically cross-trained to perform most or all the jobs in the team's area. They monitor quality, schedule work, control costs, plan, hire, interact with customers and vendors, and handle discipline. Most members need extensive training and encouragement to handle such a wide range of activities. "You have to be educated about hiring, disabilities, affirmative action—lots of things you never thought about when you took the job," says Carl Dildy, a maintenance mechanic at Lyondell and a member of a self-directed work team. Team member and lab technician Mark Bradley says, "The biggest problem is discipline. How do you tell another team member they're not pulling their load?" As Shirley Holman-Unger points out, "Empowerment forces you to deal with human resource problems. Lyondell has been very good at giving us these skills."

As Lyondell, Paul Revere, Dana, and others who are setting up self-directed work teams have learned, making the teams work involves careful planning, selecting the right team members and leaders, setting the teams up to succeed, providing extensive and continuous training, and carefully managing the shift of power and responsibility from leaders to team members.

At Dana's Minneapolis plant the transition to self-directed work teams began in 1987 when the plant spent 16 months training everyone in such areas as cell development, setup time reduction, problem-solving skills, and team skills. Even key suppliers took the 40-hour course.

The teams then organized their machines into cells. There are 8 to 10 people on each team, "but the teams are fairly dynamic," says Neusiis. "We have three shifts, so some will combine to address a major project. The teams make that call." The teams meet one hour a week to work on issues related to their cells. If a team needs input from suppliers, they are invited to participate. Four of Dana's 34 teams are office teams.

Each team can spend up to $500 with no management approval. "They don't need one more person telling them 'no,'" Neusiis says. If a team needs more than $500, it must define the return on investment (ROI) and present its findings to the area manager and Neusiis. Three people are available to help the teams with their ROIs, but they rarely get called. According to Neusiis, "About 95 percent of the teams' projects take less than a $200 investment."

Each team completes 10 to 25 projects per year. The projects focus on quality, safety, cost reduction, setup reduction, and customer/supplier issues. Although the teams have a great deal of autonomy and responsibility, they are considered semi–self-directed work teams because they do not yet do their own buying or scheduling. Pilots are underway in which teams are performing these functions as well.

Unlike most companies, Dana does not formally recognize the contributions of individual employees, choosing instead to honor team accomplishments. "Americans work well as individuals, but not as teams," says Neusiis. "We had to do a lot of team training to help people understand that what one person does benefits everyone." Dana extends this emphasis to its recognition program, helping to create an environment in which team goals come first. As a recent employee attitude survey confirmed, Dana's people now believe that teamwork and team building are the plant's biggest assets.

Lyondell Petrochemical could make the same claim. Virtually all of Lyondell's business is carried out through teams. Everyone is on at least one of the following cross-functional teams, with managers acting as coaches and consultants:

- *Quality breakthrough teams* resolve quality opportunities or problems.
- *Quality improvement teams* direct and implement process improvements.
- *Business teams* enable employees to share ideas and participate in running the business.

"We've gotten better at defining the expected outcome and parameters for our teams," says Rose Nenni, manager of employee relations for manufacturing. "Each team creates a formal charter describing the team's roles and boundaries." The charter is one of the first steps a team takes in its continuous improvement process.

Lyondell's implementation of self-directed work teams is growing. The impetus for forming such a team comes from a work unit, which investigates customer expectations, benchmarks self-directed work teams at other companies, studies information and process flows, and considers the new team's effect on quality of work life before bringing its recommendations to management. Figure 6.1 provides an overview of Lyondell's empowerment process.

Such a thoughtful approach would be beneficial for any company wishing to set up self-directed work teams:

- Start small with a pilot team that is already performing many of the tasks assigned to a self-directed team.
- Bring it up to speed slowly, adding responsibilities only after team members have been trained in the skills required.
- Make managers available as facilitators, consultants, and experts, but not as decision makers.
- Encourage the team to draw from many resources, including benchmarking successful self-directed work teams, inviting key suppliers to participate, and talking to customers.
- Expand the concept to other areas of the company, using the pilot as the jumping-off point.

THE SHIFT IN THINKING

"Everything is changing," says Paul Revere's Gardner. "Whatever we're doing could be different in six months, building on what we're doing now." Compa-

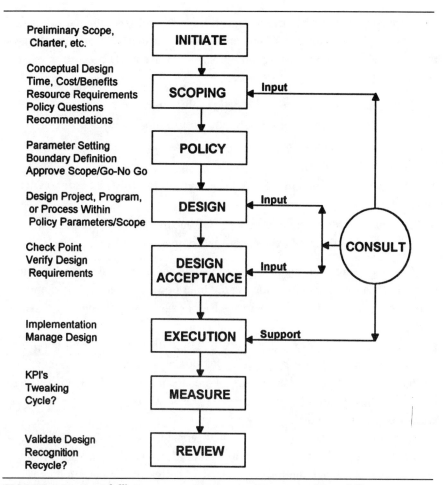

FIGURE 6.1.   Lyondell's empowerment process. (Courtesy of Lyondell Petrochemical.)

nies need to change. People need to change. Gone are the days when today's job is the same as yesterday's, when months pass with no discernible difference in people, processes, or output.

According to a study of worker attitudes and behavior headed by psychologist G. Clotaire Rapaille, Americans are threatened by change when it is imposed, but feel positive about it when they can control it. Carl Dildy, a maintenance mechanic at Lyondell, agrees: "The marketplace is constantly changing, and people need to change. Being involved in teams helps people accept this change."

Across America, companies are looking for the best approach to the demands for higher quality, the pressure of increasing global competition, the necessity to be more efficient and productive, and the effects of rapid change. To compete, companies must produce a high-quality product or service at the lowest possible cost in the shortest possible time and be prepared to change any part of that equation at a moment's notice. Successful companies believe the only way to compete is through employee involvement, because they have learned that:

- The employees who perform the tasks that produce a product or service are in the best position to ensure and improve its quality.
- The same employees are best able to lower costs by eliminating waste throughout the process.
- They are also in the best position to speed up their processes by reducing cycle times.
- They are the ideal agents of change, in touch with their processes, trained through education and experience, and empowered to act decisively.

Companies are choosing to empower people because it makes good business sense. In the process they are blurring the lines between manager and employee as they create a boundary-less company. Employees on self-directed work teams perform all the tasks formerly done by managers. They plan, schedule, buy, hire, control, and improve. They work closely with customers and suppliers. In every respect they are responsible for how well their company meets its customers' requirements. The culture of a company that understands this will be significantly different from the culture of a company that still treats its employees like commodities.

The other dramatic difference is in how employees see themselves. In Chapter 10 we will talk about a training program at Metropolitan Life called *Achieving Personal Quality*. To help serve customers better, employees are taught the fundamentals of personal quality, including treating others as you would like to be treated, taking responsibility, learning, and sharing. These are universal values, values we teach our children, values we try to live by every day. Employee involvement is another way of teaching these values.

"The biggest thing Lyondell has done for me has been to give me confidence and ownership. It even helps me work with my three teenagers as a single parent," says Shirley Holman-Unger. Her co-worker, Mark Bradley, adds, "You can go home and feel good about your day, and that spreads to your family."

In the process of empowering people companies are also blurring the lines between work and home, giving people the tools they need to succeed in all facets of their lives. That, too, makes good business sense.

7 TRAINING

Plumley Companies
Northern Trust
Globe Metallurgical

The Plumley Companies manufacture rubber hoses and ducts for the automobile industry. In the early 1980s Buick stopped using Plumley because its defect rate was too high. To address the problem, Plumley bought and installed high-tech equipment to improve the production of its rubber products.

It didn't solve the problem. Employees had trouble using the new equipment, and even when they got it running, mistakes were common. Training was the obvious solution. When the Big Three auto makers told Plumley that they expected it to use statistical process control (SPC) to improve the quality of its products, the training path seemed clear: Plumley began training its workers in SPC.

That didn't solve the problem either. Larry Moore, Plumley's director of education, remembers chairman Mike Plumley bumping into an employee who had had 30 hours of SPC training. As they talked, Plumley realized that the employee didn't know that one-quarter inch equaled 0.25 inch. A closer look at just how much its employees knew revealed that many lacked basic math and reading skills. Although new equipment and SPC training were the obvious solutions to a high defect rate, both assumed a level of knowledge that did not exist. Before Plumley could improve quality, it had to train employees in the basic skills they would need to run the equipment and implement SPC.

Training for continuous improvement involves everything from remedial reading and math to design of experiments and concurrent engineering. Without such training—and lots of it—continuous improvement is not possible. Leading companies across the country have shown that training is one of the pillars of improvements in quality and performance. Motorola spent $120 million on education in 1992. Corning expects all employees to spend 5% of their work time on training—about 92 hours per employee per year. In 1992 Federal Express spent 4.5% of its payroll on training. Solectron's employees averaged 110 training hours in 1993—all during normal working hours.

These top performers treat their workers as assets to be developed, not commodities to be used. They invest in their people because they must; their expectations of their employees are too high, their demands too great, to send them forward unarmed. Consider just a few of the things high-performance companies are asking their employees to do:

- Contribute to work unit, department, and cross-functional teams
- Solve process problems in all parts of the company
- Communicate with customers and suppliers, both internal and external
- Measure and analyze indicators of performance and improvement
- Manage processes to improve quality and reduce cycle time
- Learn a wide range of skills to improve flexibility
- Take the initiative in identifying and addressing improvements
- Assume responsibility for quality and productivity

These tasks require a host of advanced skills in such areas as teamwork, problem solving, communication, process management, and leadership. Employees cannot do any of these if they check their brains at the door—and if employees cannot improve quality, it will not get done. That is why companies that want to improve quality fire up a quality training program early in the process. When Plumley wanted to improve its defect rate, it turned to SPC training. In the process it wrestled with questions every company must answer as it organizes an effective training process:

- What kind of training do we need?
- Whom should we train?
- How do we deliver the training?
- How do we know the training is effective?
- How do we improve the training process?

In this chapter we will look at how three quality leaders are answering these questions. In the process we will examine how they use quality and related training to achieve their quality and performance goals.

MODELS OF EXCELLENCE

Plumley is a family-owned business headquartered in Paris, Tennessee. It has more than 1,200 employees at seven manufacturing facilities, with $82 million in sales in 1992. In the last few years Plumley has earned most of the auto industry's highest awards, including General Motors' Mark of Excellence Award, Ford's Total Quality Excellence status, Nissan's Quality Master rating, and Chrysler's Pentastar rating. In 1990 Plumley was one of only 16 companies nationwide to receive the LIFT Award (Labor Investing For Tomorrow) from the U.S. Department of Labor for excellence in employee training.

Northern Trust Corporation opened for business in Chicago more than a hundred years ago. Today, it employs more than 6,500 people in 45 locations in seven states, Canada, and Great Britain. Although Northern Trust has long been a leader in the trust side of the banking business, it determined in 1990 that a systematic quality improvement process would improve its position. It developed a process it calls Commitment to Absolute Quality, with the goal of consistently exceeding client/partner expectations while striving to become their ideal provider. Northern Trust is training all its employees in a 24-hour Commitment to Absolute Quality curriculum.

Globe Metallurgical is a major producer of silicon metal and ferrosilicon products, with more than 250 employees at its two plants in Beverly, Ohio, and Selma, Alabama. In 1988 Globe was the first small business to win the Baldrige Award. Since then it has earned the first-ever Shingo Prize for Manufacturing Excellence, Ford's highest award for Total Quality Excellence, and the U.S. Senate Productivity Award for Alabama. Globe is a flat organization run by self-directed work teams; of the 140 people working in the Ohio plant, only 10 are managers. Training is driven by customer and/or team needs and focuses on skills that can be put to use immediately.

DETERMINING TRAINING NEEDS

The rush to improve quality frequently leads to poor decisions about what kind of training to provide. These are some of the most common mistakes:

- A customer tells you it expects a new skill from your company, so you begin training employees in that skill without knowing if they are ready to learn it.
- You discover a competitor is implementing a certain quality technique, or you read about how such a technique turned a business around, and quickly organize your own training before finding out if it is a good idea for your company.

- You install new equipment, prepare to make a new product or offer a new service, or redesign a process and only consider training as an afterthought.
- You begin general training in broad quality concepts without knowing how each employee will apply those concepts in his or her daily work to improve quality.

The mistakes suggest a more effective way of determining your company's training needs, a process anchored in the business management model. The process begins with data and information that will tell you what skills employees now have and what skills they will need to have to achieve your short- and long-range plans, satisfy customers, improve quality and operational performance, and grow personally and professionally. At the three benchmark companies profiled in this chapter, the human resources departments gather their data and information from a variety of sources, perform an analysis, and determine training needs.

The nature of the assessment depends primarily on the size of the company: The smaller the company, the less formal the assessment. "There's no room to hide in this company," says Norm Jennings, Globe's quality director. "Everybody knows what everybody else is doing to contribute, which makes our training needs very obvious. Teams identify what skills their people need. Individual employees suggest training. Looking at what we as a company will need for the future reveals training needs. And our customers' changing expectations inspire new training."

Because of Globe's size and structure, it is able to practice more "just-in-time" training than a larger company could accomplish. The danger in this less formal approach is that training can end up being short term and reactive, a response to problems rather than a means to anticipate and prevent them. Globe avoids this by collecting, correlating, and acting on information from a variety of sources—teams, individuals, corporate goals, and customers—and by responding quickly to a training need when it is identified.

"One of our customers, General Motors, told us it wanted its suppliers to be more sensitive to reductions in lead times, cycle times, and costs," Jennings says. "We determined that the best way to continue to improve in those areas was through synchronous management [i.e., performing a series of tasks in parallel, also called concurrent engineering], and we're now doing training in that area."

Plumley determines its employees' training needs in much the same ways as Globe, but because it has more employees in more plants, it also conducts surveys to identify needs. "I try to survey one plant at a time," says Larry Moore, Plumley's director of education, "to find out what may be keeping them from improving and what other training needs they may have." As the company discovered in 1983, those needs often range from basic to highly technical.

Plumley is not the only company to plunge ahead with what seemed like the right training, only to hit a wall of ignorance that had to be broken down first. For example, Baldrige Award–winner Motorola took nearly a decade, from 1980 to 1990, to develop a training program that did what it wanted it to do. Initial executive training did little to improve quality. Motorola then developed a five-part curriculum that included courses in SPC, problem solving, and goal setting. Every employee received about 20 hours of training, but this failed because the employees were not motivated to apply what they were learning and their managers were not receiving the same training.

From 1985 to 1987 Motorola's top 200 executives had 17 days of training in manufacturing, global competition, and cycle time. The training was then cascaded down through the company. However, when Motorola converted a facility from radio technology to cellular technology, it discovered *the wall:* elementary reading and math. Only 40% of the facility's employees passed a simple math test, and 60% of those who failed could not read the questions. Motorola surveyed its 25,000 manufacturing and support employees in the United States and found that half could not do seventh-grade math and English.

When one of Northern Trust's business units wanted to learn how to attract and retain skilled, flexible employees, the company conducted a workplace study to establish benchmark performance levels and training needs. The study revealed that some of the most important skills were reading, grammar and writing, math, and problem solving.

Learning from Plumley, Motorola, and Northern Trust, a company would be wise not to assume any level of knowledge when it assesses the need for quality training. The Baldrige criteria acknowledge the need for remedial training in a note that says, "[Quality and related training] may include job enrichment skills and basic skills such as reading, writing, language, arithmetic, and basic mathematics that are needed to meet quality and operational performance improvement objectives." Whether you talk to individuals or teams or conduct employee surveys, your assessment must include the ability to identify the need for basic skills training.

Northern Trust identifies training needs by:

1. Determining what *skills* its employees will need to achieve the company's strategic quality initiative. Its 24-hour training curriculum, "Commitment to Absolute Quality," includes skill building in the four key principles Northern has identified for achieving absolute quality: unrivaled client satisfaction; continuous improvement of all processes; inspired leadership; and active involvement of all Northern people.

2. Conducting periodic needs assessments to identify *topics* to be addressed. At the time we interviewed Northern, it was assessing the training needs of all its subsidiary business units as a way of zeroing in on the kinds of training they need.

3. Using an ongoing *needs identification* process, which includes employee evaluations of courses they complete and suggestions by Northern's business units and managers for new training.

4. *Benchmarking other companies* within their industry to find out what they are doing and where their training programs are going.

The skills taught as part of the "Commitment to Absolute Quality" course target the areas Northern has identified as essential to achieving its goal. The course is filled with individual and team exercises that help employees understand and act on each of the principles listed under each of Northern Trust's four quality goals:

Unrivaled Client Satisfaction
- Client needs drive improvement decisions.
- All areas need an ongoing process for establishing client and partner requirements.
- Prevention of defects is essential to meet or exceed client and partner requirements.

Continuous Improvement of All Processes
- Everything is a process—and every process can be improved.
- Process measurements provide the facts that will guide decisions.
- To solve problems, look beyond symptoms so you can find and remove root causes.

Inspired Leadership
- Absolute quality management is achieved through attention to both process *and* results.
- We will deliver absolute quality to our clients and partners through cooperation and teamwork between areas.
- Managers can lead improvement by creating a climate of support and respect for all Northern people.

Active Involvement of All Northern People
- Everyone has a vital role in delivering unrivaled client satisfaction through absolute quality in everything we do.

- We exceed client expectations when all Northern people apply a systematic and disciplined approach to process improvement.
- Skills improvement and knowledge of the Bank are fundamental tools for Northern people.

"Our course on absolute quality is the only course we mandate for all of our employees," says Tom Abraham, vice-president of the human resource department. "We're a very decentralized organization; each business unit is responsible for running its own area, for customizing any training to its unique needs."

As with Plumley and Motorola, that training ranges from basic to advanced skills. A workplace survey of more than 200 employees revealed that fundamental reading, writing, and math skills were critical to success. At the other end of the spectrum an analysis of Northern's goals and principles pointed out the need for courses on the Baldrige criteria, benchmarking, advanced SPC, service delivery, and team skills. Northern is addressing the full spectrum through a comprehensive training program that reflects where employees are and where they will need to be.

WHOM TO TRAIN IN WHAT

All employees require some quality and related training. For example:

- Every Northern Trust employee is trained in absolute quality.
- Every Globe employee has had problem-solving training.
- Every Plumley employee learns statistical process control.

In varying degrees, these and other quality leaders train all their employees in quality awareness, problem solving, reducing waste, process simplification, teamwork, and meeting customer requirements.

It's like teaching the fundamentals to a baseball team. Learn what the fundamentals are for your company (Northern Trust's list is a good place to start), then teach those fundamentals to everybody in the company. With that foundation in place, use a variety of methods to continuously identify the additional training needs of departments, work units, teams, and individuals. The additional needs differ with each "player." In baseball all pitchers run to strengthen their leg muscles, throw in the bullpen to work on their pitches and develop a rhythm, and keep track of how other pitchers approach different hitters to learn what will get them out. The nonpitchers learn and practice other skills. Within the pitching group each individual pitcher works on additional skills only he needs, such as developing a new pitch, improving a pickoff move, or changing speeds on an existing pitch. The team's coaches work with the pitchers as a group and with each pitcher individually to improve the quality of the entire team.

The quality of a company, like the quality of a team, depends on the continuous improvement of every member. A training program that recognizes who needs what types of specific training has an advantage over the program that only provides one course in quality for all employees. "At Plumley, we print a monthly bulletin announcing the courses scheduled for the coming months," says Moore. "We'll also put together a course for any group of employees that identifies a need—and we'll meet whenever they want to meet. We're not locked into some scientific education process. We're looking to be a true learning organization."

Because of its size, Globe is quick to respond when a single employee identifies a training need. "I step in to do one-on-one training immediately," says Jennings. "If an employee wants to make his or her job easier, I'll offer some tools that may help. If someone needs insight into why a pattern on a control chart isn't random, I'll take 15 or 20 minutes to help them understand what could be going on."

"We don't put a lot of stock into evaluating this or that program," Jennings concludes. "We'd rather get out there and do things and learn on our own." A flat organization of Globe's size, dealing with an old technology employees know well, can afford to focus more on the immediate training needs of individuals and teams. Organizations that are larger, that are new to the quality improvement process, or that are involved in rapidly changing industries will need to develop a quality training program that teaches the fundamentals to all employees, then establish a mechanism, as Plumley and Globe have done, that allows them to respond quickly to specific needs.

DELIVERING TRAINING

As you would expect, Globe does not bring in consultants to conduct training for them, preferring to do it internally. However, Globe does take advantage of training offered by its customers. "General Motors, Ford, Dow-Corning, General Electric, and other customers have been very generous about training our employees," Jennings says. Whatever training is offered, the company is sensitive to the demands on its employees. "Our people won't sit still for a long time, maybe an hour or two at the most," says Jennings, "so we try to do our training on the fly. A half-hour to an hour training session is ideal."

Like Globe, Plumley does most of its training internally. "We have 34 full-time employees who are part-time instructors," says Moore. The use of internal trainers gives a company a pool of talent to draw from as it adds and changes courses—and it is less expensive than hiring outside trainers.

Northern Trust created a volunteer corps of 70 trainers drawn from its business units to teach the course on absolute quality. Only one had any experience as a trainer. "All of them had to be certified to train," says Debra Danziger, vice-president and chief quality officer. "They each had 70 hours of preparation time, during which they attended class, studied absolute quality, and practiced being a trainer during videotaped sessions. They also spent about 100 hours each customizing the training materials for their business units." An *audit team* observes the training sessions to make sure the message is consistent and to help improve the training process.

Customizing the materials for each business unit makes the information more relevant. Asking participants to apply what they are learning as individuals and teams helps them remember information. For example, one exercise in Northern Trust's "Commitment to Absolute Quality" course reinforces the steps in describing a problem. The exercise asks the participant to "define a problem in one of your processes," then list key individuals or groups to be involved, current performance on key indicators, desired performance level, and a problem statement. A subsequent team exercise after a section on identifying root causes asks the participant team to choose one of the problems described previously and construct a cause-effect diagram to help identify likely causes.

Northern closes the loop with an "Action Guide" section rife with assignments on everything from conducting an internal partner interview to developing a plan for preventing service defects to assessing team information needs. The on-the-job application of skills learned in training is spurring a fundamental change in Northern's culture. "People who have been through the course start thinking of their jobs as processes and of the need to manage those processes by fact," says Beverly Griffith, vice-president of subsidiary banks and one of Northern's certified trainers. "They're also applying what they learn to every area they come into contact with."

The on-the-job application of knowledge and skills becomes more difficult when the training is more theoretical or general, or when immediate applications are not identified and monitored. Globe typically performs its training on the job. As Norm Jennings says, "If we're going to give training and take any time out of their day, we want them to be able to use it right away."

Plumley determined that its on-the-job training was not as effective as it needed to be. Discussions with front-line supervisors resulted in a plan for standardized on-the-job training that is currently being implemented.

All three companies focus on quality during the orientation of new employees. Plumley's three-day preemployment training program includes an introduction to continuous improvement and statistical process control. New employees spend half of each day on the floor working, then return to the group to discuss their experiences.

Norm Jennings emphasizes quality system training for new Globe employees. "I describe the process from raw materials to finished product, then give them some background on the industries we serve and why. And I make sure they understand what to do with nonconforming material." After the orientation, each new employee works with a production team for three months before being left on his or her own.

Northern introduces new employees to absolute quality in a letter they receive before they start work. A half-day seminar during their first week of work includes a more detailed description. Within their first two months, new employees attend a welcome assembly hosted by Northern's chairman. He talks about his career at the bank, how the new employees fit into the process, why they were chosen, and how they carry out the bank's quality mission.

EVALUATING THE EXTENT AND EFFECTIVENESS OF TRAINING

Evaluating the extent and effectiveness of training requires the identification and use of key indicators for each.

Extent is the easy one: How much of each type of training have your employees received? "For our 'Commitment to Absolute Quality' course, we're tracking the number of training hours for each person who's taking the course," says Northern Trust's Tom Abrahams. "We keep track of all training, internal and external, for each employee. Managers use this information to plan training with their people, and the information also feeds into our evaluation and improvement process."

The number of training hours per employee varies considerably, even among quality leaders. Here are some guidelines:

- Federal Express employees average about 27 hours a year.
- Motorola employees average about 36 hours.
- Marlow Industries employees average over 60 hours.
- Milliken associates average about 76 hours.
- Corning employees average more than 90 hours.
- Solectron employees average over 100 hours.

The *effectiveness* of quality and related training is harder to measure. Many companies tie general improvements in quality to the completion of training.

Since it turned its attention to education in 1985, Plumley has had 65 employees earn General Educational Development diplomas (the adult equivalent of a high school diploma), 26 achieve Certified Quality Technician certification, and 16 achieve Certified Quality Engineer certification. The average hours of training per employee has risen from 8 in 1985 to 102 in 1993. As proof of the effectiveness of this training, Plumley points to the supplier and Department of Labor awards mentioned earlier in this chapter.

Other companies are measuring effectiveness through indicators more closely linked to the training. Such indicators offer a more immediate and traceable footprint, instead of trying to extrapolate the impact of one quality contributor from that of the whole herd. Typical indicators come from:

- Surveys of employees upon completion of a course to measure such things as how appropriate the material was and how easy it was to understand
- Surveys of employees a few weeks or months after completion of a course to determine the degree to which the course content has been retained and applied
- Questions in annual employee surveys about training needs and effectiveness
- Follow-up training sessions some time after completion of a course to discuss problems, obstacles, and successes
- The development of measures that show the application of learned behaviors and skills on the job (statistical process control, for example)

Northern Trust surveys employees at the end of each module of the "Commitment to Absolute Quality" curriculum. It is looking at surveying employees again six months after they complete the course to check on how their new skills are being applied. The company also relies on its certified trainers for input. "We tap into them about every three months," says Danziger. "They've played a major role in helping us develop and refine the course for our nonmanagement employees."

For smaller companies the measures of effectiveness tend to be more immediate. "We don't do any trending," says Globe's Jennings. "We're so lean that we can look at each other and know what areas need training. We don't need a lot of fanfare to make a change."

THE SHIFT IN THINKING

In the new business management model, a company is obligated to train its employees, to provide them with the intellectual arsenal they need to work in teams, collect and analyze data, initiate improvements, satisfy customers, and assume all the other responsibilities that come with empowerment and involvement. As the role models in this chapter and throughout the book prove, continuous improvement is possible only with the continuous and effective training of all employees at all levels.

The key to effective training is to truly understand your employees' and your company's training needs. Companies such as Globe Metallurgical, the Plumley Companies, and Northern Trust determine employees' needs through observation, surveys, testing, and listening. To find out where their employees and the company need to be, they listen to their customers, study their competitors, translate their short- and long-term goals into training needs, and solicit input from employees and teams.

Successful companies train all their employees in the fundamentals of quality as defined by their company's goals and objectives. They build on the fundamentals by tailoring more specific quality training to the needs of business units, divisions, departments, teams, and individuals.

Their training programs change constantly to reflect and anticipate changes in customer needs and expectations, new technologies, new markets, competition, and employee capabilities. They change, but they never end, for individuals or for groups of employees. Improving your organization's "system" is a continuous process fraught with obstacles to overcome, challenges to tackle, and opportunities to seize. The people in the system are in the best position to make these improvements, but they cannot unlock the possibilities without knowledge. As Anthony Carnevale, chief economist at the American Society for Training and Development, said in a *Fortune* article, "If you want to build a high-tech, high-performance, flexible organization, then you have to train your workers."

8 REWARD AND RECOGNITION

Tennant Company
GTE Telephone Operations
L-SE Steel

In the new management model the role of employee rewards and recognition—such things as performance appraisals, compensation, recognition programs, and promotion systems—is to support the achievement of the company's goals. This aspect of the system is usually not among the first to receive attention, nor should it be when a company is still figuring out how to satisfy customers, manage processes, and involve employees. Besides, it is better to get your collective feet wet in the easy stuff before diving into the treacherous waters of reward and recognition.

The treachery lies in our beliefs about what motivates people. Most managers and supervisors believe that pay is a prime motivator of performance. Research and surveys of employees suggest it is not. Traditionalists scoff at the need for pats on the back and thank-you's, pointing out that people are paid well to do well. Surveys of employees and the experiences of a few companies, however, suggest that day-to-day recognition is a powerful motivator.

In an article in the *Harvard Business Review*, former Baldrige judge Donald Berwick said, "Total quality comes not from contingencies set up by managers but from the native curiosity, pride, and desire for craftsmanship that are likely to be widespread in the workplace." The new management model supports the expression of curiosity, pride, and desire for craftmanship because they are the attributes that make continuous improvement possible. At the same time, the new model supports the use of employee rewards and recognition—Berwick's "contingencies"—to attain the company's goals. As Berwick rightly claims, rewards and recognition will not produce total quality, but the lack thereof can produce the opposite: a steady erosion of an employee's belief in the real value of quality and of his or her contribution to improving it. A company's first charge when it does turn to this area is to bring its reward and recognition approaches into alignment with its new management system.

Of all the components of the new model, employee reward and recognition may have the farthest to go. Human resource and non–human resource executives alike scratch their heads about how to send the right messages with their compensation and recognition programs. They are torn by opposing viewpoints:

- That performance appraisals help improve performance versus the view that performance appraisals undermine performance.
- That people focus on what they are paid to do versus the view that pay is not a motivator.
- That formal recognition inspires quality improvement versus the view that formal recognition is the least effective part of a total recognition program.
- That the reward and recognition approaches should be in the domain of human resources versus the view that employees should establish and improve these approaches.

In this chapter we will consider these viewpoints from the perspective of three models of excellence: Tennant Company, GTE Telephone Operations, and L-SE Steel. They were chosen because they have aligned their reward and recognition systems with their quality improvement efforts. Each has a particular strength: Tennant in the scope of its recognition programs, GTE Telephone Operations in its formal recognition programs, and L-SE Steel in its gain-sharing program. Yet none of the three are comfortable enough to leave their programs alone. "We realize we still don't have it right," says Rita Ferguson Maehling, Tennant's employee programs manager—involvement and recognition, "and we need to step out of our own paradigms."

In this chapter we will challenge existing paradigms of pay and recognition by addressing three questions:

- How can we pay employees in ways that support the company's quality goals?
- How can we assess performance in ways that support the company's quality goals?
- How can we recognize employees in ways that support the company's quality goals?

MODELS OF EXCELLENCE

Tennant Company is one of the world's leading manufacturers of industrial and commercial floor coatings, sweepers, scrubbers, and scarifiers. It has approximately 1,700 employees and is headquartered in Minneapolis. The company's recognition program has an interesting historical/contemporary flavor: Although its profit sharing, service awards, retirement parties, and suggestion system have all been in place for more than 45 years, it has added a half-dozen new recognition programs in the past decade—all developed and run by employees.

GTE Telephone Operations is the largest U.S.-based local telephone company, providing telephone service through more than 21 million access lines to portions of 40 states, British Columbia, Quebec, Venezuela, and the Dominican Republic. GTE Telops also markets telecommunication products and services and supplies computer software and data processing. It has approximately 121,000 employees worldwide. Its parent organization, GTE Corporation, is the fourth largest publicly owned telecommunications company in the world.

L-SE Steel electrogalvanizes steel to prevent corrosion in car parts. A joint venture of LTV Company and Sumitomo Metals of Japan, L-SE has 85 employees at its Cleveland plant. In 1992 its integrated process control team was awarded the RIT/USA TODAY Quality Cup for implementing a total quality management system that saved the company $2.2 million in 1991.

HOW COMPENSATION SUPPORTS THE NEW MODEL

In this corner is Dr. Michael Beer, a Harvard professor of business administration. In the *Harvard Business Review* he wrote:

> Pay's function is to create equity and fairness. It should attract people to an organization and keep them there. Pay should not be an active ingredient in promoting teamwork and motivating performance.

In the opposite corner is Quentin Skrabec, Jr., manager of quality at L-SE Company. In an interview he said:

> I've been the manager of quality control at four plants. I've seen a variety of systems used to promote quality, but gain sharing works the best. Our workers respond to pay, so we drive quality with gain sharing.

Before the debate begins, a review of the ground rules. First, pay must support a company's quality improvement process. That support may take the role of an aggressive incentive or of a loyal fan, or some role in between, but it must support quality improvement. To that end, any compensation system should follow these key principles of quality management:

1. *Compensation should be customer driven.* Pay all employees for skills that matter to the company's external customers. Doing so requires a clear understanding of what customers need and expect and what the company does to meet those needs and expectations. Internally, both employees and managers are "customers" of the compensation system. Their needs and expectations must also drive the compensation system.

2. *Compensation should be team-oriented.* Total quality management requires the extensive use of teams. If any compensation is considered "at risk"— dependent on performance or results—it should be based primarily on achieving team goals.

3. *Compensation should be measurable.* The measures used to determine any at risk pay must be the observable results of team performance. Measures must be relevant, available throughout the process, focused on what is important to the customer, and established, collected, and controlled to a great degree by the team.

4. *The compensation system should have full employee participation.* As Berwick writes, "Knowledge is in the work force." Employees, individually and in teams, must participate in setting meaningful goals, identifying key performance indicators, and monitoring and evaluating progress. The company must provide and encourage training to help employees master these tasks.

L-SE's Gain-Sharing Program

With these four principles in mind, consider L-SE Company's gain-sharing program. L-SE does not have traditional seniority pay levels. Instead, an employee's base pay is for skills, such as electrical or mechanical. Employees that start at around $19,000 a year can boost their pay to over $32,000 if they complete all the training the company offers, which can take up to four years. The company's goal is to give all employees the skills they need to serve their customers better. To reinforce the value of their skills to their customers, line employees are assigned monthly visits with L-SE's major customers.

L-SE's plant is run by teams, which the company calls committees. An employee can volunteer for up to seven committees. The committees handle everything from scheduling to hiring to gain sharing. An example of their authority: When the company needs to add a new employee, the hiring committee places ads in newspapers, interviews candidates, secures outside testing, and hires the employee. Management does not meet the new employee until after he or she is hired (although a manager is on the hiring committee).

The integrated process control (IPC) committee that won the Quality Cup is another example. This team of 13 L-SE employees focuses on standards and the improvement of compliance with standards through statistical process control (SPC) tools. Beginning in 1988 L-SE provided an average of nine days of training in SPC and IPC per employee. Employees developed process standards for all key variables, then implemented the use of SPC tools and monitored compliance to standards.

To promote compliance, the IPC and gain-sharing committees recommended that 20% of the gain-sharing payout be tied to IPC implementation goals. Other gain-sharing goals have included reducing the number of customer complaints, improving output, and increasing training. All goals are *measurable* company goals. Employees can earn bonuses equal to 25% of their base salaries if they meet the goals. Management's gain-sharing program is slightly different: It equals 6–9% of their base pay, with half based on the company's gain-sharing goals and the other half on profitability.

The gain-sharing committee sets new goals every six months. As with every L-SE committee, all gain-sharing committee meetings are open to all employees. "If employees have problems or issues to raise, they can come to our committee meetings. That happens a lot," says Skrabec. The recommendations must be approved by a consensus of employees, and the committee report must be approved by the general manager.

To tap into the knowledge in its work force and to give all employees a say in matters that affect them, L-SE conducts a quality workshop for three hours every Friday. All employees participate, receiving overtime pay if necessary. The only issues are quality and the IPC system. Problems command the attention of the entire work force, proposals are debated, and issues are examined.

New ideas are typically discussed in one six-month period, then acted on in the next period, so that any significant change gets almost a year of discussion. For example, the gain-sharing committee is currently studying the addition of a safety goal to the gain-sharing goals. "We thought putting safety into gain sharing would be a positive reinforcement, rather than the negative of safety rules and being written up," Skrabec says.

L-SE's committee approach and gain-sharing program drive quality improvement. In 1991 the IPC system was responsible for savings of 27.5% of L-SE's net income. *L-SE is the only steel company to be profitable in each of the last six years.* Skrabec notes that, compared to the same type of steel plant in Japan, L-SE excels in both quality and profitability.

The gain-sharing program is not without its detractors. Union leaders from other companies have resisted the new program because they prefer incentive-based bonuses instead. Managers from other companies fear that such a bonus system will increase their payroll. "Actually, our costs are much lower because we operate with fewer employees," says Skrabec. "We believe the pay-for-skills and gain-sharing programs lower costs by requiring fewer employees. This reduces our total payroll while maintaining high pay for our employees."

A common concern about such programs is that employees will begin to see the bonuses not as bonuses but as part of their pay; they will plan on receiving the full amount every time it is available. "We're concerned about that," Skrabec says, "but so far it hasn't been a problem—although we've had arguments about tightening up our gain sharing goals." L-SE may be able to avoid this problem because of its high level of employee involvement and open, frequent communication.

L-SE's gain-sharing program works as an incentive because it reflects the way the company works. The program was created by employees and is improved by employees. Everyone who is affected by the program has input into how it changes. It did not require a new structure, a new agenda, or new roles and responsibilities. So it works. But would it work for anyone else?

The accepted wisdom among those who have studied pay and performance leans toward Dr. Beer: Pay is like unconditional love—you give it no matter what. Unconditional pay is not a tool for change; it is the cost of having a person work for the company. Tying pay to performance invites a number of bad side effects, described by W. Edwards Deming as follows: "Evaluation of performance, merit rating, or annual review nourishes short-term performance, annihilates long-term planning, builds fear, demolishes teamwork, (and) nourishes rivalry and politics." Companies intent on following Deming's teachings agonize over how to create compensation plans, performance appraisal systems, and recognition programs that do not include the seeds of destruction.

In this area few quality leaders are far along the evolutionary path. Although L-SE's gain-sharing program may trip warning alarms for quality purists, it has been effective because it is built upon several key principles of quality management. It succeeds not as a prime motivator but as a reward for a team-oriented, empowered work force. Most companies have a lot of work to do on their quality systems before it would be natural to explore gain sharing.

When they do, many will be able to draw on their experience with another form of gain sharing: *incentive programs*. Companies have always had incentive programs for their salespeople, in many cases putting all their pay at risk as commissions for sales. Now companies are beginning to tie such incentive pay to customer satisfaction, especially for their executives. Although these programs help focus attention where it needs to be, even the best of them must be cautious about building fear, demolishing teamwork, and nourishing rivalry.

GTE Telops's Incentive Program

GTE Telephone Operations puts 20% of its executives' compensation at risk through its *Executive Incentive Program.* Of that 20%, 35% is based on customer satisfaction goals, 35% on financial objectives, and 30% on other factors.

GTE Telops surveys its customers extensively to find out how they rate their service. The surveys produce overall satisfaction ratings by region and area and are the baseline for an executive's customer satisfaction objectives. Benchmarks and other measures are used to establish expectations for each executive. For example, if an executive's overall customer satisfaction rating for last year was 88% and benchmarks of competitors showed the best to be 94%, an executive's customer satisfaction objective may be set at 92% for this year. If surveys at the end of this year show overall satisfaction at 92%, the executive receives all of the 35% customer satisfaction portion of his or her incentive compensation. If the surveys show a jump to 95% the executive will receive 150% of the customer satisfaction portion. If the surveys show no change, he or she will receive only 50% of the amount possible.

The Executive Incentive Program rewards people for improving customer satisfaction, but its ability to build teamwork, involve employees, and improve quality is unclear. GTE Telops continues to refine the program according to its quality principles to make sure it supports the division's quality goals.

The debate about the relationship of pay to quality continues to grow as more and more quality leaders turn their attention to this issue. They agree that changes in a company's compensation package should be based on key principles of quality management: It should be customer driven, team oriented, measurable, and strong in employee participation. They differ in the role money should play: At one end of the spectrum is the belief that money is a valuable incentive; at the other end is the belief that pay should have nothing to do with quality improvement. The most effective options should emerge as more companies join the debate and test compensation plans of their own.

HOW PERFORMANCE REVIEWS SUPPORT
THE NEW MODEL

Unlike the debate about pay, the consensus on performance assessments seems to be that performance reviews conducted according to the principles of quality management fit neatly into the drive for continuous improvement. The prevailing opinion among quality experts is that performance appraisals support quality improvement under the following conditions:

1. *The performance appraisal must be separate from the compensation system.*
   The purpose of a performance appraisal is to improve performance through

communication. Dangling pay like a carrot changes the emphasis from improving because it is the *right* thing to do to improving because it is the *profitable* thing to do.

2. *The performance appraisal must be based on observable, measurable behaviors and results.* The identification and use of key indicators is a principle of quality management that is just as valuable to an employee who is evaluating his or her performance as it is to an employee who is evaluating the performance of his or her punch press. In both cases the goal is to improve performance, not to criticize the performer. And in both cases the employee should help determine what to measure, then collect the data.

3. *The performance appraisal must include timely feedback.* Annual performance reviews are too infrequent to promote continuous improvement and defect prevention. Feedback should be specific, related to performance the employee can control, positive, and immediate.

4. *The performance appraisal must encourage employee participation.* The manager's role in a performance appraisal is to help the employee understand the assessment, to work with the employee to develop new goals and actions, to explore opportunities for career development, and to encourage the employee to provide feedback on the manager's performance as it relates to the employee. The employee is not a passive listener but an active participant.

This new way of reviewing performance is a natural extension of the principles that quality leaders have embraced. Employees are no longer commodities you do things to; they are *valued internal customers and suppliers* who are responsible for continuous improvement. A performance assessment that supports and encourages their contributions becomes an important tool for the quality improvement process.

HOW RECOGNITION PROGRAMS SUPPORT THE NEW MODEL

When you think about recognition programs, what is the first type of recognition that pops into your head? Formal, right? Employee of the Month, maybe, or the company equivalent of the Academy Awards: the Chairman's Award, President's Award, or Company XYZ Quality Award.

If you asked a cross-section of your co-workers the same question, you would get the same answers. If, however, you asked them what type of recognition they personally *value* most, you would probably find, as Tennant Company did, that the great majority prefer day-to-day thank-you's, praise, and pats on the back from their managers and co-workers.

In 1992 Tennant published a book titled *Recognition Redefined: Building Self-Esteem at Work*. In one chapter is a description of a survey of industrial employees conducted in 1946. Asked what factors provided the greatest job satisfaction, the workers ranked "full appreciation of work done" first. The same survey done again in 1981 and 1986 placed "full appreciation of work done" second behind "interesting work"—but still ahead of job security, good wages, good working conditions, and every other factor that contributes to job satisfaction. *Employees crave recognition.* Quality leaders take every opportunity to satisfy that craving with recognition for their efforts.

The distinction between rewards and recognition is that *rewards* are usually monetary, while *recognition* is an action or activity and is nonmonetary. Examples of rewards are bonuses, cash awards, trips, and merchandise. Examples of recognition are company awards, department or team awards and special events, individual awards, and personal thank-you's.

Based on research into human behavior and its own experiences and goals, Tennant created a *three-dimensional recognition model*: formal, informal, and day-to-day. To understand the benefits of each, Tennant identified a list of attributes that define a recognition program:

- It is *consistent*—delivered the same way every time.
- Some *cost* must be incurred.
- The recognition is *frequent*.
- The person providing the recognition uses *interpersonal skills* to give personal, specific information about the accomplishment.
- The recognition comes from *peers*.
- The goal is to recognize the highest *percentage* of total employees possible.
- Some *prestigious* awards are considered special and sought after.
- *Public display*—a high-visibility event—is involved.
- The recognition must be based on *sincere* trust and respect.
- *Specific feedback* is provided to show what the person did of value.
- The more people involved in the selection process, the more *subjective* their opinions and judgments become.
- The recognition comes from *superiors*.
- A *tangible reminder* is left behind to remind the recipient of the reason for the recognition.
- The recognition is *timely*; as little time as possible is allowed to elapse between the action and the recognition.
- The recognition is *win/win*—everyone is a winner.

Tennant then looked at each type of recognition offered—formal, informal, and day-to-day—and determined whether an attribute ranked high, medium, or low for that type. For example, the cost of formal recognition is high, while the percentage of total employees recognized is low. Tennant divided the attributes into three distinct continuums shown in Table 8.1 on page 117.

Table 8.1 reveals two insights: first, that each type of recognition has different strengths, and second, that all three types rank high in consistency, sincerity, and specific feedback. The first insight suggests that a three-pronged approach to quality recognition has a better chance of success than a program that provides only one type of recognition. The second insight suggests that consistency, sincerity, and specific feedback are critical to the success of any recognition program.

Formal Recognition

Like Tennant, most quality leaders begin with formal recognition. Intel, Carrier, IBM, Baxter Healthcare, Honeywell, and others have introduced *corporate quality awards* based on quality and/or customer satisfaction measures. The awards have two primary goals:

- To recognize employees for their contributions
- To communicate a commitment to quality and customer satisfaction at the highest levels of the company

"We wanted our recognition program to act as an accelerator, to cause employees to take responsibility and be role models for improving customer satisfaction," says Mike English, director of quality improvement for GTE Telephone Operations. The vehicle for the accelerator was the President's Quality Award, enthusiastically endorsed and supported by the president of GTE Telops, Kent Foster, who said:

> The President's Quality Awards are a proud celebration of employee excellence. Anyone can be nominated, and anyone can win. An employee's title, position, or job description does not qualify him or her for an award; creativity, teamwork, and a sense of urgency do. That's what our customers expect; that's what we must deliver. And that's what we celebrate with the President's Quality Awards.

"Foster wanted these awards to become like the Academy Awards for our people, to have that prestige level," says English—and their awards celebration has all the feel of a Hollywood production. Guests are met at the airport, taken to their hotels, and treated to a dinner and reception with GTE Telops senior executives. The next afternoon they are honored at a lavish awards ceremony hosted by NBC sportscaster Dick Enberg and broadcast to 60 satellite locations.

TABLE 8.1.   Tennant Company's recognition program attributes

Low	Medium	High
	Formal Recognition	
Frequent	From peers	Consistent
Interpersonal skills	Subjective	Cost
Percentage of total	From superiors	Prestigious
Timely		Public display
Win/win		Sincere
		Specific feedback
		Tangible reminder
	Informal Recognition	
Subjective	Cost	Consistent
	Frequent	Sincere
	Interpersonal skills	Specific feedback
	From peers	From superiors
	Percentage of total	
	Prestigious	
	Public display	
	Tangible reminder	
	Timely	
	Win/win	
	Day-to-Day Recognition	
Cost		Consistent
Prestigious		Frequent
Public display		Interpersonal skills
Subjective		From peers
Tangible reminder		Percent of total
		Sincere
		Specific feedback
		From superiors
		Timely
		Win/win

Source: Tennant Company; used with permission.

That evening the winners attend a gala theme party. "All of the people who attend the ceremonies get to rate them," says English. "We've had exceptional results in terms of how this has been received and how effective it is considered."

The President's Quality Awards recognize employees in three categories: individual, team, and unit. The goal of the awards is "to recognize, reward, and encourage those who fully meet and exceed customer expectations." Nominations are by customers, peers, or management or, in the case of units, through customer survey data.

From a group of 80 semifinalists, the 10 employees that excel in customer satisfaction receive *Individual Quality Champion Awards*. "It's clear we have some exceptional people who go out of their way to understand their customers and delight them," says English. The individual awards follow a series of awards that include rings and the employees' pictures on the company's Wall of Fame in Irving, Texas. At the awards ceremony the president honors the employee who has demonstrated the highest commitment to quality with the *President's Distinctive Award*.

Two *Team Excellence Awards*, one for external quality and one for internal quality, are presented to the members of the winning teams. Top areas and regions receive the Quality Champion Cup, Quality Improvement, and Quality Award of Excellence. The quality leader among GTE's international telephone companies is given the *International Award*.

GTE Telops gave out its first President's Quality Awards in 1987. The award task force has been refining the process annually, changing categories, adding awards, and modifying requirements based on the ceremony evaluations and employee surveys. "Our employee opinion surveys have tracked the effectiveness of the recognition program and our employees' attitudes about quality," says English. "Despite downsizing and other disruptive changes, quality, productivity, and customer satisfaction have continued to improve. We attribute this primarily to Kent Foster's emphasis on the President's Quality Awards."

The prestige of the President's Quality Awards and the hoopla surrounding their presentation tell everyone at GTE Telops that quality is a priority for their leaders and their division. With quality as the vehicle for improving customer satisfaction, the President's Quality Awards have become the kind of accelerator GTE Telops had hoped for.

Like GTE Telops, Tennant's first foray into quality recognition was in the formal arena. Candidates for the Formal Quality Recognition Award are nominated by their co-workers. The nominations for individuals and groups are reviewed and evaluated by the Recognition Committee, which is a cross-functional team of employees. An average of 30 individuals and up to 12 groups receive their awards at banquets in their honor.

To increase the number of employees recognized and spread the honors throughout the year, Tennant introduced the *Koala T. Bear Award*. To qualify for the award, an employee must do one of the following:

- Exert extra effort to meet or exceed customer needs
- Go above and beyond job requirements in a small group or special project
- Consistently meet job standards and have a positive work attitude

Candidates are nominated in writing by their peers or managers. A cross-functional employee committee selects the winners. Each month, someone dons a koala bear costume, grabs a bunch of stuffed koala bears wearing Tennant Quality T-shirts, and surprises employees at all three of the company's Minneapolis facilities. Sounds hokey, right? Some employees thought so, causing the Koala T. Bear Award committee to get rid of the bear suit and just hand out the awards. A lot of employees asked where the costumed bear went. The committee brought it back.

Informal Recognition

The second dimension of Tennant's recognition program, informal recognition, took shape as the company sought ways to help managers and supervisors uniformly recognize groups. Informal recognition is given more frequently than formal recognition and less frequently than day-to-day recognition. According to Tennant's guidelines, it depends on:

- The amount of effort the group put into the project beyond the members' regular job responsibilities
- The amount of time expended to accomplish the task
- The importance of the accomplishment to the entire organization
- The ability of the group to set and meet goals

The form of recognition usually falls into three categories:

- Parties or gatherings (pizza parties, luncheons, or coffee and doughnuts)
- Outings (tours of other companies, visits to customers or suppliers)
- Gifts or giveaways (coffee mugs, pens and pencils, or gift certificates)

Managers decide what type of recognition to give and pay for it from their company budgets.

Tennant's informal recognition program has had notable successes. One committee used informal recognition to encourage employees to wear their name tags. As a result the number of employees wearing name tags doubled from 30% to 60% over a five-year period. Tennant's informal recognition program for safety began in 1975. It includes cash awards, special dinners, small gifts, and internal publicity. The recognition helped Tennant achieve one of the lowest workers' compensation rates in the country and earn public recognition for its safety efforts.

Day-to-Day Recognition

The third dimension of Tennant's recognition program, day-to-day recognition, occurs when one employee thanks or praises another employee. The recognition can be verbal or written and can be used by any employee; it is not strictly a management tool. Research shows that people value such specific individual recognition more than any other type.

In *Recognition Redefined* Maehling describes recent surveys that support this point:

- A study of 1,500 employees throughout the United States revealed that the most preferred recognition was "spur-of-the-moment recognition from their direct supervisors."
- In studies of 5,000 employees and managers conducted by recognition experts Kathryn Wall and Rosalind Jeffries, seven out of ten people said they wanted individual recognition for a job well done.

In 1992 Maehling asked over 400 people attending recognition training to rank the three types of recognition in order of importance to them. Two-thirds said day-to-day recognition was most important, 28% ranked informal recognition first, and only 6% put formal recognition at the top of the list. Asked to rank where the company placed its emphasis, 46% said the focus was on formal recognition, 44% said informal, and 10% said day-to-day.

"The surveys show that people crave day-to-day recognition but they're not getting it," says Maehling. "They want feedback. They can't function in a vacuum anymore. We need to change our culture so that regular, positive feedback is a natural reflex." Maehling intends to close the gap by increasing awareness of the value of positive feedback and by training more managers and employees in the skills they need to give and receive positive feedback. "One of our strengths at Tennant is our willingness as a corporation to do something about this," says Maehling.

Although it is not where it wants to be, Tennant is building on a decade of attention to day-to-day recognition. The Operations Committee made positive feedback a priority in 1983 and set up a Positive Feedback Committee the next year to implement daily feedback. One of the committee's first acts was to introduce That-A-Way notes. Under a bold "That-A-Way" heading, an employee writes specific praise or thanks to another employee. Acceptance of the program is visible in the number of yellow That-A-Way notes people proudly display in their work areas.

Like Tennant, many organizations are discovering the need for and value of daily positive feedback. GTE Mobile Communications has a formal recognition program that includes discretionary awards (ongoing awards for employees, managers, and teams), annual awards presented by the business unit president or vice-president, and the President's Award. "Employees are very happy with the awards and recognition process," says Lew Castle, director of employee relations, "but our employee opinion surveys tell us they want more day-to-day, intangible recognition from their supervisors. Managers are so preoccupied with meeting schedules and deadlines that they don't celebrate the successes. We're addressing that issue now." The division formed an employee involvement team of 14 people from all regional and headquarters departments. The team studied four key issues that came out of the employee surveys, analyzing data, conducting focus groups with employees, and making recommendations to management that included more informal recognition.

As organizations listen to the "customers" of their recognition and reward programs and involve employees in improving them, the effectiveness of their compensation system and of all types of recognition—formal, informal, and day-to-day—will grow in support of their quality and performance goals.

THE SHIFT IN THINKING

The shift in thinking about rewards and recognition reflects a shift in thinking about employees as a *resource*, not a commodity. The issue quality leaders are addressing is how to align their compensation and recognition programs with their new management model so that employees are rewarded and recognized for their achievements and motivated to do even better.

The best way to begin the alignment is by using the principles of quality management to assess and improve your compensation and recognition programs:

1. Learn what the "customers" of the programs *need* and expect. You can develop effective programs only if they are based on the needs and expectations of all employees.
2. *Involve employees* in improving the compensation and recognition programs. The involvement may include:

- Participating in opinion surveys
- Setting and tracking measures and objectives for any compensation tied to quality or customer satisfaction
- Creating new types and improving existing types of recognition
- Managing recognition programs
- Nominating other employees for awards
- Providing and accepting positive feedback

3. Focus on recognizing and rewarding the achievement of *team* goals. The new management model relies on teamwork to succeed. Touting individual accomplishments when you are trying to encourage teamwork can be destructive.

4. Make at risk pay and formal recognition dependent on *measurable* performance. Even better, have the employees establish, collect, and control the measurements. Better yet, make the measurements measure team performance.

Finally, don't make it worse. In your haste to improve quality, it is tempting to create a flashy Quality Award or a pay-for-quality plan that seems to promote exactly what you are looking for. Resist the temptation. Pay and recognition address some very basic human needs, such as security, acceptance, self-respect, achievement, and appreciation. You may introduce a new reward for all the right reasons, but if you have not talked to and involved employees in the process, it is likely to fail and worse: it may leave employees feeling manipulated and controlled when you are trying to motivate and involve them.

If your existing reward and recognition programs are doing no harm, you may want to leave them alone until the new management model is in place. When your system is running smoothly, revamping or fine-tuning rewards and recognition can be just the booster needed to speed the company toward its goals.

9 EMPLOYEE FOCUS

AT&T Network Systems Group/Transmission Systems Unit
Aetna Health Plans
Ben & Jerry's

One of this chapter's models of excellence is Ben & Jerry's, the second largest producer of superpremium ice cream in the United States. The company's employee handbook includes little stories employees tell about their work experiences. The stories are funny, inspiring, and touching, giving the reader a good sense of what it must be like to work there. On one page Cathie Dinsmore from the art department wrote about meeting people and telling them she works for Ben & Jerry's:

> Right away, you feel like you've performed magic. People lean closer, their eyes light up, and they get a glow in their face.... Then they start the barrage of questions that always begins with, "Is it true that you get three pints of ice cream a day?" [*It is*]. They'll ask things like, "Is it as fun as they say it is?" and "Don't you feel good about working for a company that believes in doing good deeds and believes in social responsibility?" And I always smile and answer, "Yes."

Such stories tend to make the bottom line types cringe. They would argue that a company's social responsibility is to increase profits and that any "good deeds" or programs to cure society's ills are stealing from the shareholders. This assumes that a company's sole purpose is to make money, an assumption widely shared throughout the country—but not an assumption of Ben & Jerry's.

Since its inception, Ben & Jerry's has had a two-part bottom line: to be a successful business and a force for social change. It attempts to achieve both by integrating social concerns into its regular business operations. One way it does this as a company is by contributing 7.5% of pretax profits to charity. Another way is by encouraging employees to learn about the world around them. Its search for ingredient suppliers helped employees learn about African-American farmers in the South and rural poverty in Mexico. To understand Vermont's agreement to buy electricity from the Hydro-Quebec project, seven employees spent a week in northern Quebec living with the Cree Indians being displaced by the project. In early 1992 the company sent 10 employees to the annual meeting of the Children's Defense Fund; Ben & Jerry's was the only American company represented at the meeting. Employees share their experiences with the rest of the company, raising awareness and shaping this "force for social change."

Ben & Jerry's also happens to be a profitable business, in no small part because it has very satisfied employees. In its most recent employee survey 96% of employees said they really care what happens in the company, 88% are proud to work at Ben & Jerry's, and 90% are satisfied with their jobs.

In the new business management model, employee satisfaction is considered an indicator of operating performance and customer satisfaction. As employee satisfaction increases, a company can expect its key performance and customer satisfaction indicators to improve also.

Aetna Health Plans, another of this chapter's models of excellence, is developing a new employee survey that will allow it to make a better connection between employee and customer satisfaction. "We'll take a series of employee satisfaction indicators and set benchmarks in those areas, then correlate those to similar types of expectations on the customer side," says David Lundgren, vice-president of human resources. "That's where we think the true indicator of long-term success is."

Many would agree with Lundgren's assessment, but few actually seem to have thought through its ramifications. The transition from viewing employees as commodities to embracing them as partners in a shared mission continues to be a slow process. Recent tough economic times have led many companies, including several of this country's role models—companies that have invested heavily in training their employees and encouraged them to take more responsibility—to demand so much of their people that stress has become a major problem for many employees.

Part of the stress is fear of losing your job. A startling number of senior executives have turned to layoffs as the solution to their financial woes. In a column for the Cox News Service Dale Dauten blasts this "downsizing" trend:

[CEOs who slash jobs] ought to be getting up and saying: "We did such a lousy job of planning and hiring that we have more people than we have work. And we are so broke and so dimwitted that we can't come up with any way to get more work, so our only choice is to send a lot of good people home. I am ashamed, and I am sorry."

Senior executives surely cringe at such harsh judgments. No doubt they can rationalize laying people off, but the rationalizations do not equal sound business reasoning. According to a study published by *U.S. News & World Report*, a typical company's stock price rose by 10% after downsizing. Three years later the stock had dropped by 35%.

Companies are learning that you cannot lay people off because it erodes the foundation of the company. You cannot build teamwork when people feel they are expendable. You cannot expect people to give their best when they do not feel the company values them. You cannot rally the troops around a common vision of excellence when the troops know that the only excellence that really matters is profits to shareholders and senior executives. Leaders need to understand that layoffs are counterproductive and threaten to undermine the entire system.

In fact, few leaders seem to recognize the contradictory nature of their actions. They say customer satisfaction is the primary goal, but make short-term decisions focused solely on improving the bottom line. They say that quality is an overriding value, but sacrifice quality when it threatens to cost too much. They say that the company's employees are responsible for the company's success, then lay them off. They say that the people who make the products and deliver the services and serve the customers are the most important people in the company, then pay themselves hundreds of times more than the people they are praising.

They don't get it. None of these contradictory messages is lost on employees. If senior management says one thing and does another, employees become distrustful, anxious, and cynical. They do not become satisfied. As leaders strive to align their management system, *they must also strive to align their messages.* If customer satisfaction is the primary goal, measure your success by customer satisfaction and retention. If quality is job one, sacrifice it for nothing. If your employees are responsible for your success, institute a no-layoff policy. If everyone is important, adjust your pay—including stock bonuses—to more equitable levels. And if you don't want to make such changes, don't make contrary claims.

The mission statement of Ben & Jerry's begins: "Ben & Jerry's is dedicated to the creation and demonstration of a new corporate concept of linked prosperity." This is one of the ways it makes that linkage to its employees: It has a Compressed Compensation Ratio policy that top salaries can be no more than seven times the lowest wages paid. As the policy states: "The ratio is calculated by adding the lowest wage for a full-time employee with one year of employment and the value of benefits paid by the company. At current wage levels, this figure is $18,500. Thus, the highest wage Ben & Jerry's could pay is $129,920, including benefits."

This policy has received a lot of press in the last few years as the media search for contrasts to the obscene amounts being raked in by too many business leaders. The fact is, those obscene amounts will continue to be paid. What must change, then, is the message. The first step toward improving employee satisfaction is to *communicate clearly and consistently what is expected of employees and what they will get in return.* The leader who has the ability and courage to do this can create a powerful team of people who are proud to work there, satisfied with their jobs, and eager to improve.

In this chapter we will look at how the Transmission Systems business unit of AT&T's Network Systems Group, Aetna Health Plans, and Ben & Jerry's focus on their employees. We will address three questions:

- How do we improve our human resources functions?
- How do we serve our employees?
- How do we determine employee satisfaction?

The new management model is a *people*-focused system, driven by customers and fueled by employees. As we saw in Chapters 5 and 6, a company must involve *all* its employees in meeting customer requirements. Relationships grow in importance: the relationships between customers and employees, managers and employees, employees and other employees, employees and suppliers. Satisfied employees do better in these relationships than dissatisfied employees. For that reason alone, it is in a company's best interests to produce satisfied employees.

MODELS OF EXCELLENCE

The Transmission Systems Business Unit (TSBU) of AT&T's Network Systems Group develops, manufactures, markets, and services systems for transporting data, voice, and images over public and private telecommunications networks. TSBU is the world's second largest maker of transmission systems. Headquartered in Morristown, New Jersey, the company employs more than 10,000 people in the United States and Europe. TSBU won the Baldrige Award in 1992.

Aetna Health Plans finances and delivers health care to more than 13 million people nationwide. Headquartered in Middletown, Connecticut, this diverse health services company helps employers control their medical costs by managing physician networks, administers health benefit claims for major organizations, and provides employee benefits related to insurance coverage. Aetna Health Plans is a strategic business unit within Aetna Life and Casualty Company, the nation's largest stockholder-owned insurance and financial services organization. It has approximately 17,000 employees.

Ben & Jerry's, Vermont's Finest All Natural Ice Cream & Frozen Yogurt, was founded in 1978 in a renovated gas station in Burlington, Vermont. The company markets its products through supermarkets, grocery stores, convenience stores, and restaurants, and also franchises Ben & Jerry's ice cream scoop shops. It has 500 employees. Its mission statement says: "Underlying the mission of Ben & Jerry's is the determination to seek new and creative ways of addressing [its product, social, and economic missions], while holding a deep respect for individuals, inside and outside the company...."

IMPROVING THE HR FUNCTION

"In a general sense, our mission statement says how we're going to treat people," says Liz Lonergan, human resources manager at Ben & Jerry's. "We are developing a more specific definition of how we are going to deal with people and how you can expect to be treated as a Ben & Jerry's employee."

The impetus for these and other changes affecting employees comes from the company's president, who is charged with implementing the will of the company's board of directors, and from the company's biannual *employee survey*. Ben & Jerry's has a three-year plan. The *people* piece of that plan for 1993 focuses on:

- Diversity
- Training
- Becoming a learning organization
- Communication
- Total quality
- Customer service
- Work/life issues

The diversity issue came from Ben Cohen, the "Ben" in Ben & Jerry's. The need for training came from the board and the employee survey. "The need to become a learning organization comes from the sense that, we have the resources, we're profitable, there have to be ways we can use people's skills that we're not," Lonergan says. The other issues were also raised by the board and/or employee survey.

Larger companies often identify human resources (HR) issues through their strategic planning process. At Aetna the human resources manager participates in the strategic planning team. As the team determines key business strategies, gaps, and actions, the HR manager provides a human resources perspective. The resulting plan includes major human resources initiatives, and human resources personnel support strategies for other key initiatives throughout the organization.

Like Aetna, AT&T's Transmission Systems business unit takes its HR plan from the unit's strategic plan. The head of human resources is part of the executive board that develops the plan. In addition, each executive board member is responsible for a different major area of the business, which means that someone other than the head of human resources is responsible for raising HR issues at the board level and for overseeing the implementation of plans.

Human resources professionals are responsible for implementing the strategic plan in their areas. They typically rely on information from the employee attitude survey and from focus groups formed specifically to discuss a particular issue. They form cross-functional teams to analyze the information and develop plans of action. The teams may present their recommendations to the executive board or implement them on a trial basis. "We do a lot of things on a trial basis, then look at it for six months to see if it's working before deploying it to other parts of the business unit," says Sheila Landers, personnel services manager for AT&T Network Systems.

For quality leaders the implementation usually means pushing more of the responsibility for human resources issues to managers, supervisors, and front-line employees. We saw in Chapter 6 how employees on self-directed work teams are getting involved in hiring, training, recognition, and other functions that used to be the domain of human resources. At Ben & Jerry's, improving the development and effectiveness of the work force is primarily the job of managers and supervisors. Human resources people become facilitators, consultants, and coaches.

Aetna Health Plans sees a similar transformation. "We're preparing our managers to be strong human resource leaders, empowered to take responsibility for HR issues in their area and supported by state-of-the-art tools ," says Lundgren. "We're redefining the role of the manager, putting more emphasis on people without trading off our tremendous strengths."

Aetna Health Plans has developed a middle management council that helps identify and frame human resource issues and serves as a sounding board for senior management. The human resources department works with this council on communication initiatives and experimental HR programs. Aetna is also using focus groups to bring human resource issues to the people affected by them. For example, it has formed a focus group, consisting of doctors, nurses, and network people, to improve staffing in the medical area. "The goal is to work from the customer back," Lundgren says.

Working from the customer back is not something human resources departments typically do well. They are charged with developing their company's people, and that responsibility tends to focus all their attention within the company's walls. However, the new management model is customer-driven, and that charge supersedes all others. Human resource departments that start with customers often gain a new understanding of what employees must be able to do, and of HR's role in supporting them.

SERVING EMPLOYEES WITH BETTER BENEFIT PROGRAMS

In the last three chapters we showed how several leading companies are serving their employees by empowering, training, rewarding, and recognizing them. In this section we will examine how each model of excellence for this chapter goes beyond the basics to satisfy employee requirements.

Acting on a premise of the new management model that you can only manage what you measure, Aetna Health Plans' David Lundgren set up a human resources "dashboard" that lists eight or nine measures that represent the health and well-being of the work force. Lundgren says, "I present our performance on these measures to the senior staff every month to get them to consider human resource issues with the same intensity as the financial bottom line."

Aetna Health Plan's benefits are corporate driven, with HR people from the Health Plan sitting on the corporate human resources team. In 1987 Aetna appointed a *work/family task force* to look at services and benefits that would help as many employees as possible, be cost-effective and flexible, and help recruit and retain employees. Actions taken on the task forces' recommendations significantly improved the company's benefit program by:

- Providing more generous benefits for part-time workers
- Making it easier for employees to work at home or share jobs
- Offering work-time seminars on life issues (i.e., home alone and safe, communicating with teenagers, etc.)
- Supporting a variety of support groups
- Providing adoption benefits
- Opening family resource libraries
- Establishing a liberal family leave policy

The new leave policy demonstrates how improvements in benefits can improve employee satisfaction, and thus benefit the company. Eligible employees can now take up to six months off without pay, plus an additional six months with their supervisors' approval. Their benefits continue during the leave and their job is guaranteed upon their return. Since implementing the policy, Aetna is retaining 91% of those who took the leave, compared to 77% under its old policy. "The way we build our benefit package and the way our policies are created is to achieve a balance between work and personal life. We stress the need to keep that in some kind of equilibrium," says Lundgren.

DeAnn Anderson, assistant vice-president of quality for Aetna Health Plans, adds, "We're in the health care business, so this *should* be a strong area for us. We have a lot of programs ranging from physical fitness to flextime to Employee Assistance Programs. We want to provide the right balance so that we get the best out of people."

Aetna is a leader in its use of *flex hours*. "I've seen individual managers and supervisors really work with people, treat them like customers by asking what works best for them—and that's more productive for the company, too," Anderson says. "Our managers are empowered to make these arrangements work for the employee."

Aetna has a very aggressive *Employee Assistance Program* (EAP) that recognizes the tremendous pressure on single mothers, on couples with dual careers, and from increased work loads and demands to improve productivity. In addition, Aetna Health Plans is in the process of becoming a managed healthcare company, and that puts additional stress on its employees. The human resources department has placed a lot of emphasis on stress management, including extensive communication and training. "I believe that you can teach people to be more resilient to change. We begin to build resilience during orientation, then provide 'tune-ups' throughout their careers," says Lundgren. "I've added a measure to the dashboard on our EAP usage rate. As we give people the skills they need to handle change, we'll see if we reduce EAP usage."

Two more of Aetna Health Plans' services to employees need to be mentioned, even though the subjects are covered elsewhere in this book.

First, Aetna encourages its employees to volunteer in their communities by providing the time and support that allow them to contribute. It is a practice Aetna's chairman has fostered, similar to the attitudes of the leaders of USAA and EMD Associates (see Chapter 17 for more on this subject). What is interesting about Aetna's stance is its belief that the people who give, get something in return. "We believe that volunteerism is a part of employee well-being also," says Anderson.

The second area is Aetna's performance appraisal program, a subject we covered in more detail in the previous chapter. One of the products of this program is a *personal development plan* that focuses on closing gaps in knowledge and skills. "Our training investments are driven by feedback from AHP's personal development plans," says Lundgren. To create a learning organization, Aetna is linking the competencies that individuals need to be successful with the technology of education, including "downlink satellite services to our major facilities so people can learn without being away from their jobs and families," says Lundgren. "To close the educational loop, we're tracking performance in our certificate programs and feeding the results to our managers, who correlate them with the employee's productivity."

Like Aetna, AT&T is known for its leadership in services to employees. In partnership with unions, AT&T established *Alliance Learning Centers*, where employees can go for training in areas of interest *outside* AT&T. Transmission Systems is considered the benchmark in this area within AT&T. "If you have another occupation you're trained to do, you're less fearful of something happening here," says Landers. "We have employees learning about nursing, law, flying planes, and many other occupations." Transmission Systems works with employees to help them develop career plans. More than 2,000 nonmanagement employees now have career plans—and some of those plans will mean leaving AT&T.

AT&T excels in other areas as well. *The AT&T Development Fund*, a joint project of AT&T and two unions (CWA and IBEW), gives money to day-care providers in areas where there are large numbers of AT&T employees, to improve or expand their programs. The Fund is a $25 million project over a six-year period. Transmission Systems provides one of the safest work environments in its industry, with a host of safety awards to affirm its world-class performance. It offers its employees an *Employee Assistance Program*, tutoring programs, retirement planning, and lots of athletic leagues. It has an active *Affirmative Action* program, spearheaded by a vice-president who leads an affirmative action committee. It sponsors local chapters of support groups that are sponsored by AT&T at the national level, including a Hispanic-American group, Asian-American group, African-American group, gay and lesbian group, and women's group. "The groups have been very effective because they can raise issues and are a resource to management on related issues," says Landers.

Ben & Jerry's offers a benefits package designed to address employees' basic needs, including a health insurance plan that covers all members of the employee's family, including domestic partners. "To me, this is the best thing we do, because it gives the employee control," says Lonergan. "Who do you love? Who do you care about? Who do you live with? It's not who society says is OK, but who the employee chooses." The free health and dental insurance plan focuses heavily on preventive care and includes 80% coverage for alternative care providers.

Among its other benefits Ben & Jerry's offers a stock purchase plan; more than 60% of its employees have participated or are participating in this plan. It also provides wellness benefits, a great maternity leave policy, two weeks of paternity leave, an Employee Assistance Plan, educational assistance, and free fitness center memberships.

Beyond benefits, Ben & Jerry's serves its employees by *valuing* them for who they are. "One of the biggest benefits of working at Ben & Jerry's is that you can be yourself," Lonergan says. "I went to a conference a couple years ago where this dynamic woman speaker was talking about quitting her job: The closer she got to work, she'd turn the music down, put her make-up on, button the top button on her blouse. I didn't get it. Here, it's OK to express yourself and to be valued for being yourself, rather than fitting into what some executive thinks." While such a notion is probably more than most executives can bear, it is a refreshing affirmation of the values we try to teach our children and to live by ourselves. Many senior executives would like their employees to believe that they are free to express themselves and that they are valued for who they are; very few have actually done anything about it.

Here is one last example of the contrast Ben & Jerry's provides. Company cofounder Jerry Greenfield preaches a simple philosophy: "If it's not fun, why do it?" Acting on this philosophy, Greenfield created the Joy Gang to increase joy in the workplace. "The Joy Gang's mission is to do cool stuff that employees like," says Lonergan. "They bring masseuses to the plant and people can sign up. Every other month they do a lunch for people at a site. Every once in awhile you'll find a flower or candy with your paycheck, or they'll just hand out candy. They'll sponsor trips, like free skiing." And then there is the Name That Face Contest (employees bring in photos of themselves from the past and everyone tries to guess who is who), ping-pong contest, Elvis Presley Day, Barry Manilow Day (Manilow tunes are played in the lunchroom and other activities celebrate the singer's birthday), and a Halloween contest that encourages employees to come to work in zany, weird, and ugly costumes. The list is much longer, but the point is the same: *increasing joy in the workplace*. For companies that wish to improve service to their most valuable resource, increasing joy sounds like a good place to start.

DETERMINING EMPLOYEE SATISFACTION

Ben & Jerry's and Aetna Health Plans conduct *employee surveys* every two years. AT&T's Transmission Systems' annual survey asks 118 questions. It used to send the survey home because it wanted employees to take their time completing it, but the response rate was too low. In 1992 they had employees complete the surveys at work, after encouraging supervisors to provide adequate time. The response rate jumped to 85%.

Transmission Systems considers the results of the survey to be its best indicator of employee satisfaction. It has been tracking six key indicators of satisfaction for several years. If there is a blip in an indicator, the business unit forms focus groups to help it understand the problem and cross-functional teams to address it. The survey also includes space for comments, which are forwarded anonymously to the vice-president level. "You get a great idea of what's going on from those comments," Landers says.

In addition to its surveys, Aetna gathers employee satisfaction data through its middle management council, ongoing roundtables that include managers and employees, and regular dialogue between managers and employees on issues of common interest. The dialogue is inspired by a quarterly newsletter that introduces the subject, provides background, and suggests points for discussion. Recent topics have included health care reform, the changing role of leadership, and the creation of a learning organization. Human resources personnel communicate with managers and employees to find out how the dialogue went, as another way of understanding how people feel about the issues that concern them. As Lundgren says, "You've got to communicate if you're trying to improve quality and the workplace."

And it doesn't hurt to listen, either. Aetna Health Plans continues to seek ways to improve its understanding of the current levels of employee satisfaction, and of the steps that cause that satisfaction to go up. One way to tap into this information is to increase the frequency of employee surveys. AT&T's Transmission Systems business unit did that in 1991 when it began conducting mini surveys. Other companies have gone to annual surveys, although progress on this front is slow. "I think you'll see companies increase employee feedback through less formal channels," says Aetna's Lundgren. "When you ask for feedback, you don't always get accolades and that makes some managers uncomfortable. Enlightened managers are starting to say that this type of information is valuable because it helps them improve their leadership style."

In the new management model, relevant information is required to improve the system, not to fix blame. If a process goes out of control, information about that process is used to bring it back into control, not to seek out the responsible people and chew them out. This is true whether the process involves manufacturing a widget or managing people. It is the reason companies that embrace the new model need to do a better job of collecting information about employee satisfaction.

Consider the parallels to customer satisfaction. Companies have always assumed that they knew what their customers required. However, when they were forced by competition and other pressures to get closer to their customers, they quickly discovered that their understanding only went skin deep. Companies such as Solectron, IBM Rochester, Xerox, and Staples now work hard to stay on top of customer requirements because they know those requirements drive their business—and the requirements change.

We can apply the same shift in thinking to employee satisfaction. Companies have always assumed that they know what their employees require. However, as they are being forced to involve all of their employees in satisfying customer requirements, they are discovering that their understanding only goes skin deep. Companies that believe that employee satisfaction is an indicator of customer satisfaction know that they must do a better job of understanding and meeting their employees' requirements.

THE SHIFT IN THINKING

In the new management model, *employees make the system work*. They interact with customers, translate customer requirements into products and services, manage and improve processes, work with suppliers, determine and use measurements, compare their processes to others, contribute to their communities, and perform all the other tasks that turn a building filled with equipment into a successful business.

In this respect the new management model heads in the direction laid out by economist Lester Thurow, who has written that, "in the twenty-first century, the education and skills of the work force will end up being the dominant competitive weapon." Thurow wrote this prophecy in his book, *Head to Head* (William Morrow and Company, 1992). He pointed out that individuals, companies, and countries become rich through some combination of four factors: more natural resources, more capital, superior technologies, or more skills. Comparing the economies of the United States, Japan, and Europe, he states:

> New technologies and new institutions are combining to substantially alter these four traditional sources of competitive advantage. Natural resources essentially drop out of the competitive equation. Being born rich becomes much less of an advantage than it used to be. Technology gets turned upside down. New product technologies become secondary; new process technologies become primary.

And the new process technologies depend on people who are empowered, trained, recognized—and satisfied with their work.

The shift in thinking in this area is as dramatic as any required by the new management model. If a company truly succeeds or fails because of its human resources, *it must always act as if employees are its most important asset.* Management must serve the work force, in the sense that it must help people learn, grow, contribute, and excel.

More than 20 years ago Robert Greenleaf wrote an essay called "The Servant as Leader." A line from that essay captures the new management model's employee focus:

> The business exists as much to provide meaningful work to the person as it exists to provide a product or service to the customer.

10 CUSTOMER CONTACTS

Solectron

Metropolitan Life Insurance Company

Randall's Food Markets

Thomas Interior Systems

Satisfied employees produce satisfied customers. In the old style of management the one or two people who actually believed this statement interpreted it to mean that happy employees cared more about the quality of the widgets they were assembling than disgruntled employees did. The warning never to buy a car built on a Monday was offered as proof.

In the new management model the connection between satisfied employees and satisfied customers is much broader. Companies intent on tracking their customers' changing requirements and improving their service are encouraging more and more employees to interact with customer representatives on a regular basis. As competition neutralizes the distinctions between products, companies vie to differentiate themselves through the quality of their service.

MetLife developed a personal quality training program for this reason. We will discuss the program later in this chapter. In the videotape it used to introduce the program to employees, the narrator summarizes the importance of those "moments of truth" when customer and employee interact:

> At some point today, for some customer somewhere, whether internal or external, YOU will be MetLife, and our entire reputation as a company will be in your individual hands. In that moment, you will make an impression. The impression will either be good or it will be bad, and you will speak

more loudly than all our community involvement, all our advertising, and all our public relations put together.

MetLife recognizes the power of personal contact. Its "Achieving Personal Quality" course captures the attributes that contribute to solid customer relationships.

In fact, the attributes would be equally valuable in any type of relationship. It is striking to notice the similarities between MetLife's attributes of personal quality and the ways quality leaders such as Engelhard-Huntsville and Ben & Jerry's relate to their employees (see Chapters 5 and 9) or the way Bose relates to its key suppliers (see Chapter 13) or the ways USAA and EMD Associates relate to their communities (see Chapter 16). MetLife's attributes have the feel of universal truths, like the behaviors that contribute to a good marriage or the wisdom we wish to pass along to our children, yet they were the result of an extensive study of customer expectations. As the foundation for solid customer relationships, they are the point where our intuition and intellect meet.

If all of this sounds too touchy-feely, too bad. You can either work hard on relating to your customers at a personal level or you can watch them run off with the first company that does. Successful companies in all types of industries are doing everything they can to bring their customers into their organizations. They are reorganized to be:

- Customer focused, not function focused.
- Driven by customer requirements, not operational requirements.
- Relationship oriented, not product or service oriented.

For example (as discussed in Chapter 2), Federal Express has three cardinal rules for achieving a quality perspective:

- We must take the customer's viewpoint.
- We must emphasize the emotional issues by making the product or service emotionally attractive.
- We must look at everything that affects the customer.

These are all *relationship* issues. In this chapter we will look at how four companies improve their customer relationships. As in any relationship, the success of a customer relationship depends on how well you answer these questions:

- How do we define and carry out our roles and responsibilities in this relationship?
- How do we communicate with our customers?

Implicit in both questions is the need to continuously improve. Solectron, one of this chapter's role models and a 1991 Baldrige Award winner, has one of the best systems we have seen for staying close to its customers. It is aggressively seeking a better way. "We're as good as we're going to get with our current system," says Gary Ogden, director of marketing. While it is very good, Solectron understands what all of us need to learn, that *a customer relationship is a dynamic process needing constant care and attention.*

MODELS OF EXCELLENCE

Solectron operates one of the world's largest surface mount facilities for the assembly of complex printed circuit boards and subsystems. Its customers include manufacturers of computers, workstations, disk and tape drives, and other equipment. It has 2,500 employees in Milpitas, California. In 1990 Solectron won nine superior performance awards from its customers. In 1991 it won the Baldrige Award.

Metropolitan Life Insurance Company insures or administers coverage for more than 45 million people around the world. MetLife's products and services include life, health, disability, auto and homeowners insurance, retirement plans and related services, mutual funds, investment management and advisory services, equipment financing, and real estate sales, management, and leasing. Headquartered in New York, MetLife employs more than 57,000 people.

Randall's Food Markets, Inc. has more than $1 billion in sales annually from 48 supermarkets, 46 of which are in the Houston area. Its 12,000 employees serve more than a million customers each week. Randall's customer service orientation has helped it grow and flourish for 27 years despite the up-and-down Houston economy.

Thomas Interior Systems provides office planning and furnishings services to organizations of all sizes through three locations in the Chicago metropolitan area. It has 70 employees. The goal of the company is to be the leader in its industry, a goal it intends to reach by providing value-added office, environmental, and business tools that enhance the business productivity of its customers.

IMPROVING CUSTOMER CONTACT

MetLife's initial foray into a formal service quality improvement process occurred in the mid 1980s. The company created a network of teams centered around products and services as seen from the customer's perspective. Each team identified its major products and services, the customers for each, and the standards the team would use to monitor its effectiveness. Each team then set off to:

- Improve customer satisfaction. Every team maintains an ongoing dialogue with its customers to determine their expectations and see if the team's performance measures up.
- Reach high levels of effectiveness. As performance measures are met or exceeded, the teams "raise the bar."
- Eliminate extra processing.

The teams helped MetLife understand and fulfill its customers' expectations. To improve this process, MetLife studied the role of the individual in delivering quality service to its customers. Drawing on existing research, the company concluded that customers care about two things: how they are treated and the product or service they receive. They have expectations about these two aspects of a service: the *process* used to deliver the service and the *outcome* of that service. MetLife determined that *the quality of the process is what distinguishes one company from another,* because it is during the process that customers directly experience the service skills of a company's employees.

The direct experience is highly personal, one person to another. Company after company has tried to inspire its employees to be friendly, courteous, and helpful—and most have failed. MetLife decided to look at the issue from the *customer's* perspective.

The company invited customers to focus groups where they were asked what they expected from and valued during a service interaction. MetLife took what it learned from these groups and developed a training program, called Achieving Personal Quality, aimed at the personal aspect of quality customer service.

The cornerstones of the program are six attributes of personal quality and the underlying behaviors that exemplify them. With apologies to Robert Fulgham, reading the list is like finding out that "all I really needed to know about quality I learned in Kindergarten." Such lessons are no less valid because they are simple.

MetLife's attributes of personal quality, along with the underlying behaviors of each, show how employees should deliver high-quality service to customers:

1. Treat customers as you want to be treated when you are a customer.

   - Ask customers and co-workers how you can be helpful.
   - Listen to the concerns of others, offering support and withholding criticism.
   - Emphasize other people's strong points instead of focusing on their weaknesses.
   - Be cooperative and share credit for success.

2. Take personal responsibility to see that customers' needs are met.

   - Set clear goals and objectives for yourself.
   - Make sure that action is taken to solve the problem.
   - Follow through on commitments.
   - Become aware of your strengths and weaknesses.

3. Constantly seek to improve by learning as much as possible about your job so as to serve your customers more effectively.

   - Ask for, and be open to, feedback and suggestions from your customers, manager, and co-workers.
   - Do not be afraid to say you don't know how to do something or be embarrassed to seek help.
   - Read constantly to expand job knowledge.

4. Share your knowledge, skills, and time with others, offering help and assistance to customers and co-workers.

   - Share information gathered and lessons learned.
   - Recognize the contributions of others.
   - Treat co-workers as equals and genuine team members.
   - Worry less about who does the work or gets the credit, and more about satisfying the customer.

5. Have a positive outlook and be persistent in meeting customer expectations.

   - Take prompt action and do not procrastinate.
   - Rarely complain; instead, attack obstacles and accept challenges as opportunities.
   - Be enthusiastic about work and focus on good outcomes.
   - Find new ways to approach a task.
   - Keep your sense of humor, no matter how difficult or adverse the situation is.
   - Work hard to solve customers' problems.

6. Communicate effectively with customers and fellow employees.

   - Ask questions, especially open-ended ones that allow others to share.
   - Make statements that show your concern and understanding for other people's points of view.
   - Listen carefully and rephrase what others say to show you understand.

- Speak clearly and concisely in language that is easily understood.
- Avoid jargon.

Many companies would feel awkward trying to communicate such basic behaviors to their employees. For MetLife, the power of these attributes was that they came directly from customers. However, the company understood that people could not and would not improve in these areas unless they could learn at their own pace and in their own way. The company produced individual packets containing course materials for Achieving Personal Quality. The materials introduce the attributes and behaviors and encourage the employee to follow a six-step improvement process:

1. *Establish a vision* of what you wish to accomplish.
2. *Set goals and pinpoint* actions that will achieve them.
3. *Activate* your behavior by using cues to trigger your memory.
4. *Track* your progress.
5. *Take action* to carry out your plans.
6. *Reinforce* your progress by rewarding your efforts.

MetLife believed that people would prefer to take these steps alone. However, in focus groups held after the first pilot program, employees said they wished they could have gotten together to share and discuss the attributes and behaviors. As a result, MetLife developed discussion guides to help groups of employees talk about their experiences and opinions. Groups of ten people or so meet for about an hour at a time to discuss what the attributes mean in their own work situations.

Although the corporate quality staff created Achieving Personal Quality, it was implemented locally. "Each line of business has its own approach," says Norma Rossi, senior program consultant in corporate quality. "We created the program, but how the lines use it and what pieces they take depends on their own agenda."

A common problem for large companies with multiple business units is having to implement by persuasion rather than mandate. Smaller companies can standardize their approaches and implement them throughout the company. At Solectron the standards for contact with customers are listed in a *Customer Service Guidelines manual*. Compared to MetLife's general attributes, Solectron's specific standards sound arbitrary and rigid. However, each company's standards reflect the expectations and requirements of its customers.

MetLife's employees interact with thousands of consumers about their insurance policies. Solectron has 70 original equipment manufacturing customers. Consumers tend to be more patient than business customers. Few MetLife employees talk to the same customer twice, while Solectron's employees constantly interact with the same customers. MetLife's customers have a general sense of what constitutes good service, while Solectron's customers tell the company exactly what they expect.

Solectron has translated its customer service requirements into *standards* that include:

- If unexpected problems occur, notify the customer as soon as possible; identify the problem, impact, action, and scheduling.
- Answer phone calls within four rings; respond to messages from customers within two hours.
- Acknowledge receipt of customer problems as soon as possible; respond within 24 hours to customer problems with a solution, action plan, or date for a plan.
- When a customer calls to complain, listen carefully, do not argue, encourage the customer to talk, apologize for any inconvenience or misunderstanding, give assurance for satisfaction, ask for suggestions, and take action immediately; follow up and call back within four hours.
- The Solectron person contacted by the customer represents Solectron; do not blame Solectron's problems on any individual or department within Solectron; resolve the issue internally and apologize to the customer on the company's behalf.
- All ongoing customer partnerships must have weekly formal exchanges with the customer.

Listen. Act. Take responsibility. Meet expectations. Be courteous. Communicate. The essence of Solectron's standards fits well with MetLife's attributes of personal quality. The definition of the standards varies with customers' expectations and the organization's structure.

Randall's Food Markets is a large company, with 48 stores, that is as adamant as Solectron about anticipating and meeting customer requirements, but as flexible as MetLife in how it does it. For example, Randall's does not have a set of standards it imposes on every new store it opens. Instead, it surveys the area where the new store will be built to understand the people it will serve, then sets up the store based on its potential customers' preferences. As the store's relationship with its customers matures, it changes to more accurately respond to customer needs. "It takes a couple years for a store to adapt to its community," says R. Randall Onstead, Jr., president and chief operating officer.

Randall's is a very *relationship-oriented company.* Its employees are trained and encouraged to listen to and assist customers. For example, when a customer asks a Randall's stock person where to find an item, the stock person will not rattle off an aisle number or point the customer in the general direction. The response they have been trained to give is, "Let me show you where that is." Another example: The people checking groceries have been trained to listen carefully to the customer while they work because "they're the ones who seem to hear everything," Onstead says. If the customer has any concern or question, the employee calls over a manager to handle it on the spot.

All this listening helps store and company management stay close to their customers' changing needs. Do they want their groceries bagged for them? Do they want them carried out to their cars? Do they want to be able to rent videotapes or fill prescriptions at the store? Customers are quick to tell Randall's employees their likes and dislikes, in large part because Randall's has a reputation for listening and responding. "My job is to give the stores the tools they need to be successful," says Onstead. "We're in the business of giving people what they want."

Treat customers as you would like to be treated when you are a customer. Successful companies understand that the "Golden Rule" is just as golden for business relationships as it is for personal ones.

COMMUNICATING WITH CUSTOMERS

Good relationships require *constant communication*. As Randall's is quick to point out, an important part of that is active listening. "What differentiates us from our competitors is that we're better listeners," says Onstead. "If we didn't have a reputation for listening, we wouldn't get near the response we're getting."

In addition to the daily feedback it gets from customers, the company receives about 20 letters a day from them. It responds to every letter. About half are complimentary. The rest are requests to add, change, or fix something, or complaints. The chairman personally responds to those customers who are upset about something.

Good relationships also require *close contact*. Randall's maintains that contact because of the nature of its business, but it trains its people to take advantage of the contact by listening and assisting. Companies that do not enjoy such frequent interaction can still make it easy for their customers to stay in touch. Many give their customers lists of key employees' telephone numbers and pagers. They equip their customer-contact personnel with pagers, car phones, portable computers with fax capabilities, and access to E-mail. They encourage their customers to contact them by setting up direct numbers, "800" numbers, voice mail, and conference calls.

At Thomas Interior Systems only about a half-dozen employees do not have direct, daily contact with customers. With such broad exposure, the company recognizes the need for employees to be generalists, familiar with customer requirements and with every element of Thomas's business. It responds to the need by requiring every employee to take 40 hours of training a year in such subjects as product lines and programs with major manufacturers, specifications for major lines (i.e., carpeting, panel systems, electrical), project management, delivery and installation, estimating, design, computer issues, and business math. The company tracks who takes what courses and discusses each employee's training progress and needs during performance reviews.

In 1991 Thomas decided that some extra face-to-face contact with customers would help both sides better understand the other while helping Thomas Interior Systems improve its service. Every person in the company visited a customer. Employees did not visit customers they normally served. Each associate spent time at the customer's facility asking three questions about how Thomas Interior Systems could improve. "We got a lot of good information from this," says president Thomas Klobucher. "We took the top five expectations and revised our customer satisfaction survey to reflect them."

To capture customer feedback, Thomas relies on its customer satisfaction surveys and on employee participation in weekly cross-functional team meetings and the company's suggestion system. The company sends surveys to customers after every delivery. About one-fourth are returned. Every employee either reads or hears about every survey. Results for each question on the survey are compiled and tracked monthly.

Employees bring issues raised by customers to weekly meetings for discussion and action. They may choose to enter a specific customer request or idea into the suggestion system, which will initiate a formal process for addressing it within the company. As at Randall's, complaints that come in by letter are given to the president and his staff and handled immediately.

Solectron relies on a more formal process to communicate with its customers. It surveys all 70 of them every week, and its executive staff meets weekly to review the results. Before customers are surveyed, Solectron finds out from them who has the best information on how Solectron is performing. That person gets the survey. The company faxes its one-page *Customer Satisfaction Index (CSI) survey* to these key people every Friday. The form asks one question each about quality, delivery, communication, and service. Customers respond with a letter grade (A–D) and any comments, then fax the completed form back, usually within a day.

The CSI coordinator who receives the surveys knows from experience when one suggests a problem. He immediately contacts the responsible division to advise it of the problem so that it can discuss a plan of action during the Thursday morning executive meeting. Solectron also enters all the weekly survey information into a database to track numbers and plot trends by customer, category, division, and so on. The coordinator usually spends Wednesday evening cranking out a half-inch pile of overheads on this information for the next morning's presentation.

The Thursday morning meeting of about 100 people typically includes senior executives and customer-contact people. The meeting starts with a corporatewide summary of the previous day's quality results, then turns to a review of the week's performance using the stack of overheads. Depending on the number or severity of the issues, division managers spend a total of about a half-hour describing the problems, their analysis of the causes, and their proposed solutions. The purpose is not to put managers on the spot, but to make customer issues highly visible. "We want our customers to tell us weekly about anything they are dissatisfied with, and it doesn't matter whose fault it is," says Ogden. "We want to make the problems visible to the management at this company. Not many problems last more than a week or two."

Solectron has found that most problems are caused by poor communication. The solution is usually as simple as getting back with the customer to make sure everyone agrees on the problem, then changing the communication process so that it does not happen again.

As with all parts of the customer relationship, *communication* is the key to making customer surveys work. Companies that have tried to increase the frequency of their surveys are usually deterred when the customers complain about how much work it is or refuse to complete it. Solectron has encountered similar resistance. To persuade customers to participate, it invites them to attend the Thursday morning meetings. "When they see that they aren't filling out a form just to fill out a form, and that the information they send back is used to improve, they tend to become believers," says Ogden. If a customer still resists, a division vice-president visits the customer's president to explain the value of the process. The fact that every Solectron customer participates in the weekly survey suggests that customers believe the value outweighs the minor hassle.

Solectron's goal with every survey is "straight A's." Any grade of B or worse on a customer survey is considered a complaint and is formally logged into the company's system. Solectron sends an acknowledgment to the customer that it has received the complaint and is addressing it, then pursues one of two problem-solving modes:

- If something is out of control in the process, the company does whatever is necessary to bring it back into control. It then goes through a formal process to find out what happened and to take steps to prevent it from happening again.

- If the process is in control but the customer is unhappy, it tightens the tolerance limits on the process using statistical tools.

All complaints are tracked until they are closed. Although customers are encouraged to communicate and complain in any way they choose, this is the formal process for handling complaints.

The survey is only one of many ways Solectron stays close to its customers. *Customer focus teams* review quality and delivery to current schedules during weekly meetings. Customer executives make presentations at Solectron's weekly Tuesday morning forums. Each quarter, a team headed by the senior executive who represents the customer's interests at Solectron visits the customer to discuss ways to improve existing projects and plans for future projects. Customer executives are surveyed twice a year, and an annual third-party survey provides objective data for comparison.

As Solectron shows, constant communication and close contact are essential to building and maintaining sound customer relationships. Solectron began its weekly customer satisfaction index in 1987. In the course of five years it raised its average score from 86% to 96%. To understand how impressive that 96% is, consider that an A equals 100%, an A− is 90%, a B+ is 85%, a B is 80%, a B−is 75%, a C is worth 0, and a D equals −100. It would not take many D's to bring the average down. By surveying its customers weekly and acting on their concerns immediately, Solectron prevents B's from turning into D's, retains satisfied customers, gains new customers they refer, and grows sales at a rate of 50% a year.

THE SHIFT IN THINKING

In the new management model, companies work very hard at *bringing their customers into their organizations*. They have learned from experience that constant communication solidifies customer relationships and that such communication is much easier when:

- Customer contact is continuous.
- As many employees as possible are involved.
- A variety of communication vehicles are used.
- Formal processes are established for listening and responding to customer concerns.

The contact occurs at many points in the new model. *Leaders* are making it a part of their job to regularly visit their peers at key customer companies. Many executive staff meetings now include time for the executives to share what they learned from their recent customer visits. They also use a broader range of customer data to guide their decision making.

Some companies are including customers in their *strategic planning process*. They invite customer representatives to participate in discussions about current and future customer requirements, understanding that such requirements drive the planning process. They also encourage customers to review the plans and suggest ways they could be improved.

Many companies are setting up *customer teams* to work closely with customers on designing and manufacturing the customers' products and services. The teams interact with their customers on an ongoing basis, establishing relationships that blur the lines between customer and supplier. Customers feel that they are part of the process, welcome at their suppliers' facilities, valued for their ideas and guidance.

Successful companies use *every opportunity* to learn more about what their customers need and want. As Solectron, MetLife, Randall's Food Markets, and Thomas Interior Systems show, there are many different methods for staying close to your customers. To the extent that you use different methods in an organized, long-term way, and that the people who have contact with customers practice the attributes of personal quality, your company will develop a customer focus, strengthening the relationships that are critical to sustained growth and profitability.

11 DESIGN OF PRODUCTS AND SERVICES

Intel Corporation

IDS Financial Services

Custom Research

The design of products and services is the most customer-focused activity your company undertakes, the point where external requirements are translated into internal requirements, where customers "throw the switch" that activates your business. The design process constantly forces companies that are truly customer-driven to reevaluate customer requirements and their response to those requirements. It is a cauldron of opinions and ideas stirred by customers, suppliers, and employees throughout the company.

Popularly known as "concurrent engineering," this process encourages everyone involved in product development, including designers, engineers, customers, and suppliers, to contribute simultaneously as a team. It replaces the traditional method of passing the pot from one group to the next in serial fashion, which looks something like this:

- Sales and marketing identify a customer need and define the requirements to meet that need.
- They tell engineering what they want.
- Engineering develops a product in a series of steps that can take several years.
- When engineering finally has something marketing is happy with, it "tosses it over the wall" to manufacturing.
- Manufacturing figures out how to produce it.

The *serial design process* is lengthy and fraught with opportunities for miscommunication and rework. Decisions are made at various stages without the benefit of valuable input from affected parties. When this input is finally received, designs must be reworked, new models created, new tests ordered, and new production schedules arranged. By comparison, companies that use *concurrent engineering* find that it typically cuts the time from conception to production in half, reduces costs, and improves quality.

Intel's CEO Andrew Grove, in a February 1993 article in *Fortune*, said, "When companies lose their proprietary advantages, speed seems to be what matters most." While Intel is introducing a new chip in 1993 that is the most complex microprocessor ever built, it continues to work on its next three generations at the same time. We will look at Intel's design process in this chapter.

Involving everyone simultaneously on a design also cuts costs. Although only 5% to 8% of a product's cost is in the design phase, the decisions the designers make lock in 60% to 80% of the total costs. A change in the design that may cost $1,000 early in the process can cost millions as production nears.

Concurrent engineering improves quality by "building it in" in the early stages of development. The design process factors in the manufacturability of products and the deliverability of services to anticipate quality issues and initiate corrective action *before* the design is completed. This proactive, prevention-based approach has proven to be a far more effective way of improving quality than fixing problems along the way. Or, as Judith Corson says, "Quality pays and it's more fun. Doing things over is not." She is one of two partners who founded Custom Research, which is another model of excellence in this chapter.

Through concurrent engineering, companies strive to involve customers in every stage of the development cycle. If the point is to translate customer requirements into products and services, it makes sense to keep customers handy so that the design team can run new ideas and changes past them. Improved communication among everyone who should be involved in the design process is one of the big reasons concurrent engineering works.

The idea of forming cross-functional teams to design products and services is equally applicable to service companies. They too share the goals of reducing cycle time, cutting costs, and improving quality. The primary difference is that the variability of a service is often in the hands of the person or team providing it. For example, if a customer sits down with a bank's loan officer to talk about borrowing money, the loan officer determines from the customer's requirements what type of loan to recommend. Through his or her relationship with the customer, the loan officer learns what the specific requirements are, then translates those requirements into a loan package that is most appropriate for the situation.

The loan officer chooses from a list of options the bank has generated during its loan design process, which may have used an approach similar to concurrent engineering. However, the officer's relationship with the customer is often more important to satisfying and retaining that customer than the loan itself. As this chapter's third model of excellence, IDS Financial Services, has discovered, its clients' primary requirement is for a long-term relationship with one financial planner. IDS is currently redesigning its entire organization to improve this relationship.

In this chapter we will use the experiences of three models of excellence, Intel, IDS Financial Services, and Custom Research, to look at the design process in the new business management model. Each offers new insights into key questions:

- How do we translate customer requirements into product and service design requirements?
- How do we ensure design quality?
- How do we reduce design-to-introduction cycle time?
- How do we improve the design process?

We will answer these questions a little differently here than in other chapters. Because each of our three models has a distinctive design process, it would be confusing to jump from one to the other in order to draw general conclusions. Instead, we will present Intel's process first, followed by IDS's process and Custom Research's process. Although we use Intel to discuss translating customer requirements into design requirements, all three of our models address this critical point. All three also touch on design quality, reducing cycle time, and improving the design process. We have tried to point out these connections throughout the chapter.

MODELS OF EXCELLENCE

Intel Corporation is the world's largest semiconductor company. Almost every PC uses at least one Intel chip, beginning with the 8088 chip and including the Intel 386™ chips, the Intel 486™ chips, and the new Pentium™ processor. That roughly translates into 100 million people who rely on Intel chips. Head-quartered in Santa Clara, California, Intel employs more than 26,000 people. In 1993 Intel put $2 billion into research and development and capital outlays, an amount equal to 43% of its 1992 revenues. Intel has developed 18 of the last 25 major inventions in the semiconductor industry.

IDS Financial Services celebrates its hundredth anniversary in 1994. A subsidiary of American Express, IDS offers financial planning and other investment advisory services to individuals and businesses across the United States. Its products include more than 100 financial and investment choices, including mutual funds, life insurance, annuities, and securities brokerage services. It employs 4,000 people at its headquarters in Minneapolis and another 1,400 at its regional offices, and supports 7,439 financial planners. Total assets owned or managed by IDS exceed $85 billion.

Custom Research provides marketing research services to *Fortune* 500 companies. Custom Research professionals work with their client counterparts to design research projects that will provide information the clients need to make good business decisions. Most of the projects deal with new product research and development, including testing new concepts, products, packaging, advertising, and pricing. Headquartered in Minneapolis, Custom Research has 81 full-time employees and 170 part-time employees. It received a Baldrige site visit in 1992.

INTEL: DESIGNING TO CUSTOMER REQUIREMENTS

When Intel introduced the Pentium processor in 1993, experts hailed it as the most important product in the company's history. For a company whose previous generations of chips are being used by 100 million people and that was already working on the next three generations of chips, "most important" is a transitory title. It is like a pro football coach getting attached to his star quarterback when he has his eyes on a few college prospects he knows are the key to his team's future. The star is the star until someone better is developed. And someone better *will* be developed.

Intel develops its next stars through a design process that relies heavily on input from three sources: the people who use computers run by Intel chips; its customers; and the architects, engineers, marketing people, and other experts at Intel.

The company has a formal process for soliciting the views of its end users: a consortium, consisting primarily of information systems managers, that meets every four months in the United States and Europe and every four to six months in Asia. "We ask them what they are looking for in their products, what they are looking to do with their computers, and what applications they're going to be using," says Pamela Olivier, strategic planning process manager for Intel's processor products group.

Intel talks to its customers constantly. "We believe in treating our customers as full partners," says Michael Wood, field product planning manager. "We directly contact a reasonable percentage of customers to determine such things as their distribution channels, geographic considerations, the ways they sell their products, and other critical information, because we want to find out what their needs are and why they're important."

Intel's internal experts combine this customer and end user input with their own experience and knowledge to brainstorm possible design solutions. "At first, we tend to float our ideas past our field applications force," says Wood. "Most of them have computer science or electrical engineering degrees with at least five years' design experience. All of them work closely with our customers. We'll talk to them to get their opinions about how they think customers will respond to our ideas."

Intel begins the design process by posing open-ended questions to its assembled experts. As their ideas are narrowed to specific types of products, Intel begins to bring customers back into the design loop to test the experts' perceptions. "We are very hesitant early in the planning stages to take ideas out to our customer base," Wood says. "The issues we are dealing with are so advanced that most of our customers haven't usually thought about them yet." Having said that, Wood is quick to point out that Intel takes new product ideas to its customers earlier than it used to, citing customer involvement early in the development of the Pentium processor.

That involvement with key customers occurs at many different points within Intel. *Everyone* who is participating on a product design team has direct responsibility for dealing with the customers that have been pulled into the process. "In our industry, we need to limit the number of customers involved in the definition phase, but then deal with them in a very open and closed-loop fashion," says Wood. "This helps maintain very strong customer relations, which is extremely important to us."

Intel involves customers and end users in *establishing* their requirements, then involves them again in *evaluating* Intel's responses to those requirements. Companies with less sophisticated products and services are striving to involve their customers at every phase of the design process, from conception to production. Such involvement improves communication, keeps the focus on customer requirements, and adds a valuable outside perspective to the process.

High-performance companies are also bringing more internal groups into the design process. At Intel, "Everybody gets involved in the definition of a product," says Olivier. "If a product crosses into other organizations, they become part of the product development team." Companies striving to create more horizontal organizations call this "laying the silos on their sides," because the first time a company does it, it must overcome the functional "silos"—the marketing department, the engineering department, the manufacturing department, and so on—that have dictated how the company operates. Some companies have gone as far as to pull together people from these different silos into one physical area to work on a specific product, product line, or service. (We will describe how IDS is doing that in the next section.) For manufacturing design, these cells become the hub for the company's concurrent engineering activities.

Intel does not directly involve suppliers in the product definition phase. However, if a new technology is involved that affects a supplier's capabilities, the suppliers' voice is brought into the team through an internal supplier working with the external supplier. Other companies are putting external suppliers right on their product development teams (for more information on this, see Chapter 13).

Once a product has been defined, Intel moves to the design phase, which follows a product implementation plan (PIP). The PIP identifies the critical steps of the development cycle, including design completion, customer samples and approval, and product certification. Designs are reviewed regularly: weekly by the design team, monthly by management, and quarterly or semiannually by executive staff. An ongoing review makes sure the product remains on target—continues to meet specifications, is still manufacturable, will still perform as expected—so that when it is actually produced, it will meet all customer and internal specifications.

Intel relies on a team to improve its design process by reviewing and marrying the definition and design phases. It also conducts regular postmortems after a product is introduced to check the design process as well as the new product. The teams involved in these activities include people from marketing, design, the field, and management.

Intel benchmarks other companies to spur improvements in its design process. "I think there are people at Intel who are better at bringing the voice of the end user to the process. Strategic planning is trying to figure out how to learn from that," says Olivier. "I think we're very good at bringing Intel's ability to innovate to the process."

The results with its new Pentium processor indicate that Intel is rapidly improving its design process. When the first manufactured Pentium processor was plugged in and "booted up," the process took only 10 minutes, compared to five days for its predecessor, the Intel 486. Intel ships the first batch of chips to computer makers so that they can test them for bugs. Of all the glitches found in the Pentium processor, customers identified only 10%, compared to about 40% for the Intel 486. Despite these advances, Intel is working hard to improve the process for the next generations of chips. "We are the most highly self-critical company I've seen," says Wood. "We're working to understand the changes we make, to measure them, and to assess their implications. You can be sure that whatever we have in place now will be improved next year."

IDS FINANCIAL SERVICES: IMPROVING DESIGN QUALITY AND REDUCING CYCLE TIME

Whereas Intel has a cultural propensity for change, IDS Financial Services has a mandate. *IDS 1994* is a project so sweeping that its goal is to create a new IDS that could put the old one out of business—before a competitor tries to do just that.

Financial planning is a relationship-oriented activity in which people trust the achievement of their financial goals to an IDS financial planner and the company that supports that planner. IDS knew as early as 1986 that it needed to focus on this relationship to succeed. It got serious about it in 1990.

By then IDS had made several sincere efforts to improve its client relationships, but none had taken root, and although IDS was good by industry standards, it was not as good as it wanted to be. Senior management decided that the only way to break through the barriers to change was to redesign the entire system and the best way to drive the change was through a new cross-functional team created solely for this purpose.

The 31-person team consisted of 17 field organization members, including 10 financial planners and 13 IDS people ranging in rank from entry-level clerk to vice-president and representing all parts of the company. The team focused on four objectives:

- Retain 95% of clients
- Retain 80% of financial planners through four years of service and 97% of veteran financial planners
- Achieve annual revenue growth of 18%
- Bolster IDS's position as industry leader

To learn about the system it was chartered to change, the team spent two weeks tracking the company's *primary processes* from beginning to end. It watched as planners picked up the phone and called prospective clients, observed meetings with clients, followed documents from planners to headquarters, trailed the documents through different functions, and returned to the planners' sides to see the results. The team learned firsthand where the processes broke down and how early choices affected subsequent steps.

During the next year, the 1994 team interviewed clients, planners, management, and staff to find out more about the existing system. They benchmarked companies such as Motorola, Microsoft, and Wal-Mart to find out how other companies handled similar processes. The team pulled together all it discovered and discussed into a list of recommendations that will transform IDS.

First, the recommendations are very *process* and *system* oriented. "We've always known that financial planning is a process, but we have sold it like it's a one-time event. Our new system treats the whole process," says Neil Taylor, the vice-president in charge of the *IDS 1994* project.

Second, the recommendations are *driven by customer requirements.* As the recommendations are implemented, IDS will shift from being product and function driven to being customer driven. This radical shift will fundamentally change IDS, including what people work on, how they work, how they interact, and what their goals are.

Many of the team's recommendations focus on the primary client requirement for a long-term relationship with one IDS financial planner who is knowledgeable about relevant financial issues. The greatest obstacle to meeting that requirement is the planner turnover rate. IDS hired 1,837 financial planners in 1989; only 514 remained in 1993. Its four-year planner retention rate is 28%. To achieve its goal of 80% retention (which it knows from benchmarking is possible), *IDS 1994* is improving the hiring process for new planners, including putting them through simulations of planning situations with clients to see how the new planners respond. The team is also having all new planners spend their first four months with the company in training. Previously, new planners took all their training before they started, which meant they could be sitting down with clients as a planning professional during their first week of work. After the four months of training proposed by *IDS 1994* the new planners will be accompanied by an established planner or planner coach for all client meetings during the next year. This mentoring relationship will allow new planners to learn the client skills and work habits of successful planners.

The team is also addressing the client relationship issue by motivating planners to form group practices. "One of this company's strengths is that our clients love their planners, especially after working with them for more than three years," says Taylor. "When our team dug into this issue deeper, we heard clients saying that they wished their planner knew more about certain financial areas. We realized that few planners could have the broad level of knowledge clients seemed to want, so we looked closer at our planner base and noticed that we usually had all the necessary skills in geographic areas."

To serve clients' needs, IDS is asking planners with different areas of expertise to form groups. Each client will still have a primary planner, but if the client needs more specialized information about a particular topic, such as taxes or education funding, the primary planner can bring in another planner from the group with that expertise. When the planner is not available to assist the client, someone else from the group can take over and provide the assistance required. IDS is also relocating the groups so that planners are closer to the majority of their clients.

The goal is to retain more clients, to improve client satisfaction. To that end, the *IDS 1994* team proposed another major change: using technology to empower planners to provide more services, more quickly, to their clients. "Our process has been relatively rigid compared to what our clients need," says Taylor. "We assumed every client always needed a plan for six financial areas. Even if a potential client had a question about just one of these areas, say, retirement, our planners reviewed all six, gathered information about all six, and requested a plan for all six—which the planner presented about six weeks after taking the information." The team recommended giving planners a tool called "Financial Scan" that will allow them to explore actual client needs, then target only those that really exist. The planner can then use the computer technology he or she has to develop a plan and present it to the client within 48 hours. *IDS 1994* has effectively reduced the design-to-introduction cycle from 42 days to 2.

By connecting planners to data bases that contain investment information as well as their clients' investment performance, IDS is putting almost everything a planner needs to serve clients at his or her fingertips. Previously, planners could not perform basic service functions, such as name or address changes. They had to complete forms and forward them to headquarters, then wait for the change to be made. Now that information, and the ability to change it instantly, is available to planners on-line. Once it is entered, the planner does not have to reenter the same information for subsequent transactions.

The technology also gives the planner the flexibility to tailor a financial plan presentation to the client's preferred way of receiving information. By pressing a key, the planner can choose to present information using numbers or pie charts and graphs, to use longer or shorter explanations, to add additional information in an appendix, or to employ other options that make it easier for clients to understand their financial plans.

Clients also want to know how they are doing once their plan is in place. Part of IDS's mission is to do just that, but it could not actually track clients' progress toward their goals until now. The *IDS 1994* team has recommended a tool called "Goal Tracking" that will enable the planner to tell clients at any time where they are in relation to their financial goals.

With *IDS 1994* every IDS financial planner becomes a designer. He or she may bring other experts into the design process, including other planners and headquarters personnel, and IDS provides the necessary tools and support, but it is the planner's role to understand customer requirements and define and design the plan that will meet those requirements.

Much of that support comes from IDS's field managers. With *IDS 1994* the role of managers is changing to one of working with their planners to understand their needs and find ways to assist. Improvements in planner retention will free up time managers had to spend with new planners and allow them to spread their efforts over more of their planner force. To help them understand and explore this changing role, IDS is providing special skills training for its field managers.

IDS is also redesigning its processes and products to improve service to its clients and planners. Client service processing is an example. IDS used to have a different service area for nearly every type of product it sold. If clients or planners had questions, they might be passed to several departments before they got one that could help. To improve service, IDS looked at this process from the client's perspective. "We created service teams that could answer all product service questions from clients and planners in one call," says Dan Foslid, quality project manager. "We also organized each team around a geographic region so that their operating hours match the regions they serve. Now our planners can build working relationships with the teams that support their clients."

In addition to its functional silos—marketing, finance, legal—IDS also has *product silos*. The life insurance group develops its own products, as do the annuity group, the mutual fund group, and the other product groups. *IDS 1994* is changing the way IDS designs its products, bringing together the product design people from these various groups to form a team responsible for designing all IDS products. The new design team uses client information gathered from surveys, focus groups, planners, and other listening posts to develop products that meet the requirements of IDS's target markets.

All these major changes are driven by the company's desire to satisfy client requirements. In the process, IDS is redesigning not only its processes, products, and services, but the entire company and culture. The cultural change began in 1993 with the implementation of the *IDS 1994* team's recommendations at two development sites. It will be rolled out to six to ten pilot sites in 1994, then to the entire company. The speed of the transition will depend on when it can spend the money that is required to create a customer-driven organization—and to lengthen its lead in the financial planning industry.

CUSTOM RESEARCH: IMPROVING
THE DESIGN PROCESS

According to independent surveys, Custom Research Inc. (CRI) is also a leader in its industry. Unlike IDS, however, it has no plans for a major redesign of its organization. It has been customer driven since it was founded in 1974, and that customer focus permeates its design process.

Like many small companies, Custom Research is responsible for a piece of a much larger organization's process. In CRI's case, that piece frequently fits into the client's design process. Custom Research does market research for large companies that want to find out more about their customers' preferences before they make any expensive decisions. CRI's clients have four key requirements: they want their research to be accurate, on time, and on budget, and to meet or exceed their expectations. For every research project it accepts, the project team assigned to carry it out works with the client to define what these four criteria mean for their project.

Almost all of Custom Research's work involves custom-designed research. It is the service company equivalent of a "job shop." Since each project is unique, each project's design phase is critical to making sure CRI clearly understands its clients' requirements.

The design begins when a senior executive and the account manager who works directly with the account meet with the client to find out specifically what the client requires. A summary of the meeting is circulated to team members who work with that client. The senior executive also summarizes the client's requirements in a letter that is sent to the client, who verifies that CRI heard what the client said. The letter, revised to reflect client feedback, becomes the basis for planning and action by the project team and for the team's service standards and account plan.

Communication between customer and supplier is nothing new, but for small service companies like Custom Research—law firms, advertising agencies, and medical practices, to name a few—defining specific client requirements on paper and verifying their accuracy with the client is rarely done with any consistency. CRI does it every time, establishing a *project design* based on the client's expressed requirements that will guide the project team's efforts.

Those requirements are translated into a more detailed project design by the account manager and project team. They prepare a *plan of action* that includes the research design, questionnaire design, data collection, data tabulation, statistical analysis, report, timetables, responsibilities, and cost estimate.

A critical element in the success of the research process is the design of the questionnaire. The project results are useful only if the client knows they accurately reflect what the target audience thinks and feels about the subject. Custom Research uses templates to ensure consistent design, then checks proposed questionnaires with computer-generated responses. "We've identified four to eight fatal flaws that can render the project useless," says partner Jeffrey Pope. "We have checkpoints that will reveal if any of these flaws are present."

Questionnaires are also pretested with a small sample of people to evaluate the effectiveness of the design, looking at such issues as whether the methodology can be implemented or whether the questions solicit the necessary information. Clients review proposed questionnaires and offer their suggestions. "We have a lot of checks and balances built into the design process," says partner Judith Corson, "such as having the client review the questionnaire, determining how to code any open-ended questions, and finding out what the client wants in the survey report."

When the data collection has been completed, CRI checks to make sure the accumulated data are correct, then generates reports directly from those data to avoid rekeying errors. The account manager presents the report to the client and refers to the plan of action generated earlier to find out if the report and CRI's performance met customer requirements.

CRI's steering committee reviews the company's performance on its clients' four key requirements every quarter. Account teams review performance on key accounts quarterly. This relentless drive to measure and analyze its performance, together with the company's constant communication with clients, has produced exceptional customer satisfaction. In CRI's fiscal year 1991, 96% of its projects met clients' requirements, and 51% exceeded those requirements.

Custom Research's experience offers three lessons for similar firms:

1. *Be explicit about what your clients expect.* "We've sat down purposefully and periodically with our clients to discuss their requirements. It's rare they don't tell us something we need to learn," says Pope.

2. *Measure customer satisfaction.* CRI measures it through a short questionnaire sent to every client on every project that asks for the client's overall level of satisfaction, through a survey of major clients conducted by telephone, and through independent competitive surveys.

3. *Tie internal measures to customer requirements.* CRI has established such internal measures as Project Quality Recap Reports. On a daily basis, every team member documents problems or errors on questionnaires, data tables, reports, and timing. Similar companies (law firms, ad agencies, etc.) like to claim that what they do cannot be measured. Custom Research shows that it can. (For more discussion about this topic, see Chapters 5 and 14.)

THE SHIFT IN THINKING

In the new business management model, the design process has been commandeered from the hands of an elite corps of engineers and delegated to a host of internal experts. People from marketing, engineering, manufacturing, and other rapidly disintegrating silos come together to address every aspect of design, production, delivery, and service during the design process. They invite customers into their teams to better understand what customer requirements really are and how well their ideas respond. They pull key suppliers into the process to benefit from their special knowledge and to assess their capabilities. The new design process is a *freewheeling exchange of information and ideas* that has some very specific goals: meet or exceed customer requirements, design quality in, and get the new product or service to customers faster than before.

IDS and Custom Research are achieving these goals by putting the responsibility for service design in the hands of the people who work with clients. The financial planner or project team uses information gathered directly from the client to shape the service. The design process is repeated for every client. Each produces a plan unique to that client. Compared to the traditional "one size fits all" mentality, the new design process is able to translate individual customer requirements into products and services that meet those requirements *exactly.*

Such a process is not limited to service companies. For example, a Japanese man in the market for a new bicycle can go to his local bike shop and get fitted for the exact bicycle he wants. He can choose from among more than 11 million variations on 18 different models. The National Bicycle Industrial Company can build the bike to his requirements in three hours.

Meeting customer requirements. Improving quality. Reducing cycle time. In the new management model, the design process has the most critical role in achieving these goals.

12 PROCESS MANAGEMENT

Texas Instruments Defense Systems & Electronics Group
NCR Corporation
New England Mutual Life Insurance Company
Alphatronix

In the late 1980s, when the New England Mutual Life Insurance Company decided to look for a program that would help it improve quality, the company's focus was on providing full financial services. It thought of itself as a *full financial services company*. As its pursuit of quality led it to understand that quality is a business strategy, not a program, the company's focus changed as well. The New England is now a *customer-responsive company*.

The difference in focus is much more than a few words. As a full financial services company, The New England organized employees with similar skills into functional groups that produce, deliver, and support its services. As a customer-responsive company, The New England is organizing employees around key processes that respond to customer requirements. One is vertical, the "silos" we discussed in the previous chapter. The other is horizontal, cutting across the vertical silos, as in The New England's case, or laying the silos on their sides, as IDS Financial Services is doing.

This move from vertical to horizontal is an essential part of the new business management model. As The New England discovered, it is very difficult to serve external customers well when the company is organized to serve internal managers. The *customer-driven company* has no choice: It must look at itself from the customer's perspective, then reorganize to improve the processes that feed the customer's requirements.

In this chapter we will look at how four companies—The New England, Texas Instruments Defense Systems & Electronics Group, NCR, and Alpha-tronix—satisfy their customers through *process management*. In all four companies process management and improvement is a cornerstone of their quality improvement processes. The New England fell in love with process improvement at first sight. "It was a no-brainer," says James Medeiros, vice-president of quality commitment. "Process improvement fit into the strategy we were trying to shape, it was quick to install, and we got immediate results. I think process management is the key to the whole thing." His company's chairman and CEO concurs. At a speech to the Canadian Life Insurance Association, Robert Shafto identified seven key premises of The New England's quality improvement efforts, the first of which was: "All work is a process, and by definition, processes cut across vertical slices of the functional organization. To succeed in quality, an organization has to determine what are its core business processes that add value to customer satisfaction, and improve their effectiveness." Some have called this "process innovation," "core process re-design," or "reengineering." By whatever name, process management affects every person in a company and every task performed.

MODELS OF EXCELLENCE

Texas Instruments Defense Systems & Electronics Group designs and manufactures advanced defense systems and electronics technology for the U.S. Department of Defense. Formed during World War II, it has grown to become the country's eighth largest defense electronics contractor. Employing approximately 15,000 people, the company operates eight manufacturing, testing, research, and distribution facilities in North and Central Texas. TI-DSEG won the Baldrige Award in 1992.

NCR Corporation, a subsidiary of AT&T, manufactures computers, automated teller machines, cash register and point-of-sale systems, and communication processors. Headquartered in Dayton, Ohio, it has more than 52,000 employees in 120 countries.

The New England is the broader enterprise name that includes the New England Mutual Life Insurance Company. It has approximately $60 billion in assets under management. Founded in 1835, The New England is the nation's first chartered mutual life insurance company. It offers a broad array of insurance and investment products and services to individual and business customers through a national distribution network of 3,000 representatives. It also has 13 regional Employee Benefit offices for sales and service of its group life, health, and pension product lines. The New England has approximately 2,650 associates at its Boston headquarters, not including its investment company, NEIC.

Alphatronix is an information storage company that makes complete systems and software to store and manage large amounts of data. It was the first company in the world to ship these systems, the largest of which can hold the equivalent of a million file cabinets of information. With headquarters in Research Triangle Park, North Carolina, Alphatronix employs 65 people. Founded in 1988, it is one of the fastest growing companies in the country, in part because it has the best quality record in its industry.

IDENTIFYING A PROCESS

Before examining how our four benchmarks manage and improve their processes, we need to be clear about basic terms and concepts. By definition, a process is a group of related tasks that yields a product or service to satisfy a customer. Demonstrated graphically, a process would look like Figure 12.1: the COPIS model, which shows the relationship between customers, output, processes, input, and suppliers. The COPIS model keeps the process customer driven.

Texas Instruments Defense Systems & Electronics Group (TI-DSEG) visualizes the process in another way; see Figure 12.2. It encourages all employees to implement this model in their jobs.

Unlike The New England, TI-DSEG began working on process management after it was well into its quality improvement process. It was turned onto the concept when it completed its first Baldrige Award application. "Going into Baldrige, we thought our business was different, especially in customer satisfaction," says Mike Cooney, vice-president and manager of quality assurance. "That was wrong. We believe we're an excellent defense contractor, but Baldrige taught us, so what? It challenged us with the idea that everything is a process, and that all processes are basic, regardless of the business."

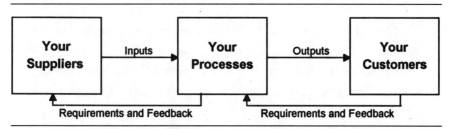

FIGURE 12.1.   COPIS model: How processes satisfy customers.

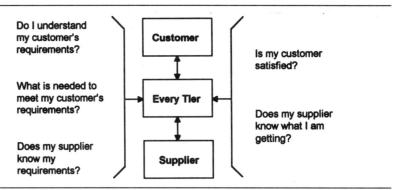

FIGURE 12.2. The customer-supplier relationship at Texas Instruments Defense Systems & Electronics Group. (Courtesy of TI-DSEG.)

The idea that "all processes are reasonably the same" is hotly disputed by people who are not used to having their processes analyzed and measured. Service companies claim that process management is a manufacturing concept; The New England demonstrates that it is not. All types of companies encounter resistance from marketing, sales, and other support functions, which are usually the last to buy into the concept. Leaders who have seen the system work throughout their organizations will tell you that such objections are groundless.

"When you start talking about quality and processes, most people think about manufacturing processes," says Dr. Robert Freese, president and CEO of Alphatronix. "Very few people think about applying the same tools and procedures to all aspects of their organization." As we will describe later in this chapter, Alphatronix is measuring, managing, and improving the processes that make up its business.

NCR has been training people in process management since 1986. It breaks down the simple process models shown in Figures 12.1 and 12.2 into nine elements. As with the COPIS acronym, NCR's list starts with the customer because the customer judges the quality of what the process produces. The key process elements are:

1. *Customer.* The internal and/or external recipient of your product or service.
2. *Output requirements.* Agreements negotiated with the customer that define in measurable terms the product or service that the customer needs.
3. *Output.* The product or service you provide to satisfy the output requirements.
4. *Work activity.* The work you perform within a given process.
5. *Tasks.* An action or defined sequence of actions that adds value.

6. *Input requirements.* Agreements negotiated with suppliers that define in measurable terms the product or service you need from the supplier.
7. *Input.* The product or service the supplier provides to satisfy the input requirements.
8. *Supplier.* The person or organization who provides you with a product or service.
9. *Boundary.* The area of the process owner's responsibility as defined by the customer/supplier relationships.

NCR graphically represents these nine elements in the process management model shown in Figure 12.3.

Process management is about delighting customers by managing and improving processes. NCR defines process management as a methodology that "empowers employees to take responsibility for their work activities. Each will be able to define, measure, control, and improve the processes for which he or she is responsible." The goal of process management is to provide superior products and services or to achieve excellence in execution. NCR's five dimensions of process management are the following:

1. *Ownership.* The person with the responsibility for and authority to manage a process.
2. *Definition.* The act of identifying and documenting the nine elements of the process.

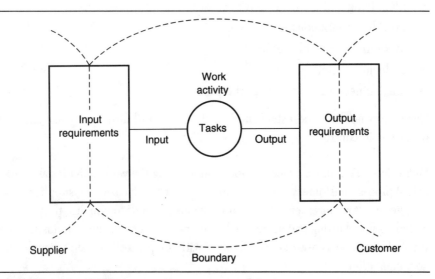

FIGURE 12.3.   NCR's process management model.

3. *Measurement.* The act of collecting appropriate and useful data that helps control and improve the process.

4. *Control.* The act of ensuring through the analysis of data that a process continuously conforms to requirements.

5. *Improvement.* The act of modifying a process to increase its efficiency and effectiveness without compromising customer satisfaction.

MANAGING AND IMPROVING PROCESSES AT NCR

When NCR decided to implement process management, it began with a week-long *Process Management Workshop* Train the Trainer course. It initially trained 140 employees, who then became trainers for subsequent workshops throughout the company, in every major country in the world.

The primary tool used in the workshops is a comprehensive, easy-to-understand *manual* that defines process management, then takes participants through its five dimensions.

Ownership   One of the key points emphasized during the training is the need to identify process owners, subprocess owners, and process users. The process owner is responsible for:

- Identifying customers and suppliers
- Planning and managing the work activity
- Identifying and eliminating root causes of process problems
- Providing continuous improvement
- Maximizing available resources
- Reducing operating costs
- Making necessary changes to the process

Ownership needs to be established so that responsibilities are clear and the process is in control.

Definition   Defining a process involves identifying the work activities and tasks in that process, customers, output requirements for each customer, suppliers, and supplier input requirements. Teams use various methods to visualize the process, including flowcharting and narrative documentation. The documentation may be verified by asking a co-worker not familiar with the process to "step through" the documentation.

Measurement   Measurement is necessary to control and improve the process. Measurements of input, work activity, and output need to be understandable, broadly applicable, subject to uniform interpretation, economical to apply, suited to numerical expression, periodically taken, flexible enough to accommodate change, accessible to people who need the information, meaningful, accurate, and useful.

Control   Whereas the first three dimensions help document the existing process, the objective of this dimension is to bring all aspects of the process into conformance with requirements. NCR's six-step closed-loop corrective action process is used to prevent and solve problems and verify that they are corrected. The six steps are:

1.   Define the problem.
2.   Accept responsibility for resolving it.
3.   Investigate and determine its cause.
4.   Determine a corrective action to eliminate the problem.
5.   Implement the correction.
6.   Verify that the corrective action has eliminated the problem.

Improvement   The first four dimensions deal with managing the existing process. This dimension focuses on improving the process, which means modifying the process to increase its efficiency and effectiveness without compromising customer satisfaction. The steps to improvement are:

1.   Identify an opportunity or establish a need.
2.   Formulate a plan of action.
3.   Identify the changes and their potential impact.
4.   Implement the plan.
5.   Monitor the improvement results.

The manual uses case studies to demonstrate key points and has participants identify their own processes to manage and improve. The manual is part of a training kit NCR developed that also includes transparencies, slides, and a videotape introducing the idea of internal customers. The tape, called "The Customer Is Always Dwight," was produced by British actor John Cleese's company, Video Arts, and has been purchased by companies around the world to teach the "internal employee" concept.

NCR began teaching process management in 1986, training more than 12,000 people over the next half-dozen years. It also developed a one-day *Quality Improvement Seminar* that introduced process management to more than 3,000 NCR executives and members of their staffs. As with every aspect of the quality improvement process, "management commitment and leadership" needs to come first.

To recognize teams that have dramatically improved key processes, NCR presents *Outstanding Process Improvement Awards*. The 12 awards given in 1991 included recognition for the following:

- A large accounting function focused on the process for intercompany reconciliations and transaction processing. Its achievements included a substantial gain in customer satisfaction survey results, aged reconciling items reduced 99.6%, the reconciliation workload reduced by over $1 million annually worldwide, and NCR's 1991 financial results enhanced by $2.4 million.

- An NCR facility reduced cycle time by coordinating improvements in the order management process with reductions in manufacturing cycle times. Its achievements included a 55% reduction in total inventory, work-in-process inventory reduction of $6.7 million, and a 25% improvement in on-time delivery.

- A team at a midwestern facility improved its engineering change control process. Its achievements included a 99.9% measured level of internal customer satisfaction, a 500% reduction in staff over four years, and a 308% improvement, over two years, in the average time to process development releases.

QUALITY IMPROVEMENT AT ALPHATRONIX

Alphatronix can point to achievements similar to NCR's, but on a far different scale. As a small company Alphatronix has had to rely on significantly fewer people than NCR to implement its quality improvement process. Its successes can be attributed to a focus on quality from the day it was founded in 1988. In fact, Alphatronix's president and CEO, Dr. Robert Freese, preaches the advantages a small, emerging company has in implementing quality:

- It is easy to start at the formation of a company.
- It is easier to establish a quality attitude in employees than to change old habits.
- It provides an opportunity to hire quality-oriented employees.

- It offers a big competitive advantage, since most competitors neglect quality improvement early on.
- It is easier to establish a reputation for quality than to change a reputation for poor quality.
- It is easier to plan for quality from the beginning rather than to integrate it later.

Alphatronix uses a five-step improvement process:

1. Involve all key people at appropriate levels.
2. Identify and quantify the problem.
3. Seek and identify solutions from employees, consultants, customers.
4. Implement a key solution that solves the problem forever.
5. Monitor performance through feedback.

To get people involved, Freese presents the concept of quality improvement within a framework they understand. "They're familiar with the concept of the customer and producing goods for that customer, and they're very familiar with suppliers," he says. "We ask, 'Who are you providing goods and services to?' The key is to get people thinking about who their customers and suppliers are, then to make sure all goods and services they provide and receive are 100% quality. Then they can go through the next steps in our improvement process."

Freese relies on the improvement process to achieve Alphatronix's ambitious goals:

- Achieve 100% quality product/100% yield.
- Double inventory turns: achieve positive cash flow.
- Introduce one new computer product per month, on time.
- Have customers pay on time.

Experts told him the goals were unrealistic. Alphatronix proved them wrong. Customer delivery times have been reduced from one month to ten days, its factory turns twice the industry average, it has introduced one new product every month for three years, and it has a positive cash flow.

To understand how Alphatronix is using process improvement to achieve its goals, consider one process that affected its fourth goal, to "have customers pay on time." Freese explains:

Almost every company has an issue associated with their accounts receivable and payable. When we first started Alphatronix, cash flow was one of the biggest issues we faced. Everybody said watch out for the Days Sales Outstanding (DSO); ours was around the industry average. We needed to improve that, so we did a series of experiments measuring why our DSO was at 60 days. It took a month to investigate, with the clerk writing down the reasons why people paid late. Then we asked what the solution was, and after some study, it was obvious: the number one reason people said they paid late was because they didn't receive our paperwork. We asked the clerk what the permanent solution to the problem was. She said she would call everyone ten days in advance to make sure they received our paperwork. I haven't heard of anyone else doing that, but she did it. As a result of that single step, our DSO is now 34 days. By reducing our DSO from 60 days to 34 days, we saved $3 million in cash flow in 1991 and again in 1992, and our bad debts have almost vaporized—0.1% compared to the industry average of 1%.

This seemingly simple solution to an ineffective process illustrates several key points about process management. The first is the value of *process ownership*. "The key to the solution is almost never with people like me," Freese says. "The solution is with the people whose primary responsibility is to do that job. We remind people every quarter that it is their responsibility to be constantly working to fix problems and improve productivity and job functions. Most people blossom with that type of instruction. The second key part is, whatever solution they come up with, it should be a permanent solution." Process management is not a short-term fix; it is a long-term, prevention-based solution. NCR describes it as verifying that the corrective action has eliminated the problem. Alphatronix says it should solve the problem forever.

Another key point involves the *use of measurements*. In just this one example Alphatronix tracks days sales outstanding, cash flow, and bad debts. As for what should be measured, Freese believes that employees know best. "Ask the employees how they should be measured. They all know what their output is; they can come up with their own measures."

Freese is adamant about the need to measure. "Marketing communications is one of the most challenging areas I've come across. They think we should advertise to improve our image, but they also say we can't measure our image. Well, if you can't measure it, it's not worth doing, so I ask how they're going to measure it. You can do internal surveys of image, hire independent consultants, have the magazines you advertise in do a survey for you—but there has to be a measure. Anything worth doing is worth measuring." (For more about establishing key measures, see Chapter 14.)

STRIVING FOR "SIX SIGMA" QUALITY AT TEXAS INSTRUMENTS DEFENSE SYSTEMS & ELECTRONICS GROUP

Resistance to process ownership, improvement, and measurement is not exclusive to small companies. Texas Instruments Defense Systems & Electronics Group has encountered similar objections. "We've found that you have to come up with several different ways to explain this," says Tony Geishauser, manager of media relations. "Process improvement is most difficult in creative areas, but it's not impossible, and we've found that the fear of process mapping is going down." As for measuring improvement, "we're planting the seed that your job *can* be measured, to the point that we now have administrative areas measuring sigma," says Mike Cooney.

Sigma is the measure of a process's capability to perform *defect-free work*. The sigma value indicates how often defects are likely to occur. The higher the sigma value, the less likely a process is to produce defects. TI-DSEG's goal is to achieve six sigma quality, which roughly translates into no more than 3.4 defects per million opportunities. The group's approach to process improvement is based on Six Steps to Six Sigma:

1. Identify the product you create or the service you provide. *What do you do?*
2. Identify the customers for your product or service, and determine what they consider important. *For whom do you do your work?*
3. Identify your needs to provide product/service so that it satisfies the customer. *What do you need to do your work?*
4. Define the process for doing the work. *How do you do your work or process?*
5. Mistake-proof the process and eliminate wasted effort. *How can you do your work better?*
6. Ensure continuous improvement by measuring, analyzing, and controlling the improved process. *How perfectly are you doing your customer-focused work?*

Like NCR's five dimensions of process management and Alphatronix's five-step improvement process, the Six Steps to Six Sigma is a process for improving processes. Its purpose is to help employees define, measure, control, and improve their processes. However, even after a process has been improved, it is still subject to significant variations known as "out-of-control occurrences." NCR uses a closed-loop corrective action process to solve these kinds of problems.

TI-DSEG applies a process called the *QC Story*. Companies worldwide use this eight-step process to identify the root cause of a problem and implement improvements. The process is:

1. Select the problem.
2. Understand the current situation.
3. Identify the root cause.
4. Plan improvement.
5. Execute improvement.
6. Confirm results.
7. Standardize the improvement.
8. Study remaining problems/make future plans.

TI-DSEG is currently applying the Six Steps to Six Sigma and the QC Story to its major processes and subprocesses. Beginning in mid-1992, the group identified its top-level business processes and determined how they related to customer needs. Figure 12.4 provides an overview of TI-DSEG business processes. TI-DSEG is using Figure 12.4 to guide the creation of flow charts and analyses of critical processes, which will help identify the subprocesses that need improving.

Each of the major processes (business strategy, business development, and so on) has an executive process owner. The subprocesses that make up each major process are being modified through customer feedback to ensure that the customers' needs are being met. Specific improvements are being identified and implemented and metrics developed to measure progress.

IMPROVING PROCESSES AT THE NEW ENGLAND

As at TI-DSEG, The New England's first step was to identify its core processes. At the same time, the company trained 75 associates in a nine-step process analysis technique methodology and gave all 2,650 associates four days of quality core training.

The New England uses two types of teams to improve its processes: *process analysis teams* (PATs) and *quality improvement teams* (QITs). PATs address horizontal processes, core processes, or subprocesses that cut across divisional and departmental boundaries. It calls these "value-adding delivery chains." QITs primarily focus on subprocesses within one of these chains and on tasks typically performed within a specific division or department. Figure 12.5 shows how PATs and QITs interrelate.

Process Analysis Teams

Process analysis teams use a nine-step process divided into three phases:

- *Commitment:*
  1. Decide to form a PAT.
  2. Identify the boundaries of the process.
  3. Write a document stating objectives, methodology, and schedule.

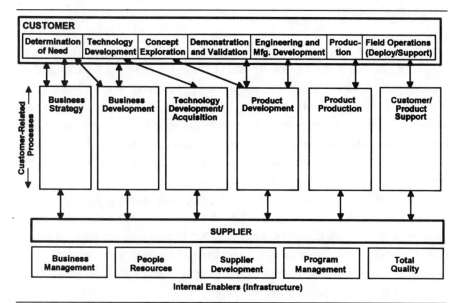

FIGURE 12.4. Overview of business processes at Texas Instruments Defense Systems & Electronics Group. (Courtesy of TI-DSEG.)

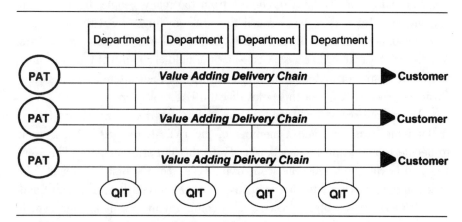

FIGURE 12.5. The New England's quality improvement process.

- *Information Gathering:*
  4. Understand the existing flow of work activities.
  5. Meet to share information.
  6. Interview task experts throughout the process.
- *Analysis and Implementation of Revisions:*
  7. Analyze existing process and look for improvement opportunities.
  8. Test the revised process.
  9. Decide to implement.

The process can take anywhere from 8 to 20 weeks, depending on the complexity of the analysis. For its first PATs, The New England turned to the core process map it had developed, choosing two areas primarily because the managers of those areas recognized the value of process analysis. One of the areas was New Business, the core process that involves responding to applications for insurance. The cross-functional New Business PAT included 11 associates. Its major objective was to improve agent satisfaction with the New Business process.

The team had its work cut out for it. Agents—the primary customers of the process—had been complaining that New Business was not an easy place to do business with and that the process was taking at least two or three weeks longer than it should. New Business had valid reasons for this, but as John Small, senior vice-president in charge of New Business, points out, "The bottom line was, so what, our customers were not happy!"

Before forming the PAT, Small and his staff studied the problem. First, they considered that the problem might be in the customers' minds, but realized that too many complaints were coming from too many people, both external and internal. Next, they wondered if the problem might be with New Business personnel, but more than 30 of its people had won the company's Extra Mile Award for extraordinary service—and the field claimed that the personnel were holding the place together. They then turned their attention to the New Business process. It was at this point that the PAT took over.

"We started saying we should do a New Business PAT," says Maura Howe, senior issue consultant and a member of the PAT. "It took us about a week to decide it should be broken down." From this initial experience, The New England learned to narrow the scope of its PATs. "For the first PAT, you should pick something critical to the company, then get buy-in from the CEO and other leaders," says Scott Andrews, quality commitment consultant. "Start small though, not with 16 processes."

The New Business PAT used the quality improvement model shown in Figure 12.5 to identify regions as the vertical "departments" and Large Amount, Regional Underwriting, Fast Track, and Pension Issue as the horizontal "value-adding delivery chains." It then identified the points where the process broke down and established goals, measures, and actions for those points. Maureen Leydon, second vice-president of New Business Services, describes the results of a PAT recommendation to put the variable life product on Fast Track. (Fast Track is a process by which an application that meets certain criteria can be approved within 96 hours of receipt.) "We couldn't do that because we needed a registered signature approving the application, which usually meant a senior vice-president—and they weren't always available. The PAT said someone *should* be available. The solution was to register one of our Fast Track underwriters— and now the product is on Fast Track."

The PAT completed its work in five months. New Business continues to implement the team's recommendations. Major achievements to date include:

- *Fast Track Processing:* Percentage of qualifying cases has improved from 14% to 22%, with a goal of 30%.

- *Non-Fast Track Processing:* Percentage of successful laboratory tests matching on the first try increased from 50% to better than 70%.

- *Large Amount Processing:* Average speed of processing time has improved by more than 20%.

"What the PATs have done best is crystallize the process by mapping it out," says Scott McInturff, second vice-president and actuary, "and they have required managers to change their approach to one of management, not decision-making. Managers don't make all the decisions, as they did in the past. Now it's the associates who make decisions, and the managers facilitate that process. We manage the process, and associates are responsible for the results. Our role now is to set expectations for such things as deliverables and dates, meet with the associates to make sure they are clear about the expectations, then hold people to them."

Quality Improvement Teams

The New England also uses quality improvement teams to manage and improve its smaller, department level processes. In the case of New Business, the PAT recommendations led to the creation of 21 QITs.

QITs follow a process that is similar to the PATs. For example, in July 1991 Michael Bachand, second vice-president of office services and printing, formed an Image Scanner and Output QIT to address a problem with his department's image scanning process. "They initially spent a lot of time on discovery and getting buy-in before looking at the whole process," says Bachand. "Everybody on the team was apprehensive going in, but now they're very proud of their finished document." The document is a 19-page report that traces the process the team followed, from identifying the problems to the methodology used to arrive at its recommendations to the recommendations and action plan. The document reflects the team's understanding and use of statistical tools:

- A fishbone diagram shows the problems that were identified.
- A Gantt chart shows who was responsible for what activity and when.
- A process map defines the interdependent components of the image scanning process.

Bachand and his staff began implementing the recommendations and action plan at the end of 1992.

As The New England's PATs and QITs touch more and more of the company's processes, functions, and tasks, the company will transform from a vertical organization focused on satisfying the boss to horizontal process management focused on satisfying the customer.

THE SHIFT IN THINKING

The customer-driven company must be organized around the *core processes that meet customer requirements*. As our four role models show, such organization depends on

- Understanding customer requirements
- Defining the processes that serve those requirements
- Identifying process owners and teams
- Mapping the process
- Establishing measures
- Bringing the process under control
- Developing and implementing a plan to improve the process

The new business management model demands *process-oriented thinking*. It forces companies to ask what their processes are for understanding customer requirements, communicating customer and quality requirements throughout the organization, determining and tracking key measures, strategic planning, involving employees, managing processes, measuring and improving customer satisfaction, and all other key elements that define the company's "work."

How do you do what you do? What's the process? The new model asks these questions relentlessly. In our experience only those companies that think in terms of processes and that have identified and sought to improve their processes are capable of providing answers.

Such a shift in thinking ripples throughout the organization. Because all work is part of at least one process, a process orientation changes how people think of their work. Employees need to be trained in this new model. They need to learn the team and problem-solving skills required to manage and improve their processes. Leadership must empower them to apply their new skills and align the reward and recognition programs to support their efforts. Leadership must also direct their efforts, using its vision of the company's future to prioritize the company's process improvement initiatives.

Finally, the company must understand its customers' requirements. Core processes aim at the bull's-eye of customer satisfaction. Remove the bull's-eye and process management becomes a hit-or-miss proposition.

13 SUPPLIER QUALITY

Ford

Pacific Bell

Bose Corporation

A critical point in process management is *managing the handoffs*, those points at which a person, team, or department completes its work and passes it along to the next one. Companies seek fewer, faster, defect-free handoffs, from supplier to customer until the process is complete. As the last chapter concluded, such handoffs must first be identified, then refined relentlessly to improve quality.

This chapter is also about handoffs, supplier to customer, except that the suppliers we are talking about are external. The good news is that identifying the handoffs is much easier because they exist wherever an outside vendor provides a product or service. The bad news is that improving the handoffs—as well as the quality of the products and services being provided—is often more difficult because you are dealing with another company.

High-performance companies attack this problem by blurring the lines between supplier and customer. Ford provides its suppliers with clear and extensive direction, training, appraisals, and recognition. Pacific Bell works with suppliers to identify key requirements and measurements, then reports on the suppliers' progress monthly. Bose Corporation brings supplier representatives right into its plants and empowers them to act as buyers for Bose. As discussed in earlier chapters, quality leaders rely on training, recognition, teamwork, and empowerment to dramatically improve quality and performance. The role

181

models in this chapter show that such initiatives are equally effective with suppliers.

The importance of improving supplier quality and performance grows as companies pare down to their core competencies. Companies that want to be lean and nimble in ever-flatter organizations strive to do only what they do best and to outsource the rest, without sacrificing quality, schedule, or cost. This is possible only when a company abandons its adversarial relationship with suppliers and establishes long-term partnerships. We will describe how three successful companies are doing just that.

We invite those who cannot shake their preoccupation with price to consider how improving supplier quality inevitably leads to lower prices—or to steady prices for higher quality goods. "Our goal is to drive costs down every year," says Lance Dixon, Bose's director of corporate purchasing and logistics. "All my material costs are frozen at the beginning of the fiscal year based on the last price paid, so year after year we're fighting our own success. But we still reduce our prices every year."

To find out how Bose, Ford, and Pacific Bell improve supplier quality and performance, we will address two questions:

- How do you define your requirements, communicate those requirements to your suppliers, and make sure they are being met?
- How do you improve your purchasing/supplier processes?

This chapter focuses on the relationship between a company and those who supply it with products and services, since all companies have such relationships. However, some companies have other relationships that could be classified as supplier relationships, including those with distributors, dealers, contractors, franchises, and strategic allies. They can be thought of as suppliers because they supply goods and services during some stage of production, delivery, and use of a company's products and services. We have chosen not to address issues specific to these types of suppliers because a narrower range of companies is affected by them and because the general ideas and strategies presented in this chapter apply equally well to all types of suppliers.

MODELS OF EXCELLENCE

Ford is the fourth largest industrial corporation in the world, the second largest producer of cars and trucks worldwide, and one of the largest providers of financial services in the United States. Founded in 1903 by Henry Ford in Detroit, Ford is also active in electronics, glass, electric and fuel handling products, plastics, climate control systems, automotive service and replacement parts, vehicle leasing and rental, and land development. It has 325,000 employees in more than 200 countries and territories.

Pacific Bell is a subsidiary of Pacific Telesis Group, a worldwide diversified telecommunications corporation based in San Francisco. Pacific Bell's 52,800 employees provide the vast majority of California's 30 million residents with telecommunications products and services through a public telecommunications network of more than 14 million access lines.

Bose Corporation designs and manufactures high-quality audio products for home and commercial use. Founded in 1964, the company has more than 3,000 employees at manufacturing locations in Massachusetts, New Hampshire, Michigan, Canada, Mexico, and Ireland. The concept of JIT II, described later in this chapter, originated with Bose.

TELLING SUPPLIERS WHAT YOU WANT—AND GETTING IT

Ford has long been the benchmark for defining and communicating requirements to suppliers. Its *Q-101 Quality System Standard* spells out exactly what Ford expects for any parts that are going into a Ford vehicle or that will be used as service parts. Those expectations reflect the same standards Ford sets for its internal processes, another example of how companies are blurring the internal/external lines. Q-101 has requirements in five general sections that cover the supplier's entire design and manufacturing process:

- Planning for Quality
- Achieving Process and Product Quality
- Documenting Quality
- Special Requirements for Control Item Products
- System and Initial Sample Approvals

Each of these sections contains "quality system evidence requirements" that Ford can use to evaluate quality. For example, the requirements for the "Documenting Quality" section are:

- Written quality procedures
- Quality system and performance records
- Drawing and design change control methods
- Part/process modification control
- Process change control methods

Ford communicates these requirements in an easy-to-understand *Q-101 document* and through books that support each section. For example, the 110-page *Planning for Quality* guides suppliers through the steps in the quality planning process.

All Ford suppliers must be Q-101 certified. Ford helps them achieve certification through its worldwide *Supplier Quality Engineering program*, in which it works with suppliers to assess their capabilities and systems before they implement Q-101. Once suppliers are certified, they can perform this assessment themselves.

What sets Ford's supplier relationships apart from those of other American companies is Ford's extensive experience with Q-101. Ford first published its supplier standards in 1964 with two goals:

1. To give outside suppliers appropriate excerpts from Ford's internal quality procedures.
2. To reorient Ford's purchased part quality program from receiving inspection to supplier quality assurance.

These two goals foreshadowed such key tenets of the new business management model as promoting partnerships with suppliers and building quality in rather than inspecting it in. Ford has nearly three decades of experience developing partnerships, refining its requirements, improving communication, and assuring conformance.

In 1990 Ford completely reorganized Q-101 to integrate the concepts of advanced quality planning and continual improvement. Advanced quality planning takes place concurrently with engineering at the component level. People from purchasing, design, and manufacturing work with suppliers to develop control plans for the characteristics that engineering and manufacturing feel are significant. Suppliers of new parts must have these control plans and must document their manufacturing process. "We want this evidence so that we have confidence in the quality of the products we are purchasing," says Dan Whelan of Ford's corporate quality office.

Ford's interaction with suppliers requires far more trust and cooperation than an adversarial relationship would allow, which is why Ford focuses on long-term partnerships. Ford has substantially reduced the size of its supply base over the past decade, with the most capable suppliers enjoying a larger share of Ford's business. In many cases, Ford is selecting suppliers for key components in future models prior to the initiation of the models' designs. This involves the suppliers in optimizing the designs for their manufacturing processes and achieving affordable targets jointly developed by Ford and the supplier.

Supplier Recognition Programs

Like many companies, Ford also defines and communicates its requirements through supplier recognition. Its Q1 Award is given to suppliers with excellent ratings for their quality systems, statistical methods, and ongoing quality performance. Higher customer expectations require Ford to go beyond traditional product quality and think in terms of total organizational quality. As a result, Ford's Total Quality Excellence (TQE) Award recognizes outstanding supplier performance in product quality and in delivery, engineering, the business relationship, and overall commitment to continuous improvement.

Pacific Bell calls its supplier recognition program the *Quality Partner Plan*. The goals for the program could be considered goals for any new customer/supplier partnership:

- To communicate to suppliers that their internal quality processes and performance results are critical
- To demonstrate that quality pervades all aspects of the business relationship
- To share expectations and information to build partnerships toward world-class performance

The fourth goal, of course, is to recognize a supplier's overall quality. Pacific Bell offers three levels of recognition:

- *Bronze Award.* The supplier is meeting all product/service standards, has action plans in place to continually improve quality, and has begun to implement these plans.
- *Silver Award.* The supplier is meeting or exceeding all Pacific Bell product/service standards and has mature, continuous quality improvement processes in place.
- *Gold Award.* The supplier exceeds all customer needs by providing superior products/services and has been "delighting" Pacific Bell through total quality efforts and customer service for more than one year.

Supplier Quality Reports

Pacific Bell communicates its standards and needs through regular quality reports. For its top dozen or so suppliers Pacific Bell and the supplier agree on a contract that defines their objectives for the next year. Senior managers from both organizations meet twice a year to review reports on progress, agree on areas for improvement, and outline actions to be taken.

Suppliers that are not part of Pacific Bell's core businesses but that are very important to its day-to-day operation (a total of about 75 suppliers) receive a one-page Supplier Quality Report every month. Pacific Bell and the supplier agree on which components to measure, although some areas, such as on-time delivery and invoicing accuracy, are consistent from supplier to supplier. The supplier begins the month with 100 points, then loses points according to the criteria in the Supplier Quality Report. Table 13.1 provides an example of a Pacific Bell Supplier Quality Report.

On the actual report the lower right corner shows the supplier's monthly point trend, with a block in the lower left corner for signatures from the supplier and Pacific Bell. "We usually send these reports to the supplier's CEO or COO," says Joseph Yacura, executive director of contracting and supplier management. "We want to give them fast, immediate feedback on their performance. Between the contracts with our major suppliers and the quality reports to our next tier of suppliers, we've captured close to 80% of our supplier dollar transactions."

The quality report sent to senior management adds legitimacy to Pacific Bell's requirements. Suppliers usually call back within a week if they get anything less than 93 points to discuss how they are addressing the problem. "In many cases, I've had suppliers bring their last two or three quality reports to talk about what they're doing," says Yacura.

TABLE 13.1. Example of a Pacific Bell supplier quality report

Component	Criteria	Score	Issues/Corrective Action
Product/Service Quality Reliability	1 point deducted for each hotline case, customer complaint, corrective action step, and Returned Material Disposition.		
Delivery Delivery	1 point deducted for each number of shipments received past contracted interval.		
Support Satisfaction Invoice exceptions	1 point deducted for each number of invoicing errors for bills paid during month.		
Support Satisfaction Supplier/QA mgr. intervention	1 point deducted for each hour of supplier manager's and QA manager's time to resolve quality issues.		
Support Satisfaction Responsiveness	1 point deducted for each untimely response and for each nonconformance to a Product Change Notice.		
	Total for January:		**of a possible 100 points**

Pacific Bell is now working with its suppliers to implement *just-in-time (JIT) delivery.* The company used to have three levels of inventory: large warehouses, miniwarehouses, and the 11,000 vehicles it uses to serve its customers. Its goal is to create 11,000 miniwarehouses by having products delivered from the point of manufacture (the supplier) to the point of consumption (the vehicles) just in time. The goal requires even higher levels of supplier quality, which is a major reason Pacific Bell is developing a certified supplier program.

BRINGING SUPPLIERS IN-HOUSE

One of the companies that both Ford and Pacific Bell have benchmarked to learn more about supplier partnerships is Bose Corporation. In 1987 Bose began using a concept it called *JIT II.* "For eons there have been sellers selling and buyers buying, and it's basically been adversarial. For me to win, I had to pull on my end of the rope," says Lance Dixon, director of corporate purchasing and logistics. "We determined that we had sellers selling to us and they weren't really selling; we had been sold on their companies for years. And we had buyers who weren't really buying. I knew there had to be a better way to do this."

Dixon's better way was to have representatives of key suppliers work full-time in Bose's facilities. The representatives operate at the buyer level and are empowered to use Bose's purchase orders to place orders at their own companies. They are invited to attend any design engineering meetings involving their companies' product area, with full access to Bose's facilities, personnel, and data. JIT II eliminates the buyer and salesman as the in-plant representative becomes the link between Bose's planning department and the supplier's production plant.

The only limitations on these in-plant representatives are the same limitations placed on Bose's own buyers. They place orders for standard cost items whose price has already been calculated, and each representative has a purchase limit. Orders above that limit require a signature from a purchasing supervisor. As Dixon points out, "The normal controls that the typical purchasing systems and purchasing manager place on a buyer function quite well."

Bose is currently using JIT II with nine suppliers. The nine suppliers provide 12 in-plant employees and are responsible for 30% of Bose's outside purchases and 65% of its transportation expenses. Bose implements only one JIT II supplier per commodity, although it continues to have competing suppliers in the same commodity. The indicators that suggest a supplier may be a candidate for JIT II status are:

- General supplier excellence: the best in a given commodity
- Dollar volume over $1 million

- Good quality already being achieved
- Good delivery record
- A substantial number of purchase order transactions
- Offers evolving technology, but not at a revolutionary pace
- Good cost levels already being achieved
- Operates in a Bose area that does not involve key trade secrets or sensitive technologies
- Already provides good engineering support

Both Bose and the supplier receive incentives for beginning a JIT II relationship: The participating supplier's business with Bose typically increases by 35 to 45%, while Bose's savings in overhead alone are about $1 million a year. For example, when Bose moved from a JIT relationship to a JIT II relationship with one supplier, it reduced inventories to one-eighth of the already low levels achieved through JIT.

The key to making JIT II work is the in-plant representative. He or she is part of Bose's system, spending much of the time getting information, analyzing and critiquing Bose's plans and working with Bose's engineers on product development. Dixon calls them "a living, breathing standards program," because they are constantly pushing standard parts and processes with the design engineers.

"You want engineers to design state-of-the-art, innovative, exciting products using routine, standardized parts, which goes against human nature. The idea of calling in suppliers to contribute to concurrent engineering also goes against human nature, because engineers get busy, they move fast, and sometimes they don't take the time to talk to outside people. And if you bring in the suppliers too late, it's not concurrent engineering. Now imagine a dozen people, all experts in their given commodities, roaming engineering and offering their assistance." As an example, Dixon points to one in-house supplier that Bose asked to evaluate the design for a speaker-enclosure. The supplier suggested a resin change that saved Bose $50,000 annually.

After Bose established its in-plant representatives, it discovered that they improved not only purchasing, but also planning, engineering, importing, and transportation. For example, Bose's three JIT II transportation suppliers give it access to their computer systems controlling material movement. For 98% of manufacturers, material en route to their factories is considered material in the pipeline. Bose considers it inventory, because it can track that material anywhere in the world. As Dixon says, "When material flowing toward Bose from locations offshore can be located and routinely accessed, the material functions as inventory, just as effectively as such inventory in our plant or warehouse."

At the other end of the pipeline, suppliers who used to keep secret piles of buffer inventory have gotten rid of it because their in-plant representatives know exactly what is needed, when.

Bose's success with JIT II has generated a great deal of interest. Most of its suppliers use it in their marketing with other customers. Companies such as Honeywell, Intel, Ford, AT&T Bell Labs, and Du Pont have already implemented it with key suppliers. The academic community, including Harvard and MIT, are using Bose as a case study. Professional societies have endorsed JIT II as a leap ahead in customer-supplier relationships.

Companies that take the leap can look forward to a host of benefits, as outlined by Dixon in an article in *Purchasing* magazine. Benefits for the customer include:

- Purchasing staff is liberated from purchasing and administrative tasks, which enables them to cultivate other skills.
- Communication and purchase order placement improve dramatically.
- Material costs are reduced immediately and on an ongoing basis.
- Supply standards are created.
- It provides a natural foundation for EDI, effective paperwork, and administrative savings.
- Concurrent engineering is increased dramatically, with resulting benefits.

Benefits for the supplier include:

- It eliminates the sales effort (although the cost is offset by having a full-time person at the customer's location).
- Communication and purchase order placement improve dramatically.
- The volume of business increases at the start of the program and is ongoing as the in-plant person gets involved with new products.
- The agreement is an evergreen contract—no end date and no bidding.
- The supplier can sell directly to engineering.
- It provides efficient invoicing and payment administration.
- On-site personnel have a dual career path: They can advance in their company or at Bose after one year.

IMPROVING BOTH ENDS OF THE CUSTOMER-SUPPLIER PIPE

Bose's in-plant supplier representatives do not blur the lines between customer and supplier, they obliterate them, setting aside "the pipe" in favor of working side-by-side on issues of mutual interest. They redefine customer-supplier partnerships by the levels of trust, cooperation, and empowerment both sides need and expect. As the widespread interest in JIT II suggests, many high-performance companies recognize it as another step in the unavoidable progression from adversarial relationships to partnerships.

However, most suppliers will not qualify for JIT II status. Bose has only nine out of hundreds of suppliers, purchasing 70% of its materials from non–JIT II suppliers. For these suppliers, "the pipe" still exists, and quality leaders are working just as hard to improve their own procurement activities as they are to improve supplier performance.

Pacific Bell uses formal quality reports to improve the supplier end of the pipe. Their focus at the procurement end is on making it easier for suppliers to communicate because, as Yacura says, "Two-way communication around quality is absolutely essential." For example, Pacific Bell established an "800" number that suppliers and potential suppliers can call to find out Pacific Bell's requirements, such as the need to have EDI and bar coding for every deliverable product. "It helps them understand whether or not we need their product or service and who they should talk to," says Yacura.

Pacific Bell also encourages suppliers to tell it how it is doing, something they are often reluctant to do. It hired an outside agency to survey suppliers about their relationship with Pacific Bell, and it asks suppliers to give it a one-page report on Pacific Bell's performance, although few have responded. "That's a big leap of faith," says Yacura. "Suppliers are always leery of telling customers about their problems." To increase the response, Pacific Bell is considering making the reports a requirement for being certified.

Another form of communication Pacific Bell promotes is training. Like Ford, Pacific Bell believes that its procurement managers and its suppliers need the same training to continuously improve both ends of the pipe. To that end, Pacific Bell worked with the University of California in Berkeley to develop and fund an Applied Total Quality program. The program includes six 30-hour courses that teach total quality management tools and their application to customer-supplier relationships. All of Pacific Bell's procurement managers will complete the program. Suppliers have been invited to participate at no cost.

Each class begins with an intensive two-day overview that summarizes the course's content. Everyone attends the overview, after which the supplier representatives return to their work (which is often in other parts of the country) while the Pacific Bell managers complete the course. However, each procurement manager works with a supplier representative on identifying and addressing a strategic quality initiative for the duration of the program. They must drive the initiative to resolution or near completion over an eight- to nine-month period, presenting their conclusions to an advisory board.

This substantial commitment on both sides produces immediate and long-term benefits:

- Participants learn about total quality management concepts and techniques and their practical application through a real-world quality project.
- Participants have the opportunity to study the issues involved in implementing a quality program.
- The program provides common ground for Pacific Bell staff and suppliers who seek to develop partnerships.

The search for common ground is another sign of the transition from adversaries to partners. When Pacific Bell treats its suppliers as an extension of the company, when it values their knowledge and input, it nurtures long-term partnerships. When Bose brings suppliers right into its plants full-time, it demonstrates the kind of supplier relationships it is seeking. When Ford involves suppliers early in concurrent engineering, it is telling them that it needs their particular expertise. All these initiatives benefit both customer and supplier; none is possible in an adversarial relationship.

An example of just how far customer-supplier relationships have come involves Ford, General Motors, and Chrysler. At a 1990 conference, suppliers told the Big Three that they were driving the suppliers crazy with their total lack of standardization. The auto makers took their concerns to heart, bringing together members of the quality and supply staffs of the Big Three to form a Chrysler, Ford, General Motors Supplier Quality Requirements Task Force.

Operating under the auspices of the American Society for Quality Control and the Automotive Industry Action Group, the task force produces joint procedures and guidelines aimed at simplifying and standardizing supplier-manufacturer requirements. The common standards are communicated to suppliers in book format, similar to Ford's supplier books described earlier. "When you're talking about tens of thousands of parts and the complex paperwork involved, this is truly a win/win venture," says Ford's Whelan.

But the improvement will not stop there. Auto parts suppliers are now asking for a common assessment to these common standards, a supplier quality rating system that would be recognized by each of the Big Three. "We said we'd take a shot at it," says Whelan. "We know it's got to have savings—and ultimately, to improve quality."

THE SHIFT IN THINKING

One of the characteristics of the new business management model is its *universality:* Strategic planning guides and permeates all activities; continuous improvement in any area depends on employee involvement; process management techniques work for any type of process; employee satisfaction is linked to customer satisfaction. The basics of improving quality and performance remain the same, no matter what the issue or people involved.

On a macro level your company's management model whirs and buzzes and spits out products and services through the ongoing efforts of employees, customers, and suppliers alike. Poor connections between or within these groups sabotage the system and impede improvement.

On a micro level the attributes of personal quality—treating people as you want to be treated, taking responsibility, improving yourself, sharing your knowledge, having a positive outlook, and communicating effectively—apply whether you are dealing with other employees, customers, or suppliers. You cannot succeed with one set of values for customers, another for employees, and yet another for suppliers. Your values for all people in and affected by your company must be consistent or the disparity, like poor connections, will sabotage the system.

Suppliers have borne the brunt of any disparity, but as our role models show, that disparity is waning. The lines between customer and supplier are blurring as companies get horizontal, their focus on core competencies elevating suppliers' roles and importance. The very term "partnership" implies equality, the sharing of risks and rewards, a focus on mutual goals. You cannot create an adversarial partnership.

That is a shift in thinking, in the same way that high-performance companies are shifting their thinking about their employees. Suppliers, like employees, are not commodities to be handled as you please. They are not children to be bribed, chastised, threatened, and punished. They are *partners in a joint venture*, members of a bigger system, allies armed with technology, knowledge, and insight your company can use to improve.

Like your company, your suppliers must be on the leading edge of their businesses to compete, and you can benefit from that. Like your company, they read books such as this to learn more about improving their systems and their relationships with their customers. Like your company, they are committed to continuous improvement and are aggressive about meeting and exceeding their customers' expectations. In fact, your best suppliers are so much like your company, they tend to make excellent partners.

14 DATA COLLECTION AND ANALYSIS

Carrier

AT&T Universal Card Services

Kennametal-Solon

AMP

When AT&T decided to get into the credit card business in 1990, it chose the Baldrige criteria as the new subsidiary's management model. It called the subsidiary Universal Card Services (UCS). Quality, defined as "customer delight," was its foundation from the first draft of its business plan. Every part of the business was designed to focus on the continuous improvement goals targeted by the Baldrige criteria. *Constant measurement* against the goal of customer delight became a normal part of every business operation.

"The biggest thing in our business is the concept of listening to customers, really working at listening to what they want," says Robert Davis, chief quality officer. "The other piece is, once we listen, how do we measure that? We are very good at the scope and use of measurements."

In this chapter we will describe how UCS translates key customer satisfiers into *more than 100 internal process measurements*. It tracks these measurements daily. Not only that, it reviews the measures and *initiates improvements daily*. It's no surprise that 96% of all UCS associates feel that the company's commitment to quality is demonstrated daily throughout the business (compared to 50% for U.S. companies and a 75% average for high-performing companies).

That commitment to quality attracts and keeps customers. In its first two-and-one-half years of existence, UCS gained 16 million customers. It is now second in its industry. More than 98% of its customers rate UCS's overall service as better than the competition.

The "brain center" of the new management model is a comprehensive data and tracking system that produces actionable data that are easily accessible to those who can use it to improve. High-performance companies understand that they can manage only what they can measure—and that is as true for such areas as marketing, administration, and legal as it is for manufacturing. As Fred Smith, chairman and chief executive officer for Federal Express, said, "We believe that service quality must be mathematically measured." The better the measurement system, the better the quality.

This chapter's role models use excellent measurement systems to acquire company-level data they then use to:

- Translate customers' requirements into process parameters.
- Monitor key processes.
- Identify problems.
- Analyze trends.
- Observe the impact of improvements.
- Delight customers.

From the perspective of our new management model, *the measurement system helps them align and integrate their quality systems*. As Joseph M. Juran wrote, "Once we have established a system of measurement, we have a common language or metric. We can use that language to help us at each and every step."

But first we need to understand the steps to establishing an effective measurement system. We will use the experiences of AT&T Universal Card Services, Kennametal-Solon, Carrier, and AMP to address these questions:

- How do you know what data and information to collect?
- How do you know they are accurate, reliable, and useful?
- How do you aggregate and analyze these data to improve customer satisfaction, quality, and operational performance?
- How do you evaluate and improve your data collection and analysis?

MODELS OF EXCELLENCE

AT&T Universal Card Services (UCS) is headquartered in Jacksonville, Florida. UCS markets and supports the AT&T Universal Card, a combination general-purpose credit card and long-distance calling card. In less than three years,

UCS grew from a concept team of 35 people to the second largest bank credit card program in the industry, a profitable billion-dollar-plus concern employing 2,500 associates, two-thirds of whom have direct contact with customers. AT&T Universal Card Services won the Baldrige Award in 1992.

Kennametal's Solon, Ohio, plant manufactures high-quality tool holders for customers who machine metal. Nearly 550 employees work at a state-of-the-art facility Kennametal built in 1988. The new plant combined two existing operations (neither of which was doing very well) into one facility organized into manufacturing cells that are run by *self-managed work teams*. This team approach has produced significant improvements:

- On-time delivery of special tooling products rose from 53% in 1989 to 95% in 1992. For standard products, performance improved from 82% to 99%.
- Average lead time improved from 42 working days to 24 over the same period.
- Cost reductions exceeded $1 million annually from 1990 through 1992.

Carrier is the world's leader in heating and air conditioning products. The company's founder, Willis Carrier, started an industry when he invented an "apparatus for treating air" in 1902. Carrier is a subsidiary of United Technologies and is headquartered in Farmington, Connecticut. The company has 28,000 employees (10,500 in its North American Operations) and manufacturing operations in 17 countries.

This chapter also describes the Quality Scorecard system AMP uses to analyze its data. AMP, headquartered in Harrisburg, Pennsylvania, is the world's largest producer of electrical and electronic connecting devices. It has more than 24,000 people in 27 countries.

DETERMINING WHAT DATA AND INFORMATION TO COLLECT

A company's measurement system, like its entire quality system, must be driven by its customers. As you determine your customers' requirements (see Chapter 3) and decide how you will meet those requirements (Chapters 4–13), you will want to construct a measurement system that aligns all activities with improving customer satisfaction.

AT&T Universal Card Services had the luxury of creating such a system at the same time it created the business unit. It started with the customer. First, people who had been in the credit card business came up with a list of primary customer satisfiers. Next, UCS took that list to a series of focus groups made up of credit card customers. The focus groups produced a definitive model of what would please these customers.

"We came up with a set of eight satisfiers, which has since been expanded to nine," says Davis. The satisfiers do not change often, although their importance to customers changes as UCS improves at delivering a satisfier. The only addition in the company's first three years was to break the "price" satisfier into two: "fee" and "annual percentage rate." "When we started our business, interest rates did not matter much to customers. Research indicated that rates had to drop by five points for customers to be interested," Davis says. "Now that's happened, and customers are much more concerned about it, so we made annual percentage rate a satisfier."

The eight satisfiers are main branches on a tree chart. (The full list of satisfiers is proprietary information UCS does not disclose.) Each branch has secondary satisfiers, and each of those has tertiary satisfiers. For example, "customer service" is a satisfier. It has four secondary satisfiers, including "accessibility" and "professionalism," and 27 tertiary satisfiers, including "courtesy," "takes time to help," "handles request first call," and "quick call answering." The tertiary satisfiers are the *internal actions that produce satisfied customers*, the internal measures that link to external, customer measures.

UCS has more than 100 tertiary satisfiers. "We believe we've defined 98% of what it takes to please customers," says Davis. "We've done modeling so that we know what places we can improve to bring additional profits and revenues." For example, UCS learned through its research that taking care of a request on the first call was very important to customers. By equipping associates with all the information they need and encouraging them to make decisions, UCS takes care of 95% of the requests it gets on the first call.

Based on these satisfiers, UCS identified more than 100 internal process measures. It takes these measures daily and reports on them the next day. For example, since taking care of a request on the first call is important, two internal measures of processes that contribute to this satisfier are system uptime and payments posting on the day received.

UCS has many more measures under each of these key measures that are diagnostic for them. "If I have an indicator for accuracy of calls," Davis explains, "I listen to a sample of calls every day and assess the accuracy of the information given to customers. I have a set of criteria I use to determine accuracy. The diagnostic measures under that focus on all processes that support the associate handling the calls, such as how often the associate's handbook is updated and how often the computer screen is refreshed."

An important part of the measurement system involves *taking the pulse of customers*. UCS calls customers daily to get specific information about eight key areas that touch on all types of customer-UCS interactions, including phone, mail, and 800 number calls. Internal people trained to be telephone associates contact about 4,000 customers every month through these contacter studies. UCS originally contracted an outside firm to do the studies, but brought it inside because it wanted more immediate information. "By doing it in-house, we got rid of 15- to 20-day delays," says Davis. "Now, if I find a hot item, we can act on it today."

Through its measurement system UCS aligns all activities within the company with its key customer satisfiers. "Our system allows us to change the measures any way we see fit," says Davis. "In some cases, we expand them, while others we might change three or four times a month. The number of measures changes, but it doesn't change radically."

As it implemented its measurement process and system, UCS encountered an obstacle many companies have faced: installing measures in support areas. Initially, UCS tried to roll it out to all areas at once. It didn't work. Davis remembers that his own quality team had serious reservations about their ability to measure improvement in the company's suggestion system, especially in the marketing area. The group found itself relying on customer surveys when it could not identify an internal process. It has since overcome that obstacle and now points to progress on its measures to prove the success of its suggestion system.

"Resistance to measurements is natural," Davis adds. "People say, 'You can't measure the things I do.' As we've shown how much measures help, people have joined the bandwagon. They're seeing success in one place and they want to know how they can make it work in their shop—though not necessarily in the same way."

Historically, service companies have had weak measurement systems, assuming that statistical measurement belongs to manufacturers. Even manufacturing companies with strong production metrics have failed to measure non-manufacturing processes. The problem is not that these processes cannot be measured, but that people have not tried to measure them. As Patrick Mene, corporate director of quality for Baldrige Award-winner Ritz-Carlton, said, "People who haven't measured, haven't even tried. They're making excuses." (For more about what Ritz-Carlton measures, see Chapter 5.)

When Kennametal's Solon plant got serious about measuring, it actually created the opposite problem: The plant started with too many measures. It got rid of irrelevant measures by focusing on customers' requirements and expectations. The Solon facility now has 120 *key performance indicators* (KPIs) in use throughout the operation, including support functions such as human resources.

Employee teams select their own measures. A coordinator keeps track of all the measures and works with the teams on identifying, establishing, and tracking them. Every measure must have a goal. "Measuring without a goal doesn't accomplish anything," says Paul Cahan, director of global steel operations and the Solon plant manager. "Through the use of measures and realistic goals you can improve performance."

Like UCS and Kennametal-Solon, Carrier uses its measurement system to align all efforts with customer satisfaction. Carrier believes that "we achieve customer satisfaction by focusing the entire organization on the needs and expectations of the customer." It focuses the organization through *standardized, corporate metrics* in three areas: customer satisfaction, product quality, and employee satisfaction.

"These three link together nicely," says David Gregerson, vice-president of quality. "Product quality coming out of the factory is a leading indicator of quality. Customer satisfaction is a lagging indicator. And employee satisfaction is a leading indicator, because happy, satisfied, trained employees are a prerequisite to happy, satisfied customers."

Gregerson understands the debate within large companies between the "centralized" and "decentralized" camps. People worry that a corporate measurement system will impede ownership by and empowerment of operating units. He has not seen that happen at Carrier. "I think there's a great advantage to having corporate metrics for quality. The standardization enables us to talk across countries, cultures, and boundaries and to start thinking of nonfinancial measurements as equal in importance to financial measurements." *The aggregation of data at the corporate level is critical to management's ability to assess current performance and determine courses of action.*

The comparison to financial measurements is intriguing because it points out the power of a measurement system. As noted in Chapter 1, *financial measurements* provide a common language for companies and nations around the world. This common language has become the accepted way to assess a company's strength and performance and to focus the company on what needs to be improved. If we had a similar system of *quality measurements*, we could assess strength and performance with quality as the criteria and focus the company on areas for improvement. That is what Carrier and other high-performance companies are striving to do.

Carrier's corporate metrics measure the following:

- *Customer satisfaction.* A standard customer survey has replaced a host of past surveys. The annual survey goes to about 7,000 distributors and dealers, but not to end users, because they are hard to identify worldwide. The one-page *Customer Satisfaction Index survey* asks distributors to rate Carrier on 13 items in the areas of product quality, business support, customer services, delivery, leadership, and overall. There's also space for comments. The one-page *Customer Satisfaction Research survey* asks about management team performance, what customers would pay a premium price for and why, comparison to competition, and an assessment of current products.

- *Product quality.* Product quality data are reported monthly from all Carrier facilities. The data represent three segments:

  - *Field*—the measure is "dead on arrivals," which are claims paid during the first 30 days for units installed.

  - *Factory*—factory critical defects, which are the percentage of units reworked in the assembly process that have critical defects, and audit critical defects, which is the quality level the customer will receive by checking 2% of the finished goods for critical defects.

  - *Warranty costs*—first-year warranty costs as a percent of last year's net sales.

- *Employee satisfaction.* The human resources department annually surveys all employees worldwide. The survey, more than 100 questions in 16 categories, is distributed in nine languages. In 1992 about 16,000 of Carrier's employees responded.

In addition to these corporate data, Carrier's operating divisions collect their own data. For example, North American Operations (NAO) collects additional customer data through 800 lines, focus groups, end-user surveys, and quarterly probes that address specific issues identified in the corporate survey. In the area of quality NAO focuses on process improvement, measuring cycle time, cost, and number of operations in a process. Process improvement measures are widespread, in place in such areas as financial, information systems, service parts, and human resources. "All employees are involved with measuring and using results to improve," says Gregerson.

NAO also has supplier measures, including defective parts per million by part number, number of suppliers, and number of certified suppliers. It has surveyed 1,400 suppliers in the last four years, finding that the process of surveying alone causes suppliers to cut their defects in half.

Carrier's most encompassing corporate metric is the Baldrige criteria, which it uses to assess business units that compete for the Willis H. Carrier Global Quality Award. Unlike most companies that are using the Baldrige criteria in a formal program, Carrier conducts site visits for every unit that applies. (For more information about the Baldrige criteria as a system assessment tool, see Chapter 17.)

MAKING SURE THE DATA AND INFORMATION ARE USEFUL

Once you have systems in place for collecting and analyzing key quality and performance measurements, the next step is to communicate the measurements to the people who can use them. Skimping on this step is like buying a sleek sports car without the key; it's a great-looking system, but it's not going to get you very far.

Universal Card Services makes it almost impossible to avoid its daily measurements:

- A composite of its 100+ internal process measures is posted in the cafeteria every day.
- Results for all the measures are posted individually, daily, on boards in common areas.
- Relevant measures are posted in work areas.
- Measures are posted outside elevators.
- They are electronically conveyed on TV monitors in common areas.
- They are available electronically at 7 A.M. every day through a computer system called "You Know," which provides the results of all measurements and even some of the diagnostic measurements.
- Those who don't like reading a computer screen can get paper copies.

If a daily measure indicates a serious problem, the process owner is contacted before the measures are published to give him or her an opportunity to address the problem. "It's very critical that measurements not be used as clubs to beat people up," says Davis. "That can easily happen. We try to avoid that by giving our process owners a chance to figure out what they're going to do about it." UCS uses the same approach with the monthly results of its contractor studies, building in a five-day interval between getting and publishing the results to give process owners time to react.

People often resist measuring what they do because they fear the measurement will be used to criticize their work, punish them, or control them. Quality leaders use measures to evaluate a process or system, not a person. "We don't use measures to tell people they're not performing," says Kennametal's Cahan. "We use them to tell people what's important and why."

At Kennametal's Solon plant, measures of key performance indicators are posted in highly-visible areas where the people who use them are located. The measures are updated weekly and typically show a year's worth of history in monthly and weekly bars. It takes one person one day a week to enter the data for all the measures and print out the colorful, easy-to-read charts.

Carrier uses similar processes to communicate data specific to a facility. At the corporate level the data are analyzed and communicated to executives and managers who can use this information to improve. Analysis of results of the Customer Satisfaction Research, which includes a summary of the top two or three strengths and areas for improvement, is distributed to the business unit executive committee. The committee uses the feedback in its strategic planning process (see Chapter 6 for insight into how this is done).

For the product quality measurements, Carrier analyzes the data monthly and reports to the executive staff and back to the units that provided the information. Problems are traced to their causes. If a trend at one of the operations is going in the wrong direction, corporate quality asks it to report on the reasons and what is being done to fix it, and offers its assistance.

Employee satisfaction survey data are compared to national norms for Carrier's industry and other industries. Human Resources feeds the data back to the general managers and to other levels as requested. (They can provide data for groups with as few as 25 employees.) The units that receive the data review and discuss them with employees and identify one or two items to work on for the next year.

One of the best systems for communicating key data quickly has been developed by AMP, which introduced its *Quality Scorecard system* in January 1993. Employees can turn to their computer terminals and call up a matrix that shows quality, delivery, value, and service down the vertical column and suppliers, internal AMP, and customers across the horizontal column. A number in each box shows the month-to-date measure of quality. For example, the box at the intersection of "Internal AMP" and "Delivery" might show 95%, which would represent AMP's on-time delivery percentage. Put the cursor inside a box, hit "Return," and you have a detailed system of measures that produced that single number. You can further pursue measures that compare divisions, measures for a particular division, measures for locations within a division, all late orders, and performace by customer. The data are on-line, updated daily.

"Our experience is that this type of fast response system causes great improvement," says J. Keith Drysdale, vice-president of global quality. Before powering up its Quality Scorecard, AMP had a similar system in place for four years in its logistics area. The system helped AMP improve its on-time delivery over that period from 66% to 95%. A similar call management system helped AMP improve its ability to handle incoming calls from 15% abandoned to 0.4% while reducing the number of people answering phones from 500 to 300. The

Quality Scorecard evolved from this experience and the desire to have instant access to critical measures.

"I took a systems approach to this," says Drysdale. "I wanted to see what was coming in from suppliers, see the choke points in our system and how things are going through the system, then look at how the customer sees it."

AMP trains employees in how to maneuver within the system to find the data they need to improve quality and customer satisfaction. Employees learn to *zero in on systemic, not individual, areas for improvement*. AMP sells 65,000 different parts in 400 product families. Chasing individual events would be like bailing water from a boat with a thimble. Employees use Pareto analysis (the 80/20 rule) to identify such things as the 5 tools a division is having the most trouble with, locations that are struggling, or the 10 customers that need immediate attention. "It's a big help to management because they can work on the areas that have traction," Drysdale says.

As powerful as this system is, AMP is working hard to improve it. It continues to add key measures, cover more processes, and generate more action-oriented reports. And it is working to reorganize the data to reflect activities at the team level instead of the division level. "If you can get to the team level, you will see rapid action," says Drysdale. "A division may have 3,000 problems, but a team only has a fraction of that to work on."

Not that problems are the problem. AMP uses the Quality Scorecard as a proactive tool for continuous improvement, an *instant snapshot* that shows opportunities throughout its system. After all, it's not as if AMP created the Quality Scorecard because it had problems with customer satisfaction. When the system came on line, 96% of AMP's customers were giving the company an overall rating of very good or excellent. And they have the numbers to prove it.

USING DATA AND INFORMATION TO IMPROVE

"The key to continuous improvement is keeping objectives visible, explaining what is behind the figures, and helping employees understand how they can influence the variables," says Paul Cahan at Kennametal. "There are no major breakthroughs, just thousands of little things that add up to something significant." At Kennametal's Solon plant, supervisors work as facilitators with employees and cell teams to discuss how they can improve performance to reach the goals they have set. The KPIs help promote continuous improvement because the employee teams want to meet their goals and move the trends in the right direction.

In addition to monitoring production activities, KPIs can be used in almost every part of a business. The first step is to identify the process or procedure to be improved, then communicate the data to the people who can improve it, establish measures and goals, and empower them to use the data to improve. At Kennametal's Solon facility three years of continuous, incremental improvements have cut the average manufacturing cost of standard products by 11% and have significantly increased its gross margin, making the Solon plant the company's top performer.

At the corporate level, companies need to aggregate and analyze a wide variety of data if they are to make wise decisions. This is one of the most difficult tasks a company faces. It must identify what information it needs, pull that information together in a timely manner, compare the data to determine what is happening, and put the data and analyses in the hands of decision makers in a format they can use to assess cause/effect connections and resource and financial implications and to initiate improvement.

Carrier handled this difficult process by narrowing the scope of data required for corporate decision making to three areas: customer satisfaction data, product quality data, and employee satisfaction data. It then developed *corporate metrics* that simplified data collection and analysis for these areas. The corporate quality department collects and analyzes customer satisfaction and product quality data and communicates the results to executives and managers. The human resources department does the same with employee satisfaction data.

Carrier motivates executives to use this data by tying their long-term incentive compensation to improvements in all three areas. Through its *Continuous Improvement Incentive Program,* more than 300 Carrier executives have bonus potential of $30,000 to $50,000 per year under the following formula:

- 20% is tied to customer satisfaction results.
- 50% to product quality improvement.
- 30% to employee satisfaction.

"We'd like to see corporate metrics tied to salary for all employees, but we understand the problems with this," says Gregerson. (For a discussion of this issue see Chapter 8.)

At AT&T Universal Card Services, every associate has the opportunity to receive a bonus up to 12% of his or her daily salary for each day UCS achieves it quality targets. The average associate earns $2,250 a year in direct, quality-linked bonuses. The *quality targets* and *performance standards* are mutually determined by associates and managers, aligning individual objectives with corporate and departmental goals.

Corporate-level decisions are made daily on the the basis of quality data and analysis. Every morning a group of leaders meets to look at the results of the previous day's internal process measures. The daily results also include month-to-date results to provide history. The meetings are chaired by the executive vice-president of customer services and include people from the collection center, telephone center, quality team, billing, human resources, public relations, and other departments. The first item on the agenda is quality. If the data indicate a quality issue, the group talks about what is being done to address it. Attention then turns to issues of information flow.

Data from UCS's contact survey are analyzed by a *cross-functional group*. The group meets monthly to assess results, look for trends, and identify areas for improvement. UCS also has a *Customer Listening Post*, a good-sized cross-functional team that meets monthly to pull together all customer-related data and spot "hotbeds" that need to be addressed. For example, at a recent meeting, the Listening Post learned that 10% of all the complaints in the previous week had been about the voice response unit. The team looked at attrition reports to see whether usage of the unit was up or down, comments to see if there was a correlation, appropriate satisfiers, general comments from customers, and correspondence. By comparing and analyzing all these data and information, it was able to identify possible causes and suggest improvements.

Another way UCS uses quality measurements to improve is through its "10 Most Wanted" list. Like Carrier, UCS relies on the Baldrige criteria for an assessment of its system. It prioritizes the areas for improvement identified during its Baldrige application process and from the examiner feedback, then puts the 10 hottest items on its "10 Most Wanted" list. "I have a huge board with slats for each of the 10 Most Wanted," says Davis. "We have a set of criteria that define what it takes to get on and off the list. The only way to add one is to retire another. When we take one off, we ceremoniously retire it and honor the team responsible." The "10 Most Wanted" concept has spread to areas within the company; legal, marketing, and strategic planning have lists, while customer services has two "because it's so large," Davis says. "We get real nervous when things stay on any list too long." With all the company's attention focused on specific areas that associates know are critical to customer satisfaction and operational performance, UCS rarely has cause to get nervous.

IMPROVING DATA COLLECTION AND ANALYSIS

UCS improves its data collection and analysis through its Listening Posts and through the formation of a new set of focus groups every 18 months to verify that it has the right satisfiers. Internal measures are checked through monthly business reviews.

At the same time the company is working on *improving the linkages* between internal measures and customer satisfiers. "We want more precise feedback on how a change to an internal process affects a satisfier," says Davis. "Most people already think the linkages make sense, but as we dig into it, we see parts that could be improved—plus the customers' requirements change." UCS recognizes that customer satisfaction is a matter of perception. It is hard to tell how a change in an internal process is going to change customers' perceptions, since the customers themselves do not always know precisely what they want. UCS knows that the better the correlation between internal measures and customer satisfiers, the more accurately it will be able to predict and anticipate customer satisfaction.

Carrier convenes a group of quality professionals, human resources people, and marketing people every three years to decide on refinements to its measurement system. Most of the attention is focused on the accuracy and timeliness of the data, which can be a problem for a global company. "I never had such respect for financial people until I tried to roll this up monthly," says Gregerson. "We've been working hard on this refinement for the past two years."

Quality leaders like Universal Card Services and Carrier refine their measurement systems by assessing their internal data requirements; the completeness, accuracy, and timeliness of the data; the reliability and usefulness of any analysis performed; the efficiency of communication; and the end results—how data and information contribute to sound decisions. That is the goal of an integrated data strategy, whether the decisions affect a single machine, a distinct process, or the company's strategic plans.

THE SHIFT IN THINKING

In the new business management model, management acts on the basis of reliable information, data, and analysis. For managers who already believe they are "managing by fact" the data systems of companies like AT&T Universal Card Systems, Carrier, and AMP provide a reality check. The data come from all parts of a company and from customers, suppliers, competitors, and other sources. The data are aggregated, analyzed, and used for a variety of company purposes, including process management, planning, improving customer service, and empowering employees.

Successful companies establish internal performance indicators that reflect the factors that produce customer satisfaction and quality improvement. Kennametal's Solon plant has more than 120 key performance indicators chosen by the teams that can affect them and tied to customer requirements. UCS's internal process measures are directly linked to customer satisfiers. As the Baldrige criteria state, "A system of indicators tied to customer and/or company performance requirements represents a clear and objective basis for aligning all activities of the company toward common goals."

To develop such an integrated data strategy, consider Carrier's Measurement Norms (in italics), followed by our commentary on each norm.

- *Customer focused on our performance vs. their expectations.* Measuring for measurement's sake has no value. The best measures are customer focused and goal oriented. And only measure what you can control.

- *Easy to collect, report, and understand the data.* Charts and graphs help people understand trends at a glance. Electronic communication, like AMP's Quality Scorecard, provides instant access and the ability to seek further detail. UCS uses many different methods of communication to reach its associates.

- *Management initiates, expects, and reviews the data.* Those who make decisions about improvements in the system must want, expect, and use the data that will help them with that process.

- *Work group and/or individual develops and reports the data for ownership.* The people closest to the process are in the best position to identify and gather the data. They are also in the best position to use the data to improve their process.

- *Data will be used for process improvement and not to spear the messenger.* Nothing will sabotage a measurement system faster than using data to evaluate an individual's performance. Data are indicators of a process's performance, not of people's performance.

- *Rewards by management for progress and permanent solutions.* Whether the rewards are monetary bonuses, team celebrations, or pats on the back, progress on key performance indicators needs to be appreciated.

15 BENCHMARKING

Alcoa

Ameritech

Seitz Corporation

Seitz Corporation makes the gears and bearings that move paper in such things as printers and copiers. When its largest market shriveled up in the mid-1980s, Seitz lost two-thirds of its work force and saw annual sales drop from $12 million to $5 million. It turned to benchmarking to overhaul its business. Six years later, sales had grown to $21 million, and its benchmarking process was well entrenched, with teams of employees benchmarking everything from bar coding to customer service to employee cafeterias.

Ameritech defines benchmarking as "the identification and implementation of best practices to achieve superior customer results and business performance." It has been called a power tool of quality because it can generate significant improvements in a company's key business processes.

Benchmarking itself is a process. You do not use it to prove you are best at something, but *to learn how to become the best*. Benchmarking, by itself, does not improve performance; it provides information you can use to improve. It is a discovery process aimed at exceeding customer expectations.

Alcoa built its quality improvement process on tools, one of which was benchmarking. The company made benchmarking a primary tool because it believed benchmarking could help it progress further, faster, and more efficiently toward its goals. As Alcoa sees it, the benefits of the benchmarking process are that it:

- Helps identify the topics that are most valuable to benchmark and learn ways to improve performance through internal and external study
- Reveals the strengths and weaknesses of significant operations, activities, and technologies
- Improves understanding of latent business threats and competitive positioning
- Better prepares Alcoa to meet its customers' requirements
- Helps identify opportunities to improve current processes, eliminate unnecessary processes, and create new products and services

Seitz was ahead of the game when it recognized these benefits in the mid-1980s; most companies have only been considering the concept in the last few years. Many credit the Baldrige Award program with bringing benchmarking to people's attention. The Baldrige criteria ask how your quality and operational performance results compare to competitors and world-class companies and how you use benchmarking to encourage breakthrough approaches. Early Baldrige Award winners Motorola, Milliken, and Xerox showed how companies could "borrow shamelessly" from world-class benchmarks to meet ambitious "stretch" goals.

Alcoa defines such benchmarks as "models of excellence." In this chapter we will use Alcoa, Ameritech, and Seitz as our models of excellence in the area of benchmarking. All three use this power tool to energize their efforts to improve quality, productivity, and customer satisfaction. As you will see in this chapter, size and type of business do not preclude the successful use of benchmarking: Alcoa and Seitz are manufacturing companies; Ameritech is a service company. Alcoa and Ameritech have about 65,000 employees each; Seitz around 200.

We will use our three quality leaders to answer these questions:

- How do we prepare for a benchmarking project?
- How do we gather benchmarking information?
- What do we do with the information we collect?

The questions cover all the steps in the benchmarking process, the number of which tends to vary from company to company. Xerox's process, probably the most-copied process in the country, has ten steps. A team at Alcoa spent several months studying the Xerox process and others before developing its six-step process:

1. Decide what to benchmark.
2. Plan the benchmarking project.

3. Understand your own performance.

4. Study others.

5. Learn from the data.

6. Use the findings.

By comparison, Seitz presents its process as a flow chart consisting of 14 steps, and Ameritech's benchmarking process has four phases and eight steps:

- Phase 1: Project conception and planning

    Step 1. Project conception

    Step 2. Project planning

- Phase 2: Internal and external data gathering and partner selection

    Step 3. Defining internal processes and performance

    Step 4. Selecting benchmarking partners

    Step 5. Collecting benchmarking partner data

- Phase 3: Analysis and assessment

    Step 6. Comparing internal processes with partners' processes

- Phase 4: Recommendations and action

    Step 7. Recommendations and implementation

    Step 8. Recalibration

Regardless of the number of steps, all formal benchmarking processes reflect the three stages we will address in this chapter:

- Getting ready to benchmark
- Conducting the site visit
- Using what you learn to improve

Informal benchmarking may skip the first and second steps, but its goal is still to improve. Informal benchmarking covers a range of activities that includes reading about similar processes or results in trade publications, talking to competitors or peers at other companies about shared issues or problems, checking out the competition during trade shows, and asking customers and suppliers to compare your performance with that of others. Although informal benchmarking does not require the same degree of planning and execution as formal benchmarking, it can benefit from a similar process: Know your product/service/process; find out what the other company is doing; compare and identify gaps; and initiate improvements.

MODELS OF EXCELLENCE

Ameritech, headquartered in Chicago, is a regional Bell operating company that offers local area telecommunications services to people in Indiana, Illinois, Michigan, Ohio, and Wisconsin. The company also has publishing, mobile telephone, and corporate international groups. It has nearly 68,000 employees. Ameritech is a founder and active participant in the Telecommunications Industry Benchmarking Consortium, a group of 18 telecommunications companies (representing 98% of the North American telecom industry) formed to use benchmarking to improve quality.

Alcoa is one of the leading aluminum companies in the world, with 159 locations in 22 countries. Its products are used in beverage containers, airplanes and cars, commercial and residential buildings, chemicals, and an array of consumer and industrial applications. With headquarters in Pittsburgh, Alcoa has more than 65,000 employees in 22 business units.

Seitz Corporation is an injection molder, assembler, and contract manufacturer of thermoplastic components in Torrington, Connecticut. The family-owned business employs 200 people. The company's sales increased from $5 million in 1986 to $21 million in 1992, when it won the State Blue Chip Enterprise Initiative Award as "the best example of a small business that effectively used resources to overcome adversity and emerge stronger." Seitz attributes its improvement to benchmarking.

PREPARING FOR A BENCHMARKING STUDY

Before employees can conduct a study, they need to know what benchmarking is, believe in its benefits, and feel empowered to invest the time such a study takes and act on their findings. Alcoa met these needs by making benchmarking a part of its culture and a requirement of its planning process. "Our culture is very 'can do' and 'invented here'," says Martin Leeper, manager of corporate quality. "We wanted to counteract that, so we made benchmarking one of our first three quality improvement tools, along with effective teaming and our eight-step problem-solving process. These three tools drive every quality project at Alcoa."

Alcoa did a great deal of training in effective teaming and the eight-step process, but chose not to train people in benchmarking, except for two-hour presentations on the subject. "The benchmarking process is fundamentally easy to understand. We decided to postpone training because otherwise people believe they can't do it until they take a course. We wanted them to get into benchmarking right away." Leeper and his group provide support by facilitating, coaching, and counseling the benchmarking teams.

Ameritech's internal benchmarking experts take a similar role. "Groups can start benchmarking on their own, but a good percentage of the time they come back to our group for training, contacts, site visit advice, and other assistance. We're the benchmarking consultants," says Orval Brown, manager of business process architecture and benchmarking. Ameritech made benchmarking part of the process improvement toolkit it developed to help reengineer its business. It did training in conjunction with its overall quality improvement process, including holding a number of benchmarking forums. "Other people's success stories get people interested and excited about the possibilities for improvement," says Brown.

Seitz includes benchmarking in its 33 hours of quality training, then reviews the steps when a team begins a benchmarking project.

Benchmarking projects can be divided into two types: internal and external. External projects are either competitive ("industry best") or functional ("best-in-class"). "We do a lot of internal comparisons at the department or work group level to gain 20 to 30% improvements," says Alcoa's Leeper. "But when it comes to breakthrough leadership and looking for 40 to 70% improvements in cycle time, quality, and cost, that comes from looking outside the company."

Obtain Management Commitment to Benchmarking

According to Leeper, the biggest problem people face when it comes to benchmarking is, "Where do we start?" As with any long-term management initiative, *the place to begin is with senior management.* "Most managers have a misconception about benchmarking, whether it is comparing companies and numbers or understanding processes," says Ameritech's Brown. "The whole thrust of our breakthrough leadership initiative is radical change. Most leaders understand this means radical changes with limited resources, based on comparisons with external, world-class companies. Benchmarking has helped our leaders become more externally focused."

Senior manager support is critical because they must commit time, allocate resources, remove roadblocks, and reward the effort. Benchmarking teams that proceed without this support expose themselves to second-guessing about how they spend their time, a lack of funds to complete the project, insurmountable objections by other managers and departments affected by the study, and little or no action on their recommendations. When the senior staff endorses benchmarking, these obstructions can be removed.

Senior management can also make sure the company's benchmarking efforts are coordinated. Companies that have identified their key business processes usually have a good handle on what a particular benchmarking study will do to other parts of the system. Communication among the areas affected by the study helps prevent interdepartmental conflicts and bottlenecks.

Finally, it is important for senior management and benchmarking teams to remember that a formal benchmarking study typically takes around six months to complete. There are no shortcuts. "The biggest problem is finding the time to do a study," says Leeper. If changes need to be made quickly, you will be better off choosing other tools.

Identifying What Should Be Benchmarked

So you have senior management buy-in and six months to get the job done. How do you decide what to study?

"Customers will tell you when you're messing up. They're a great place to start a benchmark," says Sharon LeGault, marketing manager at Seitz. "Internal and external sales people can also see differences. Another source is people who recognize a problem: 'We're losing money because of...'" Seitz does benchmarking in response to a gap, a suspected gap, or a problem. Once the need is identified, Seitz's senior staff recommends forming a team to address it, after which the team takes the leadership role.

Alcoa identifies benchmarking opportunities through its planning process and as teams work through its eight-step problem solving process. Two questions the teams must answer are: "Has anyone ever faced a similar problem before? What did they do about it?" Benchmarking is an obvious tool for finding the answers.

Alcoa uses the following criteria to decide if a topic is relevant and valid as a benchmarking subject:

- Is the topic important to our customers?
- Is the topic consistent with our mission, values, and milestones?
- Does the topic reflect an important business need?
- Is the topic significant in terms of costs or key nonfinancial indicators?
- Is the topic in an area where additional information could influence plans and actions?

The first question is undoubtedly the most important. *A benchmarking study must have clear, accurate objectives based on customer requirements.* "Most of our studies get customers involved, either through phone calls, focus groups, or bringing them on the site visit—to help us understand their requirements," says Brown. "Another advantage of involving customers is that when it's time to implement the team's recommendations they are based on clear, accurate customer requirements."

Topics for benchmarking studies cover any process that is critical to customer service and the company's success. Ameritech is currently conducting studies on product development cycle time, operational efficiency in its buy-ing organization, human resources staffing processes, and financial operations. Seitz has benchmarked tooling, customer service, accounting practices, and bar coding. Answering Alcoa's questions, listed previously, will tell you whether or not a topic makes good benchmarking material.

Creating a Benchmarking Project Plan

The next step in the process involves creating a plan of action. Ameritech calls this the project plan and suggests it cover the following areas:

- Goals and objectives
- Scope and resources
- Key players
- Critical success factors
- Roles and responsibilities
- Milestones and deliverables
- Performance measures
- High-level process flows

Seitz asks its benchmarking teams to select who will be leader, process guide, scribe, and timekeeper. The leader leads. The process guide maintains the rules, such as no evaluating during brainstorming and involving everyone in the discussions. The scribe records everything and distributes meeting minutes. The timekeeper keeps meetings within time limits and makes sure the team is progressing as planned.

Ameritech also uses teams. It identifies six roles required for a benchmark-ing project: executive sponsor, project manager, benchmarking analyst, bench-marking advisor, subject matter expert, and documenting analyst. These "hats" may be worn by different team members at different times during the process, but Brown notes that "the biggest problem in forming a team is finding a docu-menting analyst. That's the person the resource teams try to do without because of limited availability."

In each Ameritech benchmarking team the project sponsor assumes lead-ership or appoints a team leader. After team members are carefully selected, the next task is to refine the benchmarking purpose statement to answer these questions:

- Who are the customers for the study?
- What is the scope of the study?

- What characteristics will be measured?
- What information about the topic is readily available?

Seitz's teams use *statistical problem-solving tools* to develop their proposal. They begin by brainstorming to make sure the perceived problem exists. If it does, the team uses a "fishbone" diagram to identify the reasons for the outcome, does a Pareto chart to determine the primary opportunities, then creates a flow chart to map the process under study. "Once the team puts the brainstorming, fishbone, and Pareto together, the team's senior staff member brings the proposal to the senior staff with a request for money to implement the study," says LeGault.

Many benchmarking efforts fail because teams do not understand their company's process first. It is like deciding to buy new office furniture without finding out what employees are currently using, what they need, what existing furniture will be kept, where it will be put, what the work environment is like, how it is changing, and so on. *You cannot ask intelligent questions or collect meaningful information without a clear understanding of the existing process you wish to improve.*

Alcoa describes this step in its benchmarking booklet as follows:

> Teams examine the factors that influence performance and learn which characteristics are most important and which are less important. They also learn what data relate to important characteristics and how to collect and measure that data. In addition, the collection of internal data and the analysis of limits to performance may reveal new ways to overcome specific barriers. Finally, this internal collection of performance data creates the baseline and structure for benchmarking comparisons.

The easiest way to make comparisons is by developing *a common set of metrics* that define key elements of the process. Ameritech seeks metrics that are driven by customer requirements as a way of keeping the focus on improving the process to improve customer satisfaction. One of the problems benchmarking teams often encounter is finding a different set of metrics in use at the company being benchmarked. "The problem is getting an apples to apples comparison," says Brown. "We've been able to avoid the problem by asking, 'This is what we're looking for. How would you map to that?' It's not always easy, but it hasn't been a significant problem."

Identifying Companies to Use as Benchmarks

Once the project proposal is written and approved, the next step is to identify benchmarking prospects. Teams often struggle with this step; either they do not have a clue where to find such prospects, or they have one or two companies they have heard about and that is their list. Ameritech encourages its teams to brainstorm until they have at least 30 potential companies. Among the places you can look for leads are:

- Process owners
- Internal and external customers
- Professional organizations
- Trade shows and seminars
- Professional and trade publications
- Newspaper and magazine articles
- Industry experts
- Industry studies
- Suppliers

Small companies often have trouble finding benchmarking partners. Seitz focuses on companies of similar size, getting most of its leads from customers, newspaper and magazine articles, and trade shows. It has tried benchmarking large companies, but team members came back overwhelmed and Seitz discovered it could not afford to implement what the larger companies were doing.

The goal of the search is to find companies that are satisfying the same customer needs as the internal process and are doing it with a high degree of success. "You can identify similar, but better than you is the trick," says LeGault. "Our people make up a short questionnaire they use to ask potential companies leading questions. We try to come up with a long list of 15 companies, call them, then pick the top three or four to benchmark." The questions are specific and qualifying. Team members record the responses and ask if the target would be willing to participate.

Ameritech uses the following criteria to help determine appropriate partner companies:

- Companies that have received quality or business awards
- Top-rated firms in industry surveys
- Success stories published in periodicals
- Statements of pride in business articles
- Companies with excellent financial results
- Feedback from internal and external experts, customers, suppliers, and business partners

Ameritech uses these criteria and a series of questions to narrow its list of 30 to about a dozen. The questions include:

- For what quality process or result is the company known?
- What evidence exists to confirm the partner is an industry leader in the area of interest?
- What is the level of customer satisfaction?
- What is the company's profitability?
- What is the company's market share?
- Has the company made any contributions to the state of the art in its industry—new technology impacts?

Once it has a dozen or so qualified prospects, Ameritech uses a comparison matrix to cut that list down to six to eight partners. Their benchmarking manual includes the generic sample shown in Table 15.1.

Some of the matrix can be completed with information already collected. The rest comes from phone interviews with the potential partners. Brown has found that he usually has the name of someone he can call, identified either through his own networking, the quality department, or the industry benchmarking consortium to which Ameritech belongs. He tries to initiate all contacts because most companies prefer a single point of contact.

Companies deluged by benchmarking requests appreciate such courtesy. Quality leaders, such as those who have won Baldrige Awards, have been very visible benchmarking targets to the point that two winners, Milliken and Westinghouse Commercial Nuclear Fuel, are accepting requests only by customers and suppliers (which is why they are not in this book). However, many will still agree to participate, especially if they can learn something in return.

TABLE 15.1. Ameritech's benchmarking partner criteria matrix

Criteria	Co. A	Co. B	Co. C	Co. D	Co. E
1. Quality oriented					
2. Successful product/service reputation					
3. Service oriented					
4. Excellent cycle time					
5. 100% reliability					
6. 25% improvement yr.-to-yr. sales growth					
7. 25% improvement yr.-to-yr. profitability					
8. More than 20,000 employees					

"Companies realize they have to have their processes identified and that you're going to be in their plant for three hours. That's a lot to ask for some companies," says LeGault. "Others say they're not familiar with benchmarking and don't have the resources to deal with it. Out of our short list, 50 to 75 percent will agree to participate."

GATHERING BENCHMARKING INFORMATION

For companies willing to participate, you should agree on the time frame and length of the site visit, an agenda, your benchmarking practices, and the questions you will ask. Seitz faxes its questions to its partners so that they can look at the questions before the site visit and eliminate any they do not want to address. In its benchmarking guide Ameritech suggests the kinds of questions a team might ask to learn more about a process:

- Does the company have a defined, documented process?
- How is the process communicated to the process customers and users?
- How are the users kept up to date on the process changes?
- What is the management system of the process?
- What aspects of the process are considered to be world-class?

At Seitz, team members decide who will go to which companies, usually in groups of two or three. "We'll go in with 20 different questions and write comparisons side-by-side to see the differences in time and benefits," says LeGault. Team members are encouraged to ask anything and everything, but only if they are questions they would answer themselves. In fact, the team members should have the answers for their own process written down so that they can use it for comparison during the visit. Seitz offers to share the results of its project with all partners. Most are willing to share them, although some ask for confidentiality, which Seitz respects.

The act of opening up one company's facilities and processes for another company to scrutinize carries with it the potential for abuse. Many companies are adopting a benchmarking code of conduct to govern their activities and reassure their potential partners. Ameritech is a member of the Strategic Planning Institute's Council on Benchmarking, which created and adopted the following *code of conduct:*

1. Keep it legal.
2. Be willing to provide the same information that you request.
3. Respect confidentiality.

4. Keep information internal for your use only.

5. Initiate contact through benchmarking contacts.

6. Don't refer without permission.

7. Be prepared at initial contact.

8. Have a basic knowledge of benchmarking and follow the process.

9. Have determined what to benchmark and complete a rigorous self-assessment.

The effectiveness of a site visit depends primarily on how well prepared both sides are. If both companies understand their processes and if the benchmarking team knows exactly what it wants to learn, most visits proceed fairly smoothly. During its half-dozen years of benchmarking experience Seitz has encountered four common problems:

- *People are not prepared to actually compare gaps.* As a result, they gather information not pertinent to the project. Teams must be careful not to become tourists during the site visit.

- *People take poor notes.* "We recommend that every employee in the group has a copy of the same questionnaire. When the question is asked, everyone writes down the answer they hear," says LeGault.

- *People do not understand the purpose of the study.* LeGault talks about how one site visit backfired when a team of toolmakers returned saying they were underpaid, the target company had better equipment, and they liked their landscaping very much.

- *Senior management doesn't want to be bothered to participate on the teams.* If senior staff do not show interest, people on the team do not think it is important either.

Another problem mentioned earlier is finding information and data in a form you can use. "When making comparisons, the best way is to roll it up to a level where you get an apples to apples comparison, which is hard because people generally migrate to lower levels of detail," says Brown. "I've found myself making repeated calls to try to understand the data I've gotten." Developing a good relationship with your benchmarking partner makes this ongoing exchange of information possible.

WHAT TO DO WITH WHAT YOU LEARN

At Alcoa, teams analyze the data they have collected, quantify performance gaps, explore the implications of those gaps, and identify which pieces of information might help improve performance. They then work with the project sponsor to determine how to use the findings.

Ameritech talks about segmenting the gap between current and proposed performance into strategic and tactical actions necessary to close the gap. *Tactical changes* result in minor productivity gains. *Strategic changes* are major changes required to close the gap.

At Seitz, the benchmarking teams fill out comparison charts to clarify the differences on key points. Table 15.2 is an example from a team's study of kanban. The study led to a new inventory system at Seitz, reduced work in process in the assembly area by 15% to 20%, and depleted 90% of the inventory on the floor, allowing the company to add one-third more assembly line.

After the teams complete the comparison charts, they pull in people from other departments to review what they learned and to develop a list of recommendations, including any savings of time and money. If changes are in order, "our employees are empowered to make the changes they think they need," says LeGault. "The only time they have to go to upper management is when they need to spend more than $500."

Not every study results in change. "At times, the results are too expensive or don't work for you, so you do another type of problem-solving process," LeGault says.

One way to improve the odds of getting benchmarking results you can use is to benchmark more companies. "In the majority of benchmarking studies, we find that three or four of the companies we've benchmarked can give us 40% plus improvement," says Ameritech's Brown. "We typically include a half-dozen companies or more because there will be some companies we don't learn much from. We generally don't get all our improvements from one company, although there have been a few times when we've gotten a fair amount from one source."

TABLE 15.2. Sample of a Seitz information comparison sheet

Question: When issuing an order, how much work is delivered to the department?			
Seitz Full order amount	**Company A** 1 day's work is issued	**Company B** 1 week's work issued	**Company C** 2 days' work is issued
Results —WIP is high —Taking up large space for material storage	—No WIP —No space needed	—Lower amount of WIP —Small area for material storage	—Low WIP —Very small area for material storage

Implementing Changes that Result from Benchmarking

Ameritech recommends the following steps to implement the changes needed to close the gap:

- Select implementation alternatives
- Assign resources and create a schedule
- Establish goals
- Develop a monitoring plan
- Gain appropriate approval to alter the current practices
- Implement the plan
- Communicate the benchmarking findings

After the plan is implemented, the processes it affects must be *measured* and *monitored* to see if they are performing as expected and to continue to improve them. The final point in Ameritech's list is also important: Information gained from benchmarking is often valuable to other parts of the organization, especially in larger companies. At Alcoa, benchmarking teams are asked to identify others in Alcoa who might benefit from the work they have done. Corporate quality maintains a *benchmarking data base* that lists topics and organizations that have been benchmarked, and business units aggregate and share relevant information.

Ameritech's final step is *recalibration*, the reevaluation process. This is not a review of how the plan has worked, but the beginning of a new benchmarking process following all eight steps. As Brown points out, "The ultimate goal is for benchmarking to be institutionalized throughout the organization to ensure its continued success."

THE SHIFT IN THINKING

The new business management model promotes systems thinking, both in terms of understanding the internal systems around which your company is built and the external systems that affect it. In previous chapters we have examined the links with customers and suppliers. In the next chapter we will look at a company's responsibilities to its communities. These external influences force a company to constantly review the premises and processes on which it is based.

Benchmarking enables you to improve your internal systems by learning from external resources. As we have seen in this chapter, it is a process of discovering exactly what you are doing, what the best inside or outside your company are doing, how they compare, and what you can do to improve.

Our three models of excellence follow formal benchmarking processes, although all three processes differ slightly. The important point is that each follows a well-defined process. Another important point is that the process does not always have to be so formal. For example, Alcoa's senior management was concerned about improving in one of its values, promoting the health and well-being of its employees. It already had the best safety record in its industry, but it did not consider itself good enough and it was not improving. "We took our corporate and human resource leaders and national union leaders and did a week-long study mission. The participants learned that you manage safety like you manage quality," says Leeper. "The process opened up a dialogue among these leaders that led to common knowledge and acceptance. We emphasize that this is a mutual learning process."

Considered a power tool for quality, benchmarking is an indispensable tool for the learning organization. Without it you will never know how your company stands relative to competitors and world-class performers, you will miss out on new ways of thinking needed to achieve breakthrough improvements, and you will have no way of gauging the effectiveness of your processes or imagining how good they can be.

In the new management model, benchmarking is used to find out what is best and to guide process improvements that will make your company the next model of excellence. All with the goal of exceeding customer expectations.

16 CORPORATE RESPONSIBILITY AND CITIZENSHIP

3M

USAA

EMD Associates

For many people the connection between business management and corporate responsibility and citizenship is vague. What does business ethics have to do with quality? What do environmental issues have to do with improving performance? What is the value to our company of promoting community involvement?

When quality leaders answer these questions, their responses tend to fall into two categories: (1) you do it because it is profitable; (2) you do it because it is the right thing to do.

Consider two examples. The first is Procter & Gamble, which has taken a leadership role in responding to environmental issues—in the following ways:

- All P&G plastic bottles are coded for recycling.
- All Spic and Span bottles are made of 100% recycled soft drink bottles.
- P&G's concentrated laundry detergents reduce packaging and the amount of chemicals needed to clean by 30%.
- Downy refills use 75% less packaging material than the plastic bottle.
- New packaging has eliminated the outside cartons for P&G deodorants, saving 3.4 million pounds of solid waste each year.
- The company is donating $20 million a year to the development of solid waste composting.

P&G has done all this—and more—because consumers want to buy products compatible with their environmental concerns. At an environmental conference Deborah Anderson, P&G's director of environmental coordination, said, "If we meet this new need first and best, in an ethically sound way, consumers will buy our products in preference over our competitors'." Procter & Gamble has identified a customer requirement, which in this case involves corporate responsibility, and it is changing and improving its products to meet and exceed that requirement.

The second example is EMD Associates, which approaches corporate responsibility and citizenship from a different perspective. EMD, one of the quality leaders featured in this chapter, is an 800-person company that designs and manufactures printed circuit board assemblies. It is a company in transition, having added more than 300 people in the past year. As it struggles with the impact of such dramatic growth, it draws on its values for guidance: a passion for consensus, a natural inclination to work in teams, and a strong link to the community. "This is about personal quality transformation," says Dan Rukavina who, along with Dave Arnold, founded EMD and is a co-CEO. "To transform our business we need to create an environment that facilitates that transformation for everybody. We need to look at many different cultures and values as a team to invent our own. It's in the process of growing and being transformed that all of this means anything." Rukavina, Arnold, and their co-workers at EMD are community activists and leaders because they believe it is the right thing to do.

Every organizational "system" functions within, affects, and is affected by many other systems. Customers and suppliers have their own business systems. Markets are systems. The communities in which we work are systems, and these systems are the focus of this chapter, a business's relationships with the community at large, whether local, state, national, or global.

First, we need to distinguish between corporate responsibility and corporate citizenship. *Corporate responsibility* refers to basic public expectations, such as conducting business ethically and protecting public health and safety and the environment. *Corporate citizenship* means leading and supporting publicly important purposes, such as education, community services, industry and trade practices, and quality improvement.

In this chapter we will look at how three companies—3M, USAA, and EMD—take the lead in corporate citizenship and in their responsibilities to the public. We will use their experiences to clarify the connections between the new management model and a company's public responsibilities, as we answer these questions:

- How do we address corporate responsibility and citizenship in our business?

- How do we improve the ways we meet our public expectations?
- How do we lead as corporate citizens?

The purpose of this chapter is not to sell you on the merits of acting more aggressively in these areas, although our three quality leaders do present compelling arguments. Like the decision to make quality improvement a corporate priority, the decision to make public responsibility and citizenship a priority requires *enlightened leadership* and an ongoing *cultural transformation*. Your company must determine for itself what it can and will do for the public good. As our benchmarks show, what is good for the public can also be a good business strategy.

MODELS OF EXCELLENCE

3M manufactures more than 60,000 products for industrial, commercial, health care, and consumer markets around the world, including pressure-sensitive tapes, photographic films, recording tapes, coated abrasives, and insulating materials. 3M employs nearly 90,000 people in 52 nations. Its headquarters are in St. Paul, Minnesota. The company's Q90s quality effort, launched in 1990, concentrates 3M's entire system on satisfying customers.

In 1922, 25 Army officers founded the United States Automobile Association, better known as USAA, to provide themselves with competitively priced auto insurance. Today, USAA is the fifth largest personal automobile insurer and fourth largest homeowners insurer in the country. It has approximately 15,000 employees. In addition to auto and homeowners insurance, USAA offers its members life insurance, health insurance, annuities, mutual funds and discount brokerage services, banking and credit card services, auto leasing and buying services, travel services, and a retirement community. It sells all its products by telephone and mail. USAA received Baldrige site visits in 1990 and 1991. In May 1993 *Fortune* magazine named USAA first nationally among insurers for providing service.

EMD Associates designs and manufactures printed circuit board assemblies for original equipment manufacturers. Founded in 1974, EMD has grown dramatically in the last few years, increasing its work force from 500 to 800 in the past year alone. It has two facilities in Winona, Minnesota. In 1992 EMD received a Baldrige site visit and won the Minnesota Quality Award.

INCORPORATING RESPONSIBILITY AND CITIZENSHIP

Think of the process of incorporating public responsibility and citizenship in the same way a company incorporates quality improvement: begin with an understanding of customer requirements, then translate those requirements into a *vision, mission,* and *goals* for your company.

The major difference is in the need to be clear that the definition of "customer" includes all of an organization's stakeholders: the people who buy your products and services, stockholders, employees, suppliers, and people in the communities in which you work. Since employees also fit into this last category, a company must pay attention to its responsibilities to the community because a part of that community *is* the company. Separating work and home, business and nonbusiness activities, is tired thinking. The new management model takes a more *holistic view* of employees' roles in their company and community—and of their company's role in the community. Such a view challenges businesses to listen and be responsive to a broader range of needs and opinions, but it also rewards them by acting in and for their employees' best interests.

Concern for the Environment

In the next section of this chapter we will introduce 3M's innovative program, Pollution Prevention Pays (3P). Tom Zosel, who manages the program, emphasizes how the program takes advantage of people's desire to care for the environment. "I think the biggest hook in the entire program is giving people the opportunity to bring their environmental activism to their jobs. If you went out today and surveyed 3M employees and asked if they considered themselves environmentalists, I'd be surprised if you got less than a 90% positive response."

3M's corporate values reflect its employees' values by including a commitment to "respecting our social and physical environment." The goals 3M has identified that carry out this value are:

- Complying with all laws and meeting or exceeding regulations.
- Keeping customers, employees, investors, and the public informed about our operations.
- Developing products and processes that have minimal impact on the environment.
- Staying attuned to the changing needs and preferences of our customers, employees, and society.
- Uncompromising honesty and integrity in every aspect of our organization.

In 1975, the year 3M started its 3P program, the board of directors adopted the following *corporate environmental policy:*

3M will continue to recognize and exercise its responsibility to:

- Solve its own environmental pollution and conservation problems.
- Prevent pollution at the source wherever and whenever possible.

- Develop products that will have a minimum effect on the environment.
- Conserve natural resources through the use of reclamation and other appropriate methods.
- Ensure that its facilities and products meet and sustain the regulations of all federal, state, and local environmental agencies.
- Assist, wherever possible, governmental agencies and other official organizations engaged in environmental activities.

To turn the policy into action, 3M's senior management created specific policies, objectives, and implementation standards. The policies include going beyond regulatory requirements, preventing pollution at the source, conducting detailed environmental audits, and phasing out all ozone-depleting chemicals and PCBs. "Environmental concerns are considered at every step in the development and manufacture of our products," says chairman L. D. DeSimone. "This assures upper management that our goals of environmental protection are being met."

3M's goals and policies respond to the perceived requirements of its customers, employees, shareholders, and communities. Companies that put their values down on paper include their position on corporate responsibility and the environment. For example, EMD is guided by a set of principles that include the following:

- Be responsive to the needs of the community and the environment.
- Conduct all aspects of business with high ethical standards of honesty, integrity, and fairness.

Attention to Business Ethics

Business ethics is one of those areas every company says it promotes, but few can say how. For companies like EMD and USAA, *ethics is ingrained in their corporate cultures.* At USAA new employees are first exposed to the company's position on ethics during orientation. They are further exposed during training courses which have ethical considerations embedded in the curriculum. With employees currently receiving an average of 55 hours of formal training per year, reinforcement is frequent and consistent. In addition, the training department offers a four-hour course on business ethics and a one-hour "house call," brought right to a work area at the area's request, called "Ethical Navigation."

USAA keeps people focused on corporate responsibility and citizenship by making it part of the company's planning process. USAA focuses on six key result areas (KRAs): service, financial strength, product value, resources, growth, and public outreach. By putting public outreach on the same level as financial strength, growth, and other company priorities, USAA establishes its importance for all employees. By then developing five-year and annual plans to achieve its public outreach goals, USAA translates goals into measurable actions and objectives. That is the surest way to make corporate responsibility and citizenship a part of your company's culture.

ADDRESSING THE RESPONSIBILITY
TO PRESERVE THE ENVIRONMENT

When it comes to public responsibilities, business ethics and public health and safety are basically no-brainers. Regardless of a company's management philosophy, it should conduct business ethically and do everything possible to protect public health and safety. From a new management model perspective, that means:

- Establishing the company's expectations for these areas
- Training employees to understand and act on their responsibilities
- Identifying and measuring the appropriate indicators of responsible behavior and actions

The area of public responsibility that causes companies the most anguish is the environment. Faced with the "greening" of America, more and more businesses are boarding the environmental bandwagon with no clear sense of where it will take them. By contrast, quality leaders are grabbing hold of the reins and steering their companies toward environmental leadership by applying the principles of quality management to pollution prevention. The application is so appropriate it has spawned a new name: *total quality environmental management* (TQEM).

The Global Environmental Management Initiative (GEMI) is credited with coining TQEM. GEMI was founded in 1990 by senior environmental health and safety professionals from several major U.S. companies, including Procter & Gamble, AT&T, Eastman Kodak, and Florida Power & Light. Its goal is to provide an exchange of information on the most advanced environmental management techniques. In a speech at GEMI's first conference Gerald Kotes, director of the EPA's office of pollution prevention, said, "A basic premise of total quality management is, if a firm doesn't build waste into its product, then it doesn't have to pay to take the waste out. With pollution prevention, the premise is very similar: If the firm doesn't generate waste in the first place, then it doesn't have to pay to manage it."

3M's Zosel puts it this way: "Pollution is a defect. The goal of total quality management is to eliminate defects." 3M focuses on waste reduction to reduce defects, to cut the amount of pollution being generated. It does this by involving every employee in the effort. "To do pollution prevention," says Zosel, "you must get into a total quality management mentality—give people a goal and a method for achieving it, then let them do it."

The goals are part of 3M's global strategy for achieving excellence in every 3M business and support unit. The strategy, called Q90s, is based on the Baldrige criteria, which means it includes an assessment of how each unit improves in the areas of corporate responsibility and citizenship. Most business units have been through two or three assessments using the criteria, in addition to several mini self-audits. "As a result, our business assessment process is being integrated into the business planning process," says Ron Kubinski, quality manager. "Quality and business are becoming one plan focused on 3M's primary goals: listening to the voice of the customer, reducing time to market, and reducing cost."

3M has more than 7,000 core manufacturing processes based on about 100 core technologies. It is a customer-focused, technology-leveraged company that thrives on massive sharing about how units use the core technologies. The size and nature of its business present many opportunities for protecting the environment, opportunities 3M seized when it initiated an industrial environmental program in 1975 called *Pollution Prevention Pays* (3P). At that time the idea of applying pollution prevention companywide through a globally organized effort—and recording the results—had not been done before.

"What we did with Pollution Prevention Pays parallels the entire total quality management process," says Zosel. "When we looked at all the regulations that were coming, we knew we couldn't do it all from the end of the pipe, with pollution control. We had to design out the environmental problems, which means we had to build a pollution prevention ethic into the corporation."

Zosel and his environmental cohorts presented 3M's management with two choices: You can spend this much for pollution control, or you can tell people to prevent the pollution by designing it in up front. Management took door number two, in part because innovation and change are 3M strengths. "We wanted to be proactive on it, to address regulations in a way that is environmentally efficient and cost effective," says Zosel.

How 3M Implements Its Pollution Prevention Programs

The basic concept and goals of the 3P program have remained constant since 1975. The program is run by a 3P *coordinating committee*, which represents 3M's engineering, manufacturing, and laboratory organizations and the corporate

Environmental Engineering and Pollution Control organization. The committee establishes criteria for 3P participation and recommends employee recognition.

Most 3P projects are initiated when employees recognize a specific pollution or waste problem. A cross-functional team is formed to analyze the problem and develop solutions. The team submits a proposal to the affected operating division, which decides whether to commit funds, time, and other resources to it.

Employee involvement is key to the program's success. A 3M plant in Aberdeen, South Dakota, provides an example. The plant makes round respirator masks out of square fabric; one-third of the fabric ends up as waste that used to go to local landfills. A team of process engineers recognized the waste problem and tackled the issue with the goal of *zero* waste. Such a goal forces new thinking, because even the most efficient use of fabric will still produce waste. The team changed its thinking to see the waste as a supply of raw materials. It then reformulated the product so that the fibers in the waste could be used for a new line of 3M products used in hazardous waste cleanup. The goal of zero waste was achieved. As one engineer said, "Our goal is that everything that comes into the plant goes out as a useful item."

Such ambitious thinking is common throughout 3M. In the first 17 years of the 3P program *3M cut its pollution in half* (by more than 1.3 billion pounds) *and saved 3M approximately $650 million.* Those reductions in pollution and costs continue today.

In addition to tapping into people's desire to protect the environment 3M motivates participation through *recognition*. To qualify for formal recognition, a 3P program must meet the following criteria:

- Prevent pollution, not control it
- Offer some other environmental benefit besides preventing pollution
- Save money for 3M
- Include a technical accomplishment

3P doesn't exclude innovative improvements that are not technical or new programs that prevent pollution but cost money; however, they are not formally recognized. Depending on the innovative nature of their accomplishments, people get 3P awards, plaques, or certificates. In the program's first 14 years 2,511 projects received formal recognition.

The Pollution Prevention Pays program also makes *monetary rewards* available to anyone who runs a 3P project. To avoid competition, the name of every person who participates in a 3P project is put into a hat. Ten percent of the names are drawn, and those people receive $500 gift certificates.

In 1988, 3M expanded its 3P program to address pollution prevention in a more structured way. *Pollution Prevention Plus* (3P+) encourages technical innovation to prevent pollution at the source through product reformulation, process modification, equipment redesign, and resource recovery. 3P+ emphasizes that with or without cost savings 3M will spend what is necessary to protect the environment.

Waste minimization teams have been established in every 3M product operating division to identify source reduction and recycling opportunities and to develop plans to address them. A pollution prevention staff within the corporate environmental organization makes 3P+ happen, monitoring and reporting progress to management, encouraging the sharing of ideas, monitoring legislative and regulatory activity, and administering the award program. The objective of 3P+ is to reduce all hazardous and nonhazardous releases to the air, land, and water by 90% and to reduce the generations of waste by 50% by the year 1995, with 1990 levels as baselines. Chairman L. D. DeSimone has been quoted as saying that if 3M achieves this objective, it will "significantly cut the inflation-adjusted cost per unit of most products."

Many successful companies have stumbled onto the fact that pollution prevention can save significant amounts of money. Time after time, people change a process because it is environmentally better only to find out it is also economically better. To paraphrase Kotes, if you don't generate waste, you don't have to pay to manage it.

Successful companies recognize that *waste minimization and quality are two sides of the same coin.* Japanese companies surpassed American companies in the quality of their products during the 1970s and 1980s. A by-product of their quality improvement was a better utilization of resources and a reduction of waste. Japan now uses 50% less material and energy than the U.S. does to produce one unit of GNP, giving many Japanese products a 5% cost advantage—in addition to their quality advantage. All as a result of the quality improvement process.

Companies fail to meet their public responsibilities when they look at them from the old paradigm, as costly activities delegated to a few people to control and clean up. 3M approaches its environmental responsibilities from a new management perspective, as opportunities to satisfy customers and reduce waste and costs. It then uses a total quality management approach of involving everyone in identifying and acting on those opportunities. The results it has realized suggest that this is an effective approach to addressing public responsibilities.

BECOMING A MODEL CITIZEN

Although many companies question the extent of their public responsibilities, far more wonder about their roles as corporate citizens. You know you have to satisfy your customers, reduce waste, and cut costs to succeed. You understand that in the new business management model success means understanding customer requirements, involving people, and managing processes. But what does corporate citizenship have to do with any of this?

Our quality role models believe that taking the lead in publicly important areas is an essential part of a successful system. These areas include supporting education, volunteering for and funding community services, contributing to industry and trade activities, and promoting quality improvement.

3M actively encourages and supports employee involvement in all these areas. "In the process of giving, you get," says Kubinski. "It makes good corporate sense for us to be good corporate citizens."

The fact is, whether your motives are financial or altruistic, the results of being community leaders tend to be the same: The more you give, the more you get in return. And one of the returns with immeasurable value is the pride and satisfaction for each individual who contributes.

At community activities in the San Antonio area it is easy to spot USAA employees by the special shirts they wear. "People talk to our employees about how wonderful their company is and how much they appreciate the employees being there," says John Cook, senior vice-president and chief communication officer. "It builds pride, and they bring that pride back here, so they want to do a better job. They bring something back they didn't leave with."

Dan Rukavina, EMD's co-CEO, agrees. "I always learn more than I contribute," he says, which is saying quite a bit since Rukavina and his partner, Dave Arnold, have been very active in their community for many years. In this section we will look at how EMD and USAA act as leading citizens of their communities.

EMD: Supporting Education

"We started at the contribution level," says Arnold, "and with an interest in supporting education." When they brought total quality management to EMD in the early 1990s, it seemed natural to share what they were learning and doing with the rest of Winona, with their schools, city government, and other businesses. The result has been the evolution of a quality improvement process that has changed the community.

In 1991, at the urging of Rukavina and Arnold, 30 community leaders attended a four-day seminar conducted by W. Edwards Deming. The group included Rukavina, Arnold, the Winona city manager, a college president, a technical school president, and two school superintendents. Following the seminar, the school board members mandated that all schools form site-based teams made up of teachers, staff, administration, and parents to oversee day-to-day school activities and allocate funds. EMD facilitated the training of two of the site-based teams.

The seminar participants also spearheaded the formation of the Winona Quality Council. The council's goal is to promote quality throughout the community, in government, education, service, and industry. Members of the council, who come from all these sectors, meet every Thursday morning; part of every meeting is devoted to learning about and discussing Deming's theories of management.

The council has spawned a host of activities directed at improving quality in the Winona community:

- The Business Education Partnership, consisting of representatives from public and private schools, grades K–12 and college, was conceived to make business and education more responsive to each other's needs. Rukavina is on the partnership's steering committee.

- An outgrowth of the partnership is a quality team called the Business Education Action Team. The team, consisting of a dozen administrators, business people, students, and educators, studied quality improvement for Winona's middle and high schools. EMD provided financial support, co-worker expertise, and facilitators and facilities for 40 hours of training on team development and leadership.

- The council sponsors an annual total quality management conference. EMD organized the conferences in 1992 and 1993, and EMD co-workers were featured speakers.

- The council was instrumental in bringing regional and state science fairs to Winona. EMD co-workers volunteered many hours to these events.

In a very short time the council has become a major resource for the Winona area. For example, in the fall of 1992 the city manager and chief of police reported increasing friction in the community because of cultural diversity. A few months later, EMD, Winona State University, and the city of Winona sponsored an educational discussion about cultural diversity. From this discussion the council developed a cultural diversity task force. EMD was a founding member and is the business representative on the task force.

The community activitism of EMD's leaders infects the company's co-workers, whose involvement contributes to local schools, churches, charitable organizations, service groups, government agencies, and social events. "We encourage participation by supporting what our co-workers request," says Arnold. "I can't think of a request we've ever said 'no' to."

The long list of civic contributions made by EMD co-workers is a testament to the company's proclivity for community involvement. As co-workers volunteer time and talent, they receive new experiences, knowledge, and ideas that can often be applied to their work. The rapid growth EMD is currently enjoying will be fueled and sustained by this flexible, learning, changing work force.

USAA: Encouraging Volunteer Service in the Community

USAA is much larger than EMD, and it operates in a much larger community—with similar impact. As with EMD, the motivation for participation at USAA stems from its chief executive officer and chairman, General Robert McDermott. "He was brought up in an atmosphere where people were expected to be responsible for their communities," says Cook. "Duty. Honor. Country. He's a strong believer in the Golden Rule, and that ethic has been integrated into our corporate culture."

USAA's prime directive is service to its members, which also means service to other employees within the company. "Once you build that ethic, it's a natural step to serve the community," says Cook.

USAA formalized service to the community in 1983, when McDermott initiated the *Volunteer Corps* of USAA. In 1992 the Volunteer Corps identified more than 350 initiatives to which employees could contribute their time. Employees are notified of opportunities by newsletter and can volunteer whatever number of hours they prefer. Their service is tracked when they enter the project code and hours in a computer data base. At the San Antonio home office the corps's 2,300 members contributed more than 80,000 hours to community service in 1992. That number does not include include employee time donated to USAA's special volunteer programs, such as the Mentor and Junior Achievement Programs. USAA volunteer programs in 1992 provided services to more than 130 community organizations and assistance with 36 special events.

"A lot of hours were going unreported," says Angelo de Guttadauro, administrator of the Volunteer Corps. "We've created a software system to help us capture those hours, and we're trying to make people more sensitive to recording them. At the end of this year, we'll be able to see the hours donated, divided into eight different functional areas." The value of such measurements is that they will give USAA a clearer picture of what is being done to achieve its public outreach KRA.

USAA makes another significant contribution to the San Antonio community through the USAA *Mentor Program*. The program provides both one-on-one mentoring and Junior Achievement classroom instruction to at-risk students in ten schools. "We calculate that a high percentage of a school's population needs assistance," says Col. Victor Ferrari, director of the USAA Mentor and Junior Achievement programs. "We won't take less than ten percent of a population because we know we've got to have enough of a force there to create an impression. That's how we know how many mentors we need."

USAA offered the first mentor program in San Antonio. Building on its success, Ferrari has enlisted other organizations to participate, including the local FBI, military bases, banks, and school districts. "We now have 16 other organizations providing 2,268 mentors to 42 schools," he says proudly. USAA provides more than 850 one-on-one mentors and 110 Junior Achievement instructors.

USAA evaluates the entire program annually, comparing grades and other factors of students who are mentored with those who are not mentored. "Of the five items measured, our students improved in all areas while those who were not mentored improved in only two items," says Ferrari. Studies also showed that, in one year, the number of mentored students with behavioral problems dropped by 30% and class participation rose by 18%.

Support for Charities from USAA

USAA is also a major contributor to the United Way. Although it has only one of every 55 employees in San Antonio, USAA contributes $1 of every $5 given to United Way. "The fairest way to compare programs is per capita donations. Last year, our home office employees gave more than $250 per person," says Cook. In 1991, 98% of USAA's work force pledged over $2.25 million. USAA kicks in an additional 50% of its employees' donations.

That is not all USAA contributes. More than 100 USAA employees contact other businesses in the San Antonio area to solicit contributions for the United Way. They have always collected more than 100% of their goal. For USAA's efforts, the United Way of America presented USAA with three Spirit of America Awards in 1993.

Other community activities round out USAA's leadership and support of publicly important purposes:

- It keeps a list of charitable agencies and projects and supports them with time and money. For example, for the past four years a group of citizens has been raising money to revitalize a downtown park, securing contributions from several corporations and matching funds from the state. USAA is putting together a volunteer group to do the actual work.
- USAA's chairman started an Economic Development Foundation that has created more than 21,000 jobs to date.

- USAA promotes quality through a speakers' bureau and visitor program; the company gets 6,000 visitors each year.
- USAA works nationally to improve auto safety and advises Congress on safety issues. CEO McDermott has become a recognized national spokesman on these issues.
- USAA was among the first insurance companies to use "catastrophe teams," people on a disaster scene wearing properly marked hats and shirts to make them easy to recognize.

USAA has become a community leader because it is committed to service and organized to provide that service. The organization helps identify opportunities for service and gives employees a simple way to find out what needs to be done and to volunteer their assistance. "This provides an institutional structure," says Cook. "Once you make things available, people take advantage of them and are more than willing to help."

Supported by a corporate culture that values community service, USAA employees choose to look outward, to give freely of their knowledge and skills. Yolanda Vera is USAA's community relations director and a former member of the San Antonio city council. "When I wasn't at USAA, I was at city hall," she says. "I've worked with other companies where this attitude doesn't exist, and I've seen the difference."

The difference is one of *attitude:* Either a company believes it must serve its community or it does not. If it believes it must lead and support publicly important purposes, it must find ways to identify those purposes and to facilitate corporate and employee involvement. As USAA has shown, an *organized approach to community service* targets the areas of greatest need while attracting the largest number of volunteers.

But first the company must believe. Just as leaders talk about the commitment to quality as requiring a "leap of faith," the *commitment to corporate responsibility and citizenship* demands no less. Look at the companies who stand as our models. Look at the people who share so unselfishly. Like Yolanda Vera, you will see the difference.

THE SHIFT IN THINKING

In the new business management model, corporate responsibility and citizenship—like quality—are integrated into the way people do their jobs. In fact, the parallels between changing a corporate culture to make public responsibility and citizenship part of everyone's job and changing it to make quality part of everyone's job are striking:

- *Both require leadership's commitment.* 3M, USAA, and EMD stand as models of citizenship because their leaders clearly communicate its importance by encouraging involvement and by getting involved themselves.

- *Both demand employee involvement.* The opportunities for protecting the environment and acting ethically present themselves to individuals and teams in the course of their work. The opportunities for serving their communities are less evident but equally compelling. Employees must be empowered to recognize and respond to these opportunities.

- *Both need clear direction.* The more explicit the expectations for ethical conduct, protecting the public health and safety and the environment, and serving the community, the more focused the response will be. Leaders in this area establish values and policies for corporate responsibility and citizenship, develop objectives that act on their values, and measure their progress.

- *Both must be managed and measured.* To assume that, left alone, people will act responsibly and ethically and serve unselfishly is tantamount to assuming that, left alone, people will improve quality. Measures need to be established and processes managed for corporate responsibility and citizenship to take root and grow.

The new management model looks outward as well as inward. It recognizes that customers are more than the people who buy products and services and that all customers need to be satisfied for the company to have long-term success. Companies that approach this responsibility with open minds often discover that active corporate responsibility and citizenship make good business strategy.

As we wrote in Chapter 1, the Baldrige criteria define the system for our new management model. While the "Public Responsibility and Corporate Citizenship" part of the system accounts for just 25 of the criteria's possible 1,000 points, it is the only part that can cause the Department of Commerce to pass on a company the panel of judges has recommended. The criteria state that *award recipients are to serve as appropriate models of total quality achievement for other U.S. companies.* In other words, if the rest of a company's system is world-class but its ethical or environmental record stinks, it is not fit to serve as a model. Or to win an award for quality excellence.

17 SYSTEM ASSESSMENTS

Eastman Kodak Company

AT&T

Graniterock

In the new business management model, the role of assessments has evolved from punitive to supportive, from a hunt for problems and mistakes to a search for ways to improve, from assigning blame to offering assistance. The change in attitude reflects the enlightened view that problems with operational performance or quality are almost always due to *problems with the system*, not problems with people. To improve the system, you must first know what condition it is in and where the improvements need to be made. That is the purpose of a system assessment.

System assessments tend to be like annual physical examinations: You may check your blood pressure or cholesterol level regularly, and you may need a checkup when you are ill, but a thorough, general examination—a personal "system assessment"—comes but once a year. The same is true for an assessment of your organization's system. "We believe we should check our system annually," says Dale Myers, district manager of quality planning for AT&T. "Everyone reviews budgets and tracks financials monthly, but they are the result of all the processes that make up your quality system. It seems reasonable to check the health of that system once a year."

The subjects of the exam may disagree. Unlike an individual's physical examination, a system checkup relies on a *self-assessment* for accuracy and completeness—and the self-assessment is not a painless process. A business system is a complex set of elements. The interaction of those elements is what makes the system function, but it is also what makes an assessment so difficult. You cannot study the system by isolating and assessing one element in it, such as one functional area or one process, and ignoring how it affects and is affected by other elements in the system. For that reason an effective system assessment has two components: a *team* willing to do the hard work of performing the assessment and a *tool* it can use to conduct a valid assessment.

The tool must be capable of assessing the entire system as well as the key elements that make up that system. High-performance companies, including the three companies we will study in this chapter, have embraced the only assessment tool with these capabilities and with the credibility gained from being studied and used by thousands of organizations in the United States and abroad since its introduction in 1988: the criteria for the Malcolm Baldrige National Quality Award.

As we stated in Chapter 1, the Baldrige criteria represent a business management model that addresses every element in an organization. They have been scrutinized, debated, interpreted, and improved, but the criteria have not been replaced as the preeminent system assessment tool. As Kay Whitmore, former chairman, president, and CEO of Eastman Kodak Company, wrote in his company's self-assessment workbook, "I believe that performance against the national quality award criteria is a leading indicator of a unit's future success."

Other leaders concur. Kodak, AT&T, Intel, Carrier, Corning, Honeywell, Baxter Healthcare, and others have created internal system assessments using the Baldrige criteria as their tool. In Chapter 1, we quoted Robert Shafto, president of The New England, who said, "I've become more and more convinced that the Baldrige is a management guide for business success, and if you meet all the requirements, you'll end up satisfying the customer—hence, grow your business."

To meet all the requirements, a company must understand what they are, assess the company or unit based on the requirements, then use the findings of the assessment to improve. Each of these three steps requires a serious commitment if it is to be accomplished. In this chapter we will look at how AT&T, Kodak, and Graniterock are using the Baldrige criteria to assess their business systems. We will use their experiences to explore these questions:

- Who does the assessment?
- How do we conduct a system assessment?
- How is the assessment evaluated?
- How are the results of the assessment used to improve?
- How is the assessment process improved?

We will devote this chapter to system assessments because such assessments, based on the Baldrige criteria, are critical to a company's ability to understand and improve its management model. We understand that other quality assessments must also be done. Kodak, AT&T, and Graniterock perform frequent and diverse quality assessments that include such tools as employee satisfaction surveys, evaluations by customers, product quality testing, process analysis, and ISO certification. The key assessments are discussed in the relevant chapters of this book; for example, employee satisfaction surveys as an assessment tool are described in Chapter 9. In this chapter we will focus on how our role models assess their systems by means of the Baldrige criteria.

MODELS OF EXCELLENCE

AT&T is a global company that provides communications services and products, network equipment, and computer systems to businesses, consumers, telecommunications service providers, and government agencies. Its worldwide network carries more than 125 million voice, data, video, and facsimile messages each day. AT&T Bell Laboratories does basic research and product and service development. AT&T also offers a general-purpose credit card and financial and leasing services. It has 315,000 employees in more than 100 countries. In 1992 AT&T was the first company to have two Baldrige Award winners: AT&T Universal Card Services (one of AT&T's newest and smallest units) and AT&T Network Systems Group/Transmission Systems Business Unit (one of AT&T's oldest and largest units).

Eastman Kodak Company serves three primary business segments: imaging (photography, office imaging applications such as copiers and printers, printing and publishing, and motion picture and television); chemicals (chemicals, fibers, and plastics); and health (diagnostic imaging and information systems, clinical diagnostics, pharmaceuticals, consumer health products, cleaning and disinfecting products). Kodak has more than 132,000 employees at marketing and manufacturing operations in more than 50 countries. Its headquarters are in Rochester, New York. In 1988 the 18,000 member Eastman Chemical Company, a Kodak subsidiary, received a Baldrige Award site visit.

Graniterock produces high-quality construction materials—rock, sand and gravel aggregates, readymix concrete, and asphalt—for road and highway construction and maintenance and for residential and commercial building construction. Founded in 1900, the company markets its products in the central coast region of California, operating the largest crushed rock quarry west of the Mississippi River. It has nearly 400 employees. Graniterock won the Baldrige Award in 1992.

USING THE BALDRIGE AWARD CRITERIA
TO ASSESS YOUR SYSTEM

All three of our role models use the Baldrige criteria to assess their businesses. AT&T's assessment process parallels the Baldrige program's process, with a *board of examiners,* the requirement that those business units that apply submit a full-blown application, an evaluation and judging process that is at least as stringent as the Baldrige judging process, and several ways of sharing best practices. Kodak offers three forms of assessment to its business units:

1. A full system assessment using the Baldrige criteria
2. An abbreviated report using the Baldrige criteria
3. A self-assessment matrix based on the Baldrige criteria

Graniterock has applied for the Baldrige Award every year since 1989 and will continue to write an application every year solely for assessment purposes.

Kodak requires business units to perform assessments using the Baldrige criteria or its Baldrige-inspired matrix because the company understands that assessments using the criteria cause continuous improvement. In *The Baldrige Quality System: The Do-It-Yourself Way to Transform Your Business,* Stephen George identified the following benefits of the application (assessment) process, benefits that will be visible in the activities of the role models described in this chapter:

1. *It involves and motivates people.* To accurately assess the quality of your system, you need to explore every nook and cranny of every process, work unit, team, department, and so on. That means people to do the research and people to provide the answers.
2. *It provides a proven quality system.* A system assessment is only as good as the assessment tool, which is why so many companies are using the Baldrige criteria.
3. *It focuses on the customer.* The goal of each company—of every company's business system—is to satisfy its customers. An assessment using the Baldrige criteria shows how satisfying customers must be the focus of the entire system.
4. *It assesses quality.* Not only do the criteria identify the elements in a business sytem, but they also provide a means of assessing the quality of effort for each element and for the system as a whole. As Joe Rocca, one of the writers of IBM Rochester's Baldrige Award–winning application, said, "We

thought we had a good quality program, and now we've got one that's 10 times better for having gone through the application process."

5. *It demands data.* Without a formal system assessment, few people are able to describe with any accuracy the quality of their system or the elements in it. Instead, they offer a nice story or a good hunch or a best guess. A system assessment using the Baldrige criteria quickly dismisses such soft estimations by providing hard data.

6. *It provides feedback.* Any company that has performed a system assessment using the Baldrige criteria will tell you that the real value of the process is the feedback it provides. Graniterock's feedback reports on its first two Baldrige applications listed 110 areas for improvement. The company used the list to drive its quality improvement efforts (as we will describe later in this chapter).

7. *It encourages sharing.* The Baldrige criteria provide a common system, language, and metric that promotes sharing. AT&T has created a *Pockets of Excellence* report and sponsors sharing rallies to encourage internal sharing of best practices. (We will discuss the report and conference later in this chapter.)

8. *It stimulates change.* AT&T, Kodak, Graniterock, and hundreds of others that are using the Baldrige criteria to assess their systems understand that the goal of the assessment process is improvement. AT&T started its Baldrige assessment process to accelerate progress toward its goals. At the 1993 Quest for Excellence conference in Washington all five 1992 Baldrige Award winners stated that applying for the Baldrige Award speeded up their pace of improvement.

9. *It builds financial success.* Continuous assessment and improvement in quality must lead to the improvement of the system's products and services. As we illustrated in Chapter 1, quality improvements are directly linked to increases in customer satisfaction and shareholder value. When you improve the system, the products of that system must also improve, and this improvement results in a growing market share and improved profitability.

Companies embrace Baldrige-like assessment processes because they understand the benefits. In larger companies that understanding does not often extend to the people who must perform the assessments, who see the assessment process as a burden they must fit around their regular jobs. Whether companies dictate that assessments will be done or inspire business units to participate, the assessment process is always more effective if business unit leadership supports and is involved in the process.

GETTING COMMITMENT TO
THE ASSESSMENT PROCESS

One of the first problems a company faces as it is establishing an assessment process is *how to get buy-in* from the business units, divisions, or departments it wants assessed. "In the old days, a company's corporate headquarters dictated to a business unit that it must conduct an assessment," says AT&T's Myers. "That usually produced a half-hearted application and feedback that was useless." AT&T wanted its people to give the application their best effort, so they made applying for the AT&T Chairman's Quality Award a voluntary process.

With the trend toward decentralization and increased autonomy for business units, companies are increasingly sensitive about telling those units what to do. Like AT&T, many are choosing to *inspire* rather than *demand* participation. The benefit of relying on motivation to get an assessment done is that the participants recognize its value and conduct a useful assessment. The disadvantage is that units can choose not to participate, thus denying themselves and the company the benefits of the assessment.

Kodak both inspires and demands participation. "We have about 25 major units that must assess themselves annually using one of our three assessment forms," says George Vorhauer, director of corporate quality initiatives, "but it's voluntary for divisions, departments, and other layers. We've said all along that this isn't something different from your business; this is to make you more competitive, to add value, and to better serve the customer." Vorhauer admits that not all business units appreciate these benefits. "Early on, there was a tendency to see this as a lay-on—something you do in addition to the important job you have—rather than a way to measure and improve. We've addressed that by focusing more on the units' plans to improve rather than their score on the assessment."

WHO SHOULD DO THE ASSESSMENT?

Graniterock's executive committee reviews and approves the company's annual Baldrige application. Kodak, which requires its units to participate, created its matrix and abbreviated report format so that the executives could assess their unit or division in less time than a full application requires. AT&T, which encouraged its business units and divisions to participate, requires full Baldrige applications. In 1992, 32 of slightly more than 50 eligible units applied for the AT&T Chairman's Quality Award. Other AT&T units are using the criteria for self-assessment to guide their improvement efforts.

What these and other companies have learned is that senior management involvement in the assessment process results in *three major benefits:*

1. It establishes the system assessment process as the unit or company's primary tool for continuous improvement.
2. It creates an annual learning and improvement cycle, beginning with feedback to the assessment, that includes planning, execution, and evaluation.
3. It improves senior executives' ability to understand and improve the system they oversee.

The degree to which these benefits are realized *relates directly to the degree to which senior executives are involved in the assessment process.* Those who take the time to learn what the criteria are asking and what their company or unit is doing become "systems thinkers," able to identify the elements in their system and how those elements work together to achieve the company's goals. This holistic perspective is available to all who work the assessment process, whether they are executives or employees to whom the assessment has been delegated, but the organization gains most by executive involvement because *executives have the greatest control over the system.* Leaders who resist getting actively involved seem to believe that participating in the assessment process is not a good use of their time; the experience of our quality role models suggests they are wrong.

CONDUCTING A SYSTEM ASSESSMENT

An organization can conduct a system assessment for an internal or external deadline. Any company or unit of any size can set its own deadline at any time of the year. AT&T states the annual deadline for its Chairman's Quality Award in the application guidelines it distributes with copies of the Baldrige criteria. For small companies intent on performing a system assessment, senior management must drive the process if it is to be completed on deadline.

External deadlines offer the advantage of providing an immovable deadline. A system assessment packaged as a Baldrige application must be completed by the Baldrige deadline, which is typically in early April. Organizations can also submit their system assessments for state quality awards. More than half the states in the country now have or will soon have quality awards based on the Baldrige criteria.

The point is to identify a firm deadline, because without a deadline the assessment will never get done.

To assess your system using the Baldrige criteria, *plan on a three-month process* from start to finish. Kodak estimates that writing a full application takes around 2,500 labor-hours, which seems like a good average. Companies such as Xerox have reported spending much longer, largely because of the size of the organization represented in its Baldrige Award–winning application and because they were working on improvement at the same time. At the other extreme, consider the story of the Globe Metallurgical executive who wrote his company's award-winning application in one long weekend. How long it will take you depends on the size of your company or unit, the availability of system data and information, and the maturity of your quality improvement process. Size determines complexity, data availability determines research time, and maturity determines how easily you can match what you do with what the criteria measure.

Graniterock, Kodak, and AT&T all produce full Baldrige applications, with Kodak and AT&T evaluating those applications internally. The process of creating the assessment document, as described in *The Baldrige Quality System*, follows 14 major steps:

1. Involve senior management.
2. Establish application team(s). Teams share the work, bring different perspectives to the task, and spread the learning experience to more people.
3. Train team members. The first exposure to the Baldrige criteria can be more confusing than enlightening unless people receive some training in how to understand the criteria and apply them to their organization.
4. Assign responsibilities. The assessment process is most effective when there is clear accountability for gathering data and information, writing responses, and producing the report.
5. Collect data and information. The quality of the assessment depends on the quality of the data and information it presents. A system assessment that is vague or anecdotal or that reports glowingly on what the organization hopes to achieve is worthless.
6. Identify areas for improvement. Areas for improvement materialize in the course of conducting the assessment. The wise companies understand that these areas are the primary goal of the process, the gold nuggets that make the assessment worthwhile.
7. Communicate needs, ideas, and information. As the assessment process proceeds, individuals and teams tend to focus on a particular category, work

process, or functional area, thus losing sight of the system in which they exist. Constant communication helps to maintain a systems perspective.

8. Write the first draft. Writing responses to the criteria is an exercise in interpretation and communication that requires diligence and clarity. It is also very hard work, but the payoff, learning to think about what your organization does as a system, is worth it.

9. Begin the layout, including graphics. An essential part of clear communication is the presentation of information. Charts and graphs can help explain processes, information, and results.

10. Evaluate the first draft. The review usually includes the authors of the assessment document and the organization's senior people, if they did not write it. It may also include internal and external quality experts and consultants.

11. Write subsequent drafts. The first draft evaluation always identifies sections that are inappropriate, weak, inaccurate, and wrongly placed. Subsequent drafts can only make the assessment stronger.

12. Coordinate writing and graphics. As the deadline approaches, an individual or team must coordinate all the pieces that will make up the document.

13. Produce the final draft.

14. Print and deliver the assessment.

Almost every organization that creates a system assessment document follows a process similar to this. Major variations occur when companies assign responsibility for the document to an individual or a very small team, but even then, data must be gathered, areas for improvement identified, drafts written, and the document assembled. Kodak and AT&T have internal deadlines for their documents, while Graniterock adheres to the Baldrige deadline. You will need to set a deadline or the assessment will not get done. Expect resistance no matter what deadline you establish; the people who will be involved in the assessment process are already busy. This is when senior executive leadership becomes critical.

Leadership is also needed to use the assessment to drive improvement. People involved in the assessment are usually worn out from the process, but they are also aware of the weaknesses it revealed. Since the assessment has little value unless it is used to improve, leadership must make it possible for employees to integrate the findings with their ongoing improvement efforts. As AT&T's Myers says, "From my observations, improvement *only* happens at a significant rate when leaders are proactive."

TABLE 17.1. Kodak self-assessment matrix (described on page 252)

Rank	Leadership 10	Information and Analysis 6	Strategic Planning 9	Human Resources 15	QA of Products/Services 15	Quality Results 15	Customer Satisfaction 30
10 *Maturing*	Quality is placed equal to profits, market share, and stock price.	Measures reviewed regularly to identify improvement opportunities; data and information directly affect behaviors and impact overall results.	Quality improvement plans are totally integrated into long-term and short-term plans.	Measures and trends of employee well-being and morale show "Best-in-Class" when benchmarked against peer companies & units.	Process in place for continually reducing cycle time (the amount of time required to develop and introduce new or improved products).	Sustained (>3 years) results, clearly caused by approach (use of QLP), indicate "World Class" in major areas (supplier, product, service, and support).	"Best-in-Class" in customer satisfaction for products and services (include surveys, competitive awards, ratings by independent organization, trends in market share, trends in gaining customers).
9	Unit management demonstrate Kodak's five Quality Principles outside the company and encourage/positively reinforce employees for doing the same.	All teams derive data/informational needs to support KRAs that have been developed using QLP.	KRA improvement plans in place at all organizational levels.	QLP usage is an essential element of reward and promotion systems.	Human factors and mistake proofing used to design and continually improve job functions.	Quality levels of products, services, and processes considered "Best-in-Class."	Evidence that improvement results are caused by Quality Leadership Process approach.
8	Reward and consequence processes reinforce QLP involvement.	Process in place and used to track data and identify areas for immediate corrective action.	Rewards/consequences are based on both behaviors and results.	Training is evaluated for improvement at four levels: (1) attitude about course (content, instructor), (2) immediate knowledge gained from course, (3) application to job and performance, (4) impact on business results.	A formalized process, such as Quality Function Deployment, is used to translate customer needs during product/service development.	Significant improvement trends noted (3 years minimum) in major areas.	Customers actively involved in problem solving/improvement effort.

7	All teams have completed at least one full QLP cycle; management performance measures based on progress in meeting KRAs; decisions based on vision.	75% of teams derive data/informational needs to support KRAs that have been developed using QLP.	Planning processes are reviewed and improved at least annually.	All employees are trained in QLP; additional education and career development opportunities to support continuous improvement efforts widely available.	Cross-functional teams are used throughout product development cycle for major products and services.	Benchmark results show "World Class" in some areas.	Positive trends evident in all customer satisfaction indicators.
6 *Growing*	At least 75% of teams have completed at least one full QLP cycle.	Processes in place to improve reliability, insure consistency and validity of data, and reduce cycle time of data gathering, analysis, and dissemination.	A documented process for employee, supplier, and customer contribution to the planning process is used.	At least 75% of all employees have some QLP training and are involved in continuous improvement.	Evidence exists that quantitative measures of performance extend fully into both manufacturing and nonmanufacturing areas of the unit.	All improvement efforts and results are linked to KRAs.	Process for communicating customer information to appropriate units exists and is used.
5	At least top half of interlocking teams use QLP to guide all meetings.	50% of teams derive data/informational needs to support KRAs that have been developed using QLP.	Resource allocation is consistent with corporate/unit KRAs.	Resources are allocated for development and implementation of educational plans to support growth in core competencies.	Evidence exists that strong emphasis is placed on prevention rather than *fire fighting* and inspection; root cause analysis is used where problems exist.	Positive quality result trends exist in most major areas.	Process exists and is in use for integrating customer satisfaction data into the continuous improvement cycle of the company.

KEY: QLP = Quality Leadership Process, Kodak's process for improving quality; AOP = Annual Operating Plan; KRA = Key Result Area, a broad area of performance

(*continued*)

TABLE 17.1. (continued)

Rank	Leadership 10	Information and Analysis 6	Strategic Planning 9	Human Resources 15	QA of Products/Services 15	Quality Results 15	Customer Satisfaction 30
4	Management teaches QLP to their direct reports and serves as role model.	Data appropriately analyzed, reviewed, and disseminated to the right people in a timely fashion (e.g. trend analysis >2 years, projections, performance evaluations).	QLP used for short-term and long-term planning; every unit has a written plan.	Education and career development plans exist and are linked to business unit goals, tactics, and strategies.	Process in place for ensuring precision and accuracy of measurement systems, including traceability to controlled international standards.	Trends of quality measures exist for processes that produced the products or services (e.g. lead times, yields, waste, inventory levels, rework of products and repeat services, first-time success rates, environmental improvements).	Processes exist for identifying and using: (1) market segments and customers, (2) product/service features and their importance to customers.
3	Have unitwide plan for implementation of QLP including necessary resources.	Leading indicators developed and used for decision making and for taking preventive measures toward recurrence of problems.	AOP addresses: technology, human resources, suppliers, environmental issues, and competitive actions/reactions.	QLP training scheduled for all employees.	Process in place to ensure quality of products and services; audit process used for ensuring the total quality system; continuous improvement methods are used.	Positive results exist as a consequence of working with suppliers to improve their quality (include awards and other feedback).	Proactive processes exist for determining and improving customer satisfaction (beyond measurement of complaints, returns, and warranty rate).

2	Mission and vision defined, published, and understood by all stakeholders.	External data gathered (i.e. customer, supplier, competition, benchmark, environmental).	Process in place for linking customer/market needs with the strategic planning process.	Recognition/rewards (beyond performance appraisal) occur in specific, sincere, immediate, and personal ways.	Development and production of new products and services documented and followed /document control process in place and used.	Trends of key quality indicators exist for suppliers and their services.
						Processes exist to promptly resolve customer complaints.
1 *Beginning*	Direct interaction of management with employees, customers, suppliers, and other stakeholders regarding Kodak Quality Principles.	Internal data gathered (i.e. product, operations, processes, employees, safety, health, environmental, regulatory, quality results).	A documented long-term (2–5 years) and short-term (1–2 years) planning process is used.	Measures and trends of employee well-being and morale exist.	Customer input used to develop and produce products and/or services with required characteristics.	Trends exist in key measures of product and service quality, including incoming supplies (e.g. reliability, timeliness, accuracy, performance, behavior, delivery, documentation, and appearance).
						Contract/guarantee/warranty policy adhered to for product/service performance.

KEY: QLP = Quality Leadership Process, Kodak's process for improving quality; AOP = Annual Operating Plan; KRA = Key Result Area, a broad area of performance

ALTERNATIVES TO USING THE BALDRIGE AWARD APPLICATION

Kodak created two alternatives to help reduce the amount of time it would take to complete its assessments. The first, designed for units in the middle stages of their quality improvement process, is to respond to the Baldrige criteria with a written outline. Since the outline does not require the level of detail or the narrative style of a full application, it takes less time to produce.

The second alternative is a self-assessment matrix. "The matrix allows you to arrive at a Baldrige-like score in eight hours," says Vorhauer. "If you multiply that by the number of executives who perform the assessment, you've got 80 to 100 hours for an assessment—significantly less than a full application—and you also get a way to improve." As it developed the matrix, Kodak had units write applications and complete the self-assessment, then compared the scores. It found a strong correlation between the matrix and application scores, suggesting that the scoring aspect of the self-assessment matrix would give units an accurate picture of their systems and of the areas that needed to be improved.

The matrix shown in Table 17.1 (found on pages 248–251) describes ten "ranks" for each of the seven Baldrige categories (based on the 1991 criteria's category names and point values). Each member of the assessment team, which is usually a unit's management team, scores every cell in the matrix in the following way:

- Deployed (D) means the unit has fully applied the characteristics described in the cell.
- Partially deployed (P) means the characteristics have been applied only to major areas within the unit.
- Not deployed (N) means that application of the characteristics is minimal or anecdotal.

The ratings should be verifiable through available data. After each assessment team member has scored all 70 cells, the team meets to arrive at a consensus score for each cell and for the unit as a whole.

EVALUATING THE ASSESSMENT AT KODAK

At the Kodak consensus meeting, team members agree on what each cell (in the Self-Assessment Matrix) is requesting, then on what score is appropriate for their unit. They work on one category at a time, proceeding from Cell 1 to Cell 10. When they have scored all cells, they figure the total score for the assessment. The team begins by identifying the lowest cell in a category that received a score of N (not deployed). Each cell *below* that cell with a rank of D (deployed) is worth 1, while each cell *below* that cell with a rank of P (partially deployed) is worth 1/2. The total of D's plus 1/2 P's is the rank for that category.

For example, assume your team agreed that your unit's scores for the leadership category were as follows: Cell 10 = N; Cell 9 = N; Cell 8 = P; Cell 7 = N; Cell 6 = N; Cell 5 = D; Cell 4 = P; Cell 3 = P; Cell 2 = D; Cell 1 = D.

The lowest cell with a score of N is Cell 6. The three D's and 2 P's below that cell add up to 4.0, which is the score for the leadership category. The P for Cell 8 does not count because it is in a higher cell than the first N.

The number rank for each category is multiplied by the weight given to the category to arrive at the total rank for the category. The weights are shown in the matrix directly under each category heading. Using our example, the rank for the leadership category (4) times the weight for the category (10) equals a score of 40 points. The total of the scores for all seven categories is the unit's assessment score. (We will describe how to use the score and the rest of the self-assessment to improve later in this chapter.)

EVALUATING ASSESSMENTS THAT USE BALDRIGE AWARD CRITERIA

Evaluating a Baldrige application, whether internally or externally, also involves arriving at consensus scores; the difference is that someone outside the unit does the assessing and scoring. Many large companies have patterned their assessment process after the Baldrige process (also described in *The Baldrige Quality System*). Kodak trains about 50 internal examiners a year for its internal Board of Examiners. AT&T also created its own board of examiners, training 300 internal examiners in 1993. "The training for our examiners is based on materials from the National Quality Award process," says Myers, "but we strengthened the training on site visits and giving feedback. We also work hard to make sure each five- or six-person examiner team reflects a diversity of job levels and functional areas, such as manufacturing, finance, research and development, and so on."

Like the Baldrige application process, AT&T's process begins with examiner teams scoring the applications. Only those that meet certain thresholds proceed to the *site visit phase*, where the assessment is clarified and verified. Unlike the Baldrige Award, AT&T rewards both achievement and improvement. "If we hadn't done this, units in the 200 to 300 point range would have sat out the process," says Myers. "What we wanted most was to get everyone involved."

The descriptions of what it takes to earn each level of Achievement Award indicate what examiners look for when they evaluate an application (see Tables 17.2 and 17.3).

TABLE 17.2.   AT&T achievement awards (level of excellence)

Award	Point Score	Description
Gold	876–1,000	Outstanding effort and results in all categories. Effective integration and sustained results. National and world leaders.
Silver	751–875	Effective efforts in all categories, and outstanding in many. Good integration and good to excellent results in all areas. Full deployment. Many industry leaders.
Bronze	601–750	Evidence of effective efforts in most categories, and outstanding in several. Deployment and results show strength, but some efforts may lack maturity. Clear areas for further attention.
Crystal	500–600	Evidence of effective efforts in many categories and outstanding in some. A good prevention-based process. Many areas lack maturity. Further deployment and results needed to demonstrate continuity.

TABLE 17.3.   AT&T improvement awards (rate of progress)

Award	Point Score	Description
Gold	200 points per year	Improvement at a world-class rate
Silver	150 points per year	Improvement at an excellent rate
Bronze	100 points per year	Improvement at a very good rate

The assessment process is a straightforward evaluation of how an application responds to the criteria. When the criteria request a process—how you do something—the examiners assess the approach you are taking based on how sound, systematic, and prevention based it is, then determine how fully the approach has been implemented. When the criteria request results—the measures of what you are doing—the examiners study the direction and levels of trends in all key areas and how those trends compare to the trends of competitors and world-class benchmarks. For each item the examiners identify what you are doing very well (strengths) and what you need to do better (areas for improvement), then figure your score.

USING ASSESSMENT RESULTS TO IMPROVE

The results of a Baldrige assessment lend themselves to action. Such phrases as "process is not evident," "limited deployment," and "trends not given" are common in a Baldrige feedback report, and they always direct the organization's attention to specific areas for improvement. The problem many organizations face is how to tackle so many areas at once.

Graniterock organized the 110 areas for improvement listed in its first two Baldrige feedback reports into ten categories. It formed a *corporate quality team* to work on each category. Each team had a senior executive facilitator and five or six employees, usually including one middle manager and people from all levels of the company. "The executives' evaluations depend on the success of their teams," says Val Verutti, director of quality support, "while the vertical membership unified our purpose and our people to accomplish something. Each team has a definite mission, and they've all been reasonably successful at accomplishing what they set out to do."

The teams, with such unwieldy names as the Corporate Quality Team for the Improvement of Supplier Quality and the Corporate Quality Team for Commitment to the Community, still exist. They meet often and have broad authority to implement improvements. Subsequent feedback reports produce new areas for improvement that are doled out to the teams. Areas that do not fall naturally into a team's domain are addressed by ad hoc teams or departments. "This year, there's a line in our feedback report that says 'see no evidence of process for evaluating improvement in the area of environmental improvement,'" says Verutti. "That's never been mentioned before. But we do have an environmental department, and we just have to develop measures to show we're getting better."

This system assessment and improvement process is so important to Graniterock that it continues to write Baldrige examinations annually, even though it could not actually apply again until 1998. It hires former Baldrige examiners to score its applications and conduct site visits.

Many companies lose the value of their Baldrige assessments by not having a plan to act on the feedback. Part of the problem is that the feedback is nonprescriptive; it tells you when something is missing or weak, but it does not tell you how to fix it. AT&T addresses this issue in several ways. Its initial feedback, like its assessment process, parallels the Baldrige feedback: clear, concise, and nonprescriptive. Copies of the feedback report are given to the head of the organization and the unit's application coordinator to use as they wish. A unit's score and the data in its application are not shared with any other unit or with corporate staff. "We've been overly strict about enforcing confidentiality because we want to develop trust. We need honest sharing through the application to make the feedback helpful," says Myers.

If the applicant requests it, AT&T requires the examination team leader, the senior examiner, to give an *oral presentation on the feedback* to the applicant's senior management team. "Nearly every unit takes advantage of that," says Myers. "It gives them a chance to ask questions and clarify the written report. But we still ask the team leaders to be nonprescriptive, primarily because we don't want to undermine the quality manager in that unit." If the quality manager wants a prescription, he or she can request an advisory session with the senior examiner and other team members. The session focuses on what the team would do if it were responsible for acting on its report. However, the responsibility for actually doing something still belongs to the unit.

AT&T also uses the assessment process to spread knowledge about best practices. Representatives of the most successful units describe what they are doing to AT&T quality professionals and operational managers at one-day "sharing rallies." In addition, a *Pockets of Excellence* report identifies, for each Baldrige item, those units that scored 60% or higher. The report encourages internal sharing and recognizes those units that are excelling in specific areas.

The most coveted form of recognition is winning one of the *Chairman's Quality Awards*. To win, a unit must meet the point ranges listed in Tables 17.2 and 17.3, have the score and assessment findings substantiated by a site visit, be recommended for an award by AT&T's internal panel of judges (17 senior managers and quality experts in 1992), and be considered a role model. Judges recommend winners to the Management Executive Committee, which reviews the list to make sure everyone should be on it. As Myers notes, "All of these buy-ins and checks add credibility."

At the end of October AT&T brings in more than 1,000 people from all business units and divisions to its annual two-day AT&T Quality Conference. On the first night of the conference the Management Executive Committee hosts a private dinner for the award winners, each of which is represented by the head of the organization and the quality manager. "This accomplishes two things," says Myers. "The winners get to interact with the senior executives, and the senior executives get to learn what works."

The chairman presents the Achievement and Improvement Awards during the conference's plenary sessions. He describes each unit's major accomplishments, invites the head of the unit and the quality manager to come onto the stage, and hands them their award, after which the unit head speaks briefly. The ceremony is broadcast live to over 100 AT&T locations. Such recognition further displays AT&T's commitment to the quality improvement process—and it creates more than a little desire among unit leaders to stand on that stage.

AT&T also studies the feedback reports for all units to identify common threads that the company as a whole needs to work on. "We analyze the results to find common strengths and areas for improvement, then feed these findings to the Management Executive Committee," says Myers. "For example, the latest analysis showed a common need to consistently track and review customer satisfaction. The attributes vary from unit to unit, but the need is the same. We're addressing that now."

Kodak asks each major unit to provide senior management with its score by Baldrige category, the percent of management trained in its Quality Leadership Process, and the unit's improvement plan. Units must provide the same information no matter which type of assessment they chose. With the second year and subsequent assessments, the units must state how well they met their previous year's improvement plan. "The purpose of requesting this information is to have a baseline and an improvement plan," says Vorhauer. "We've set aggressive goals for the next five years for scores, percent of management trained, and percent of units meeting improvement plans. By tracking the results, units will be able to see if their system is working. If it isn't, they know what to fix and they have the tools to effect change."

Assessments using the Baldrige criteria give you a *detailed snapshot of your system*. You cannot realize the snapshot's value by passing it around for people to admire; it must be studied for clues about key areas that need to be improved, translated into a written improvement plan, and acted upon. Only then does the system assessment make the system better.

THE SHIFT IN THINKING

Until the Baldrige criteria came along, few organizations had ever assessed their entire business system. For one thing, no effective assessment tool existed. For another, the search for ways to improve rarely revealed the need for a system assessment. Problems belonged to departments, work groups, and individuals, not to the system as a whole. Only when the quality movement began harping about the system *being* the problem did people wonder what condition their system was in.

Companies that are using the Baldrige criteria to transform their business start with an assessment. They need a new understanding of the nature of their system, a baseline to gauge their improvement, and a sense for what must be worked on first. All this is available through a Baldrige assessment, whether that assessment takes the form of an 85-page application or an improvement plan based on a matrix score.

However, our experience has shown that the more *time* people invest in the assessment process, the more *value* that process has for them and for their company. An organization's score for a full application may correlate with its score for another type of assessment, such as the Kodak self-assessment matrix, but the benefits will not be the same. People who must wrestle with the criteria to understand what they are asking, then assemble a response that meets the criteria, become "systems thinkers" during that process. They begin to assimilate the Baldrige values—customer-driven quality, management by fact, continuous improvement, and so on—and apply them to their daily tasks. They think more critically, ask better questions, look for root causes of problems, and strive to improve.

Ironically, a broad system assessment inspires personal quality. (We will discuss this more in Chapter 18.) The system assessment also produces a roadmap for continuous improvement. Graniterock builds its improvement efforts around the areas for improvement identified in its feedback reports. Kodak uses its measurement process to drive improvement plans in each of the units assessed. AT&T improves by sharing how its internal role models excel in different areas of the Baldrige criteria.

A system assessment using the Baldrige criteria will identify strengths and weaknesses for every area we discuss in this book. By using the criteria to assess your system, you set in motion a process of discovery and improvement that can jump-start a failing system and energize a lumbering one. Just ask the Baldrige Award winners.

CROSSING THE RIVER: THE TRANSITION TO THE NEW MANAGEMENT MODEL

18

Two years minimum! That's what most companies of any size are looking at before the transition from a traditional management model to the new systems model begins to become institutionalized. Small companies can make the change more quickly, as can larger companies in crisis.

But you don't have to wait two years to realize the *benefits* of the new management model. Each of the action plans provided in this chapter offers immediate advantages. It may take two years before you have all the listening posts in place that tell you what customers are thinking, but your company will find itself getting closer to customers as each of those avenues of communication is established. It may be two years before employees feel empowered to shut down a manufacturing line or act on their own to solve a customer's problem, but the process of learning team and problem-solving skills and taking responsibility will cause steady improvement. The transition to systems management is an *ongoing process of continuous improvement* that begins when your company commits itself to managing by quality.

It is rarely a smooth transition. Roles are being redefined. Responsibilities change. Routines are scrutinized. Like each person in the company, the company itself is changing jobs, *learning to take a systematic approach to satisfying customers.*

In 1980 Marilyn Ferguson wrote about change in the workplace in her book, *The Aquarian Conspiracy.* She quoted Dick Raymond, the founder of a Bay Area network of entrepreneurs called Briarpatch, on the transition from working for someone to working for yourself. His insights are equally appropriate for people involved in the transition to the new management model:

Crossing this river is difficult: it means leaving behind some of your old ideas about work and jobs. Most of us (including myself) try to tiptoe around the pain, but it's important to talk about some of the agonies one is apt to confront.... When you start abandoning your old beliefs or values, some very primal circuits get ignited.... You may be stuck on the threshold for two or three years. Before moving on, you have to clear away all your cherished beliefs.

The process of clearing away cherished beliefs is one reason the transition to the new model takes two years or longer. This river is wide, the current fast, the riverbed strewn with rocks. Even when they can see the need to cross, people will wish they could remain on safe ground—which is why an unshakable commitment to change is essential.

Gaining this commitment is the first step in your transition, the need to marshal your forces before crossing the river. In this chapter we have organized the transition process into a logical sequence any company could follow. The sequence *you* follow depends on your company's unique situation. If you are in a hurry, you may need to jump to phase 4 and start grappling with your processes, then backfill with planning, training, and determining customer requirements. If you have more time, you may want to begin with a system assessment to determine what you have to work with and where you need to go. *There is no single course we can prescribe for your company.* You will need to use your understanding of your company's needs to construct a transition plan that will guide you toward your goals.

As you consider the transition, then move through it, remember to focus on the *system*. It is easy to get caught up in the steps, to fall in love with employee involvement or process management or any of the other all-consuming phases you will pass through. *The goal is to align and improve your system for satisfying customers.*

In Chapter 1 we introduced a diagram of the new business management model shown in Figure 18.1. Each element in this model has been explained through the experiences of the 53 models of excellence featured in Chapters 2 through 17. Taken together, our role models suggest a systematic approach to focusing all your resources on meeting your customers' expectations. They demonstrate how any company that has a clear and accurate understanding of their customers' expectations and of their system for meeting those expectations can achieve customer satisfaction.

This chapter outlines a course for gaining understanding:

- Phase 1 outlines the steps you can take to get senior management to commit to change.

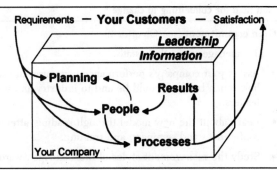

FIGURE 18.1.   The new management model.

- Phase 2 describes what you can do to determine your customers' perceptions of your company and the condition of your system.
- Phase 3 focuses on how you can institutionalize a customer focus.
- Phase 4 places the focus on your system in the areas of strategic planning, employee involvement, process management, and your measurement system.
- Phase 5 addresses the alignment of every activity to meeting and exceeding customer expectations.
- Phase 6 looks at using the Baldrige criteria to assess your system and initiate the next round of improvements.

Each of the goals identified in the tables lists the chapters where information about the subject may be found. For example, if you wonder what gaining senior management's commitment might look like (Table 18.1), you can refer to Chapter 2 for a description of how the senior executives at Corning, Federal Express, and Marlow Industries lead their companies' quality improvement processes. Their stories, like the steps listed in the tables, suggest directions your company can take as it moves toward the new management model.

PHASE 1: COMMIT TO CHANGE

Senior managers are the system's gatekeepers. If, and only if, they open the gates to cultural change will the transition begin. The leaders of world-class companies not only open the gates, they lead the transformation, putting their minds, hearts, and souls into this new management model. Table 18.1 provides an action plan for phase 1.

TABLE 18.1.   Action plan for committing to change

GOAL	Gain commitment (see Chapter 2).
Participants	Senior managers and their staffs.
Steps	• Assess your company's performance compared to your perception of how much better it could be and to industry and world-class leaders.
	• Learn about the new model through reading, attending conferences and seminars, and training.
	• Study the management styles of the Baldrige Award winners.
	• Look at your company from your customers' perspective.
	• As a staff, brainstorm what the company would look like with the new management model in place.
	• Identify the benefits, drawbacks, and obstacles of such a change.
	• Develop a new vision, mission, policies, and values that capture the company you wish to be.
	• Commit as the company's leaders to the long-term, permanent transition to management by quality.
	• Communicate this commitment throughout the company.
	• Begin work on a system of measures of senior executive and company performance based on the new management model.

PHASE 2: ASSESS YOUR SYSTEM

By the time companies turn to a new approach to management, most do not have much time for assessments. Companies, like people, resist dramatic change until they run out of options. However, even a quick assessment is better than going with the first quality program that catches your eye.

The assessment should be both external and internal, ascertaining what your customers think of your company and what your own measures tell you. The more thorough the assessments, the easier it will be to establish baselines by which you can gauge progress and to identify and prioritize areas for improvement. Table 18.2 provides an action plan for phase 2.

PHASE 3: INSTITUTIONALIZE A CUSTOMER FOCUS

Since the new management model is customer driven, there's no time like the present to put the customer behind the wheel. Unfortunately, it is not as easy as slipping the customer into the driver's seat and handing over the keys. Institutionalizing a customer focus requires getting close to customers, then

TABLE 18.2.   Action plan for assessing your system

GOAL	**Determine customer perceptions of your company** (see Chapter 3).
Participants	Executives, managers, supervisors, and other employees who have direct contact with customers, particularly members of marketing, sales, and customer service.
Steps	• Identify the primary markets and customers your new system will target.
	• Gather information from every possible source about these customers' requirements, expectations, and needs, and how your company is doing at fulfilling them.
	• Aggregate and analyze this information to determine the customers' requirements and their view of your company.
	• Run your findings past key customers to verify their accuracy.
	• Document and present findings to senior management.
GOAL	**Perform system assessment** (see Chapter 17).
Participants	Employees needed to conduct the assessment.
Steps	• Establish the assessment team, train, and assign responsibilities.
	• Collect data and information.
	• Document and present findings to senior management.
GOAL	**Develop action plan** (see Chapters 2–5).
Participants	Senior managers and their staffs, other employees.
Steps	• Compare findings with vision of where company needs to be to identify strengths and areas for improvement.
	• Prioritize areas for improvement and assign to executive owners.
	• Determine how progress will be measured.
	• Formalize a process for periodic system assessments.

acting on what they tell you. Many of the steps that make this possible will be taken again and again throughout all phases of the transition. Table 18.3, on page 264, provides an action plan for phase 3.

PHASE 4: INSTITUTIONALIZE THE NEW MANAGEMENT MODEL

The transition to the new model will remain a transition until the model is institutionalized. Companies that flit from quality program to quality program

TABLE 18.3.   Action plan for institutionalizing a customer focus

GOALS	**Establish listening posts** (see Chapter 3).
Participants	All employees, primarily sales, marketing, and customer service.
Steps	• Identify all possible sources of information about present and potential customers.
	• Formalize processes for gathering information from these sources.
	• Assess tools used to determine customer satisfaction and improve quality of information gathered, timeliness, usefulness, etc.
GOALS	**Aggregate and analyze customer information** (see Chapters 3 and 10).
Participants	Senior managers, planning process participants, members of marketing, sales, and customer service.
Steps	• Formalize a process for aggregating customer information from various listening posts.
	• Formalize processes for communicating information that needs immediate attention to appropriate units/individuals.
	• Formalize processes for analyzing the aggregated information.
	• Formalize processes for communicating this information to appropriate units/individuals.
GOALS	**Use customer requirements to drive internal processes** (see Chapters 3–6, 10–15).
Participants	All employees.
Steps	• Determine links between customer satisfiers and internal processes and measures.
	• Focus on these key processes and measures in phase 4.

with no process for weaving this into the fabric of their organizations never stray far from their old management model.

Companies convert to the new model in one or more of four ways: strategic planning, employee involvement, process management, and their measurement system. Examples of each have been described in this book. The avenues you choose depend on which are more appropriate for your company, because one does not seem to be better or more effective than another. Keep in mind that you can work toward all four of the following goals at once and that the steps toward each are often overlapping and complementary. And remember that many successful companies test everything before implementing it across the company. Use pilot projects liberally to test and fine-tune your approaches. Table 18.4 provides an action plan for phase 4.

TABLE 18.4.   Action plan for institutionalizing the new management model

GOAL	**Align all activities through the strategic planning process** (see Chapter 4).
Participants	All levels of employees, customers, and suppliers.
Steps	• Define a single strategic planning process by adapting the "best practices" of world-class companies to your organization.
	• Identify who to involve in the process, including all levels of employees, key customer representatives, and key suppliers.
	• Establish channels of communication that will feed key data and information into the planning process.
	• Determine the vital few long- and short-term goals necessary to improve customer satisfaction and operational performance.
	• Assign executive ownership for each goal.
	• Decide on measures for each goal.
	• Deploy the plan to all employees, verifying that the activities of divisions, departments, teams, and individuals are aligned with corporate objectives.
	• Formalize processes for assessing progress and helping groups not performing to plan.
GOAL	**Involve all employees in continuous improvement** (see Chapters 2, 5–7).
Participants	All employees.
Steps	• Communicate vision, goals, requirements, and expectations to all employees (by executives, managers, and supervisors).
	• Formalize processes for ongoing communication of corporate values to all levels of employees.
	• Clarify management's role in the new system, and provide training and support to assist in the transition.
	• Train employees in the skills they need to assume responsibility for their processes and results.
	• Formalize processes for providing employees with the feedback they need to assess and improve performance.
	• Train employees in the skills they need to participate in teams.
	• Initiate the use of teams to manage and improve processes and solve problems.

(continued)

TABLE 18.4. (continued)

GOAL	**Manage and improve all key processes** (see Chapters 11 and 12).
Participants	All employees.
Steps	• Identify core processes that link directly to customer requirements.
	• Train employees in process management and improvement.
	• Assemble cross-functional teams to analyze key processes that cross departmental boundaries.
	• Formalize processes for using teams' findings to manage and improve processes.
	• Reorganize the company around its core processes.
	• Formalize processes for managing and improving processes involving suppliers.
	• Assign responsibility for addressing processes within departments.
	• Formalize processes for managing and improving these processes and for solving problems within these processes.
	• Establish methods of communicating feedback to teams and results to the whole organization.
GOAL	**Establish a system of measurement** (see Chapter 14).
Participants	All employees.
Steps	• Use information about customer and company requirements to identify key measures.
	• Measure only what you can control.
	• Make sure all measures are easy to collect, report, and understand.
	• Train employees in taking, analyzing, and using measures to improve.
	• Formalize processes for collecting and reporting data.
	• Formalize processes for reviewing, analyzing, and using the data to improve.

PHASE 5: ALIGN AND EXTEND
YOUR MANAGEMENT GOALS

One of the primary goals of the new model is to align every division, department, team, individual, function, process, plan, product, and service to meeting and exceeding your customers' requirements and your company's performance goals. Once the fundamentals needed to do this are in place, you can turn your attention to less urgent, though equally important, areas of your system. The transition to the new model begins with the areas that have the greatest impact on customers and the company, then spreads out to encompass all that the company does. Now is a good time to remind yourself of the implications of managing the system, to place everything that is going on in your company in a holistic context.

Think of it as staging a play. You have chosen the play, assigned parts, begun practice, and booked theaters. Your attention now expands to include creating a set, designing costumes, and publicizing the events. You still work hard to fine-tune the performances, but you understand that the performances are only the most visible part of the production and that each area you neglect has the potential to detract from or undermine your efforts.

Phase 5 focuses attention on four areas that have had to wait: rewards and recognition, employee health and well-being, benchmarking, and corporate citizenship. Table 18.5 provides an action plan for this phase.

TABLE 18.5. Action plan for aligning the system

GOAL	**Align compensation and recognition programs with new management model** (see Chapter 8).
Participants	All employees, particularly human resources professionals.
Steps	• Survey employees to understand their expectations and requirements for compensation and recognition programs.
	• Form cross-functional teams that represent your employee base to assess and improve existing programs and develop and implement new ones.
	• Work with the teams to clarify the purpose of such programs, with the focus on doing no harm first, then promoting the company's mission and goals second.
	• Establish measures of each program's performance and contribution to the company's mission and goals.
	• Study the issues affecting compensation to determine the best course of action for your company.
	• Involve employees in running the company's recognition programs.
	• Make at-risk pay and formal recognition dependent on measurable performance, preferably team performance.
	• Formalize processes for regular review and improvement of all compensation and recognition programs.
GOAL	**Treat employees as the company's most important asset** (see Chapter 9).
Participants	All employees, particularly senior executives and human resources staff.
Steps	• Determine from employees what they require and expect in their work environment to be healthy and satisfied.
	• Align the goals for employee health, well-being, and satisfaction with the company's mission and goals.

(continued)

TABLE 18.5.   (continued)

	• Develop ongoing measures of employee health, well-being, and satisfaction.
	• Formalize processes for reviewing and improving employee health, well-being, and satisfaction.
GOAL	**Establish a benchmarking program** (see Chapter 15).
Participants	All employees.
Steps	• Involve senior executives and other decision makers in learning about what benchmarking is and what benefits it offers.
	• Formalize your company's benchmarking process, including defining who is involved, the steps in the process, and the expected results.
	• Train employees in the benchmarking process.
	• Use input from customers, suppliers, and employees to identify benchmarking opportunities, then prioritize those opportunities and assign responsibility.
	• Empower benchmarking teams to organize and conduct the studies and present their recommendations.
	• Formalize processes for translating recommendations into action plans, and for evaluating and improving the benchmarking process.
GOAL	**Provide leadership and support for publicly important purposes** (see Chapter 16).
Participants	All employees, particularly senior executives.
Steps	• Establish your company's mission, goals, and values in the areas of public responsibility and corporate citizenship.
	• Communicate these values throughout the organization, orally, through involvement in relevant activities, and by supporting employee participation in community affairs.
	• Develop measures for employee and company involvement in such areas as waste minimization, environmental responsibility, volunteerism, charitable contributions, and community service.
	• Formalize processes for reviewing and improving performance in these areas.

PHASE 6: REFINE YOUR SYSTEM

The new management model focuses on continuous improvement. The only way to continuously improve is to periodically look at where you are, compare it to where you want to be, and change course, speed up, or leap ahead. System assessments give you the information you need to decide what to do next.

They also help you develop the discipline of "refinement." Most companies, including many of the role models in this book, fail to close the loop on their processes by leaving out the refinement cycle. They develop a terrific approach, deploy it throughout the company, then move on without leaving behind a process for regularly evaluating and improving the approach. The same concept applies to the entire system; the approaches you are taking need to be evaluated and improved on a regular basis.

We recommend an annual assessment based on the Baldrige criteria (see Chapter 17). No other tool on the market is better at helping you explore, understand, and improve your entire system.

CONCLUSION

We understand that this is an imposing list of steps. The transition to the new management model cannot be done in haste or without thought. We hope, however, that the list will not deter you from stepping into the river of change.

At the beginning of this chapter we quoted Dick Raymond's thoughts about crossing this river. He concludes with an observation that captures the promise for each individual who sets foot on the new land:

> The people I know who have successfully made this transition are the most joyful, the most outgoing, the most well-rewarded people I know.

This is the ultimate benefit of total quality management for the people involved, from senior executives to front-line workers. *In our experience, the companies that involve everyone in continuous improvement, that make customer satisfaction their top priority, that value people for who they are, and that see their systems as treasure chests filled with endless opportunities—these companies have the most joyful, outgoing, and well-rewarded people we know.* Their enthusiasm is infectious, their commitment inspiring. They invariably seem more alive and fulfilled and challenged than the millions who just go through the motions day after day. They stand on the riverbank called total quality management and shout out the wonders of working together for the good of all.

We invite you to join them.

Resources

To get a copy of the Baldrige criteria and/or the requirements for applying for the Baldrige Award, contact:

United States Department of Commerce
Technology Administration
National Institute of Standards and Technology
Route 270 and Quince Orchard Road
Administration Building,
Room A537
Gaithersburg, MD 20899

To learn more about the Baldrige Award program, the criteria, and the application process, read:

The Baldrige Quality System: The Do-It-Yourself Way to Transform Your Business by Stephen George, 1992, John Wiley & Sons.

To contact the authors:

Stephen George
3416 Library Lane
Minneapolis, MN 55426
612-927-7437

Arnold Weimerskirch
Honeywell
Vice President, Corporate Quality
P.O. Box 524
Minneapolis, MN 55440
612-951-0225

To find out more information about the companies featured in this book, write or call the contact people listed in this section. If you wish to explore specific topics, please review the benchmarking process described in Chapter 15 before contacting these companies.

3M Corporate Quality Services
Ron Kubinski
Quality Manager
Building 525-5E-02, 800 East Minnehaha
St. Paul, MN 55144-1000
612-778-7584

Aetna Health Plans
H. David Lundgren
Vice President of Human Resources
151 Farmington Ave.
Hartford, CT 06156
203-636-5695

Alcoa
Martin Leeper
Manager, Corporate Quality Group
1501 Alcoa Building
Pittsburgh, PA 15219
412-553-4102

Alphatronix
Robert Freese
Chief Executive Officer
P.O. Box 13687
Research Triangle Park, NC 27709
919-544-0001

Ameritech Services
Orval Brown
Manager, Business Process Architec-
ture/Benchmarking
2000 West Ameritech Center Drive
Hoffman Estates, IL 60196-1025
708-248-4373

AMP Inc.
J. Keith Drysdale
Vice President, Global Quality
470 Friendship Road
Harrisburg, PA 17111
717-564-0100

AT&T
Dale Myers
District Manager, Quality
Planning
AT&T Corporate Quality Office
One Oak Way
Berkeley Heights, NJ 07922
908-771-2156

AT&T Network Systems Group
Sheila Landers
Personnel Services Manager
1600 Osgood Street
North Andover, MA 01845
508-960-6712

AT&T Universal Card Services
Robert Davis
Chief Quality Officer
8787 Baypine Road
Jacksonville, FL 32256
904-443-8875

Ben & Jerry's
Liz Lonergan
Human Resources Manager
P.O. Box 240, Rte. 100
Waterbury, VT 05676
802-244-6957

Bose Corporation
Lance Dixon
Director, Corporate Purchasing
and Logistics
The Mountain
Framingham, MA 10701-9168
508-872-6541

Cadillac Motor Car Division
William Lesner
Superintendent of Manufacturing
Detroit/Hamtramck Assembly
Center
2500 E. General Motors Blvd.
Detroit, MI 48211
313-972-6745

Carrier Corporation
David Gregerson
Vice President, Quality
P.O. Box 4808
Syracuse, NY 13221
315-433-4102

Corning
Martin Mariner
Director, Quality Management
HP CB 067
Corning, NY 14831
607-974-7970

Custom Research
Jeffrey Pope and Judith Corson
Partners
10301 Wayzata Blvd., P.O. Box 26695
Minneapolis, MN 55426
612-542-0800

Dana Corporation
Mobile Fluid Products Division
Thomas Neusiis
Plant Manager
P.O. Box 1313
Minneapolis, MN 55440
612-623-1960

Eastman Kodak Company
George Vorhauer
Director, Corporate Quality
Initiatives
343 State Street
Rochester, NY 14650-0543
716-724-9819

EMD Associates
Daniel M. Rukavina
Co-CEO
4065 Theurer, P.O. Box 25
Winona, MN 55987
507-452-8932

Engelhard
Joseph Steinreich
General Manager
9800 Kellner Road
Huntsville, AL 35824
205-464-6232

Federal Express
Anne Manning
Senior Marketing Specialist,
Business Logistics Services
2005 Corporate Ave.
Memphis, TN 38132
901-395-3470

Ford
Dan Whelan
Quality Strategy, Corporate Quality
Office
The American Road, P.O. Box 1899
Dearborn, MI 48121
313-594-4293

Globe Metallurgical
Norm Jennings
Quality Director of Foundry
Products
P.O. Box 157
Beverly, OH 45715
614-984-2361

Graniterock
Val Verutti
Director of Quality Support
P.O. Box 50001
Watsonville, CA 95077-5001
408-761-2300

GTE Telephone Operations
Michael English
Director of Quality Improvement
W03B68
700 Hidden Ridge Drive
P.O. Box 152092
Irving, TX 75015-2092
214-718-7446

IBM Rochester
Greg Lea
Director, Market-Driven Quality
3605 Highway 52 North
Rochester, MN 55901-7829
507-286-4711

IDS Financial Services
Neil Taylor
Vice President, IDS 1994
IDS Tower 10
Minneapolis, MN 55440
612-671-1794

Intel Corporation
Pamela Olivier
Strategic Planning Manager,
Microprocessor Products Group
220 Mission College Blvd.
Santa Clara, CA 95052
408-765-4285

Kennametal
Paul Cahan
Director of Operations
6865 Cochran Road
Solon, OH 44139
216-349-5511

L.L. Bean
Catherine Hartnett
Media Specialist
Freeport, ME 04033
207-865-4761
Ext. 4507

Louisville Redbirds
Dale Owens
Vice President and General Manager
P.O. Box 36407
Louisville, KY 40233
502-367-9121

LTV/L-SE Steel
Quentin Skrabec, Jr.
Manager of Quality Control
3100 East 45th Street
Cleveland, OH 44127
216-429-7138

Lyondell Petrochemical
Jackie Wilson
Director, Public Affairs
1221 McKinney, Suite 1600
P.O. Box 3646
Houston, TX 77253-3646
713-652-4596

Marlow Industries
Ray Marlow
President
10451 Vista Park Road
Dallas, TX 75238-1645
214-340-4900

Metropolitan Life Insurance
Company
Norma Rossi
Senior Program Consultant,
Corporate Quality
One Madison Ave.
New York, NY 10010-3690
212-578-4547

Motorola Inc.
Paul Noakes
Vice President and Director of
External Quality Programs
1303 E. Algonquin Road
Schaumburg, IL 60196-1065
708-576-7272

NCR Corporation
John Wise
AVP, Marketing & Staff Quality
Systems, Corporate Quality
1700 South Patterson Blvd.
Dayton, OH 45479
513-445-2202

The New England
Scott Andrews
Consultant, Quality Commitment
501 Boylston Street
Boston, MA 02117
617-578-3049

The Northern Trust Company
Debra Danziger
Vice President and Chief Quality
Officer
50 South LaSalle Street
Chicago, IL 60675
312-444-7701

Pacific Bell
Joseph Yacura
Executive Director, Contracting
and Supplier Management
2600 Camino Ramon, Room 1E 051
San Ramon, CA 94583
510-823-0390

Paul Revere Insurance Group
Diane Gardner
Quality Consultant
18 Chestnut Street
Worchester, MA 01608-1528
508-799-4441

Plumley Companies, Inc.
Mike Plumley
Chairman and Chief Executive
Officer
100 Plumley Drive
Paris, TN 38242
901-642-5582

Randalls Food Market
Randall Omstead
President
3663 Briapark, P.O. Box 4506
Houston, TX 77210
713-268-3462

The Ritz-Carlton Hotel Company
Patrick Mene
Corporate Director of Quality
3414 Peachtree Road, N.E.
Atlanta, GA 30326
404-237-5500

Seitz Corporation
Sharon LeGault
Marketing Manager
212 Industrial Lane,
P.O. Box 1398
Torrington, CT 06790
203-489-0476

Solectron
Gary Ogden
Director of Marketing
777 Gibraltar Dr., Bldg. 5
Milpitas, CA 95035
408-956-6689

Southern Pacific Transportation
Company
Kent Sterett
Southern Pacific Building,
Suite 660
One Market Plaza
San Francisco, CA 94105
415-541-2318

Staples Inc.
James Forbush
Vice President, Marketing
100 Pennsylvania Ave.
Framingham, MA 01701
508-370-8500

Tennant Company
Rita Ferguson Maehling
Employee Programs Manager—
Involvement and Recognition
P.O. Box 1452, Mail Drop 31
Minneapolis, MN 55440
612-540-1402

Texas Instruments Defense Systems
& Electronics Group
Mike Cooney
Vice President, Manager of Quality
Assurance
P.O. Box 660246, MS 3124
Dallas, TX 75266
214-480-3002

Thomas Interior Systems
Thomas Klobucher
President
192 Spangler Ave.
Elmhurst, IL 60126
708-832-4200

USAA
John R. Cook
Senior Vice President
USAA Building
San Antonio, TX 78288
210-498-0949

Xerox
John Swaim
Vice President, Quality and
Customer Satisfaction
Xerox Square, 100 Clinton Ave. S.
Rochester, NY 14644
716-423-4834

Zytec
Ron Schmidt
President and Chief Executive
Officer
7575 Market Place Drive
Eden Prairie, MN 55344
612-941-1100

Index